Late-medieval England

CONFERENCE ON BRITISH STUDIES
BIBLIOGRAPHICAL HANDBOOKS

Editor: J. JEAN HECHT

Consultant Editor: G.R. ELTON

Late-medieval England
1377-1485

DELLOYD J. GUTH

CAMBRIDGE UNIVERSITY PRESS
CAMBRIDGE
LONDON · NEW YORK · MELBOURNE
for the Conference on British Studies

Published by the Syndics of the Cambridge University Press
The Pitt Building, Trumpington Street, Cambridge CB2 1RP
Bentley House, 200 Euston Road, London NW1 2DB
32 East 57th Street, New York, NY 10022, USA
296 Beaconsfield Parade, Middle Park, Melbourne 3206, Australia

First published 1976

Printed in Great Britain
at the University Printing House, Cambridge
(Euan Phillips, University Printer)

Library of Congress Cataloguing in Publication Data

Guth, DeLloyd J 1938–

Late-medieval England, 1377–1485.

(Conference on British Studies bibliographical handbooks)

Includes index

1. Great Britain – History – Richard II, 1377–1399 – Bibliography. 2. Great Britain – History – Lancaster and York, 1399–1485 – Bibliography. I. Title. II. Series: Conference on British Studies. Bibliographical handbooks.
Z2017.G87 [DA235]   016.94204   75-23845
ISBN 0 521 20877 7

CONTENTS

To my parents

ANGELINE GLODOWSKI GUTH and FRANK L. GUTH

PREFACE

Fifteenth-century studies continue to thrive, as this annotated bibliography proves, even when discouraged by the ways we periodize our past. Whether we label it late-medieval, as I have done, or early modern, pre-Reformation, early-Renaissance, and pre-Tudor, the fifteenth-century must be allowed independence and integrity. It invites everyone to enjoy an unlimited range of vivacious personalities, unpublished and even undisturbed sources, piquant conundrums, and fresh perspectives. My hope is that this book will aid and encourage all who use it to build anew on past scholarship.[1]

Although I have been limited to 2500 entries, my annotations, cross-references, and nominal index are an attempt to provide directions to related and useful publications. There is also a brief topical index, leading the user into my cross-referencing system (see *Explanatory Notes*, p. x). All bibliographies must be measured by the efficiency, breadth, and accuracy that they offer to their users, and I have tried to keep to these priorities. I apologize to scholars whose books and articles I have omitted or, more likely, either combined into a single entry or included only in an annotation. Many works cited within annotations have been shortened to author and date of publication. But the nominal index includes every author and editor whose work is cited, even if only in an annotation. The gathering, sifting, evaluating, and organizing of all materials have been solely my own work. If asked whether or not I have read everything cited, I borrow my answer from a friend: 'Some of them twice!'

I have chosen to emphasize printed, available sources and those writers and editors who best use these and the many unpublished sources. The focus is on England and Wales, with some related materials for Scotland and Ireland. Because this bibliography is part of an established series, I follow its formula for dividing entries into fourteen sections and several subsections. The first two sections barely reveal the range of reference materials with which diligent compilers facilitate our labours. Virtually all public, and many private, research libraries, archives, and museums have published guides to their collections and I suggest only a few of the more important ones.

Although I follow the formula for fourteen sections, I have devised my own criteria when sorting entries into these sections. For 'Constitutional and Administrative History' I limit materials to royal and local government, including parliament, the law courts, and offices, but excluding ecclesiastical jurisdictions (Section XII). 'Political History' contains materials more personally related to monarchs, their households and officers, and to their rebels. This section shares diverse chronicles and topics, like royal marriages, with those more appropriate to the 'Foreign Relations' section.

1 I have recently synthesized this bibliography's contents and drawn diverse conclusions about fifteenth-century scholarship, in (10).

PREFACE

'Social History' includes materials about the family, household (other than royal), and community, while 'Economic History' has been defined broadly to include estate management, domestic and international commerce, industry (also under 'Fine Arts'), and local production and marketing. 'Religious History' overlaps several sections (e.g. through architecture, papal administration, theological literature, or monastic economy) and it is the largest section for fifteenth-century scholarship. 'Intellectual History' has been defined narrowly to include formal education, the scriptoria, and the printing press.

The formula for this series makes it necessary to exclude literature *per se*. For late-medieval England and Wales this means cutting away an especially important and abundant evidence. Chaucer, Lydgate, Gower, and innumerable writers of ballads, mystery and morality plays, carols, polemics, and placards do not appear in this book. I have also omitted most articles by antiquarians that exemplify a single source (e.g. a will, letter, or object), contributions in 'notes and queries' periodicals, genealogical items, student theses and dissertations, and items containing only extracts or paraphrased snippets from other sources. Only a few editions of cartulary and muniments have been cited directly because their chronological range is usually broad, even when muniments in a collection originate before 1377.

I stopped this compilation in December 1974, at which point the General Editor, J. Jean Hecht, had finished his scrutiny of my final draft. He has carefully supervised all of this work and helped me to avoid countless mistakes. What errors remain are strictly my responsibility, and I welcome comments from all users regarding omissions, errors, and midjudgements. I have had patient help from librarians in the university libraries of Michigan (Ann Arbor), London, and Bristol, and in the Institute of Historical Research (London). Professor Bertie Wilkinson and Charles D. Ross have given me their time and criticisms at important stages of the work. And Professor G.R. Elton, who suggested the task to me, has sustained his confidence, and mine, in the project and given vigorous counsel at all times. The Horace H. Rackham School of Graduate Studies, in the University of Michigan, awarded me time and aid to initiate this project, through their Alfred H. Lloyd Post-Doctoral Fellowship in 1969, and both Donald Stokes (Dean) and Ralph B. Lewis (Associate Dean) have continued this institution's support, particularly with aid for typing expenses. JoAnn Staebler typed most of the several rough drafts, and Margaret A. Griffith typed the final, press copy.

All of these people remain my creditors for their time and concern. I owe another debt for two attributes essential to a bibliographer: to my father, for the book-keeper's instinct, and to my mother, for patient persistence.

Kingsdon, Somerset, February 1975   DELLOYD J. GUTH

ABBREVIATIONS

AgHR	*The Agricultural History Review*
AHR	*The American Historical Review*
AJ	*Archaeological Journal*
AJLH	*American Journal of Legal History*
AntiqJ	*The Antiquaries Journal.* Being the Journal of the Society of Antiquaries of London.
Arch	*Archaeologia*
ArchAel	*Archaeologia Aeliana*
ArchCamb	*Archaeologia Cambrensis* (Cambrian Archaeological Association)
ArchCant	*Archaeologia Cantiana* (Kent Archaeological Society)
BBCS	*Bulletin of the Board of Celtic Studies*
BIHR	*Bulletin of the Institute of Historical Research*
BJRL	*Bulletin of the John Rylands Library*
Bristol-Gloucs	*Transactions of the Bristol and Gloucestershire Archaeological Society*
CHJ	*Cambridge Historical Journal* [later the *HJ*]
CHR	*The Catholic Historical Review*
CQR	*Church Quarterly Review*
DevonA	*Report and Transactions of the Devon Association for the Advancement of Science, Literature, and Art*
EcHR	*Economic History Review*
EETS	Early English Text Society
EHR	*English Historical Review*
e.s.	extra series
EssexT	*Transactions of the Essex Archaeological Society*
HJ	*Historical Journal* [earlier the *CHJ*]
HMC	Historical Manuscripts Commission
HMSO	Her Majesty's Stationery Office
JBAA	*Journal of the British Archaeological Association*
JEH	*Journal of Ecclesiastical History*
Lancs Antiq	*Transactions of the Lancashire and Cheshire Antiquary Society*
Lancs Historic	*Transactions of the Lancashire and Cheshire Historic Society*
LeedsS	*Proceedings of the Leeds Philosophical and Literary Society: Literary and Historical Section*
London-Midd	*Transactions of the London and Middlesex Archaeological Society*
LQR	*Law Quarterly Review*
NA	*Norfolk Archaeology* (or miscellaneous tracts relating to the antiquities of the county of Norfolk)
n.s.	new series
PBA	*Proceedings of the British Academy*
SaltS	William Salt Archaeological Society, Collections for a History of Staffordshire
ShropsT	*Transactions of the Shropshire Archaeological (and Natural History) Society*
SomersetP	*Proceedings of the Somerset Archaeological and Natural History Society*

StPaulS	*Transactions of St Paul's Ecclesiological Society*
SussexS	Sussex Archaeological Collections (relating to the history and anti-quities of the county)
ThorotonS	*Transactions of the Thoroton Society of Nottinghamshire*
TRHS	*Transactions of the Royal Historical Society*
UBHJ	*University of Birmingham Historical Journal*
WHR	*The Welsh History Review*
WiltsMag	*Wiltshire Archaeological and Natural History Society Magazine*
YorksJ	*Yorkshire Archaeological (and Topographical) Journal*
YorksRS	Yorkshire Archaeological Society, Record Series

EXPLANATORY NOTES

1. Citations to periodicals and monograph series have been abbreviated if the same citation appears more than five times in this bibliography. Otherwise, and whenever there is potential for confusion, I provide the complete citation.

2. Where no place of publication is cited it is London, and this includes any work published in London and elsewhere.

3. Wherever possible, the author or editor is given with his first and surnames in full, plus middle initials. Except for a few authors, double and hyphenated surnames have been reduced to the second name, following the British Museum's *General Catalogue* policy. In such instances, the first part of double and hyphenated surnames will appear simply as a middle initial.

4. Annotations contain descriptive information, some criticisms, relevant authors and editors whose particular work is not cited elsewhere, and cross-reference numbers (always given within parentheses) for books and articles cited elsewhere in this book.

5. The cross-reference numbers given parenthetically in annotations are an attempt to point out some relationships between entries. The major, cross-referenced topics can be found in the list given below:

Architecture and construction: 2189, 2206

Arts (illuminations, woodwork, sculpture, glass, painting): 2223, 2230, 2238, 2251, 2278

Bishops and episcopal administration: 1613, 1977

Borough government and courts leet: 128, 264

Chancery: 127

Church law: 1756

City and town government (except London): 117

Common law: 286, 357

Devotional and church literature: 1610, 1635, 1642

Estate economics and lay governance: 1235

Exchequer: 158

Foreign commerce: 1189, 1202

Humanism, books, and libraries: 2444, 2468, 2419

Ireland: 1, 133

King's Bench and crime: 255

Legal profession and literature: 124, 280

Lollards: 1634

London: 130, 626, 1481

I. BIBLIOGRAPHIES

1   Asplin, P.W.A. *Medieval Ireland, c. 1170—1495: a bibliography of secondary works.* Dublin, 1971. Much pertinent material for English history; regarding Scotland, see Philip Hancock, 1960, 2 vols., for scholarship from 1916 to 1950. For Ireland see (133, 877) and for Scotland (629, 856, 863), with surveys of each that are reliable (92, 107, 108).

2   Bateson, Fredrick N.W. (ed.). *The Cambridge bibliography of English literature, I, 600—1660.* Cambridge, 1940. Also, vol. V, ed. by G. Watson, which supplements Bateson to 1957; see Arthur G. Kennedy's earlier bibliography to 1922; and for comprehensiveness, see R.C. Alston's ten volumes, 1965—73; finally, see the *Bibliography of medieval drama*, by Carl J. Stratman, New York, 2nd ed. rev., 1972, 2 vols.

3   *Bibliotheca Celtica: a register of publications relating to Wales and the Celtic peoples and languages.* Aberystwyth, 1909—66, 28 vols. And (12, 85, 88, 97, 139); the best survey of Welsh history is (1953).

4   Coulter, Edith M. and Melanie Gerstenfeld. *Historical bibliographies. A systematic and annotated guide.* 1965. And see Harry F. Williams's index to *Festschriften* published before 1946 in medieval studies. Often useful is the annual *International bibliography of historical sciences*, first published for 1926.

5   Courtauld Institute of Art. *Annual bibliography of the history of British art, 1934—.* 1936—. For painting see (2278), woodwork (2230), manuscript illumination (2223), sculpture (2238), and glass (2251).

6   Cowley, John D. (ed.). *A bibliography of abridgements, digests, dictionaries and indexes of English law to the year 1800* (Selden Society). 1932. See Beale (280), Nicholson (287), Winfield (295, 560), Soule (287), Francis (21); also, William L. Friend's general bibliography, 1944.

7   Emmison, Frederick G. and F.W. Kuhlicke (eds.). *English local history handlist* (Historical Association, no. 69). 1965. A concise, thorough bibliography organized by topics; also, Joyce A. Youings, *Local record sources in print and in progress 1971—72*, Historical Association, no. H85, 1972; and (120, 1182).

8   Farrar, Clarissa P. and Austin P. Evans. *Bibliography of English translations from medieval sources.* New York, 1946. Organized by author's name, and still useful; now continued by Mary A. Ferguson for publications 1943—67. Louis J. Paetow's *Guide to the study of medieval history*, 1931, will soon be supplemented for 1930—70, under Gray C. Boyce's direction.

9   Gross, Charles. *The sources and literature of English history from the earliest times to about 1485.* 2nd ed., 1915. Must be consulted, especially for political history and descriptions of basic chronicle evidence. A revised edition, compiled by Edgar B. Graves, extends the survey through December 1970, Oxford, 2 vols. in one, 1975.

10   Guth, DeLloyd J. 'Fifteenth-century England: recent scholarship and future directions', *British Studies Monitor*, VII (1976—7). Survey of work published between 1963 and 1975, following Hastings (11), but with a general analysis of the field, including topics and sources that require scholarly study and a quantitative critique of this bibliography.

11   Hastings, Margaret. 'High history or hack history: England in the later middle ages', *Speculum*, XXXVI (1961), 225—53. Reprinted in Elizabeth Chapin Furber (ed.), *Changing views on British history: essays on historical writing since 1939*, Cambridge, Mass., 1966, pp. 58—100. This brings the original article's coverage through 1963, provides an intelligent commentary, and is the single most important essay for the period, supplemented by Guth (10). And see Chrimes (389), Trautz (19), and (21, 1409, 1436).

12   Jenkins, Rhys T. and William Rees (eds.). *Bibliography of the history of Wales.* 2nd ed., Cardiff, 1962; *BBCS*, XX (1963), 126—64; XXII (1966), 49—70; XXV (1972), 75—90. See (3, 97, 139).

13   Kellaway, William. *Bibliography of historical works issued in the United Kingdom 1957—1970.* 1962—72, 3 vols. Invaluable and well indexed for

recent scholarship, with (22). Also consult *The International Medieval Bibliography* for recent articles, compiled at the University of Leeds.

14 Lancaster, Joan C. *Bibliography of historical works in the United Kingdom, 1946—1956.* 1964. And see the four volumes compiled by Milne (22) covering 1938 to 1945.

15 *Modern language association international bibliography.* Published annually for the preceding year in *Publications of the modern language association*, and important for scholarship in literary and intellectual topics. Also, the *Annual bibliography* published by the Modern Humanities Research Association.

16 Peddie, Robert A. *Conspectus incunabulorum; An index catalogue of fifteenth-century books, with references to ... [diverse] bibliographies.* 1910—14, 2 vols. Also his concise guide and bibliography, published 1913, as *Fifteenth-century books*; and, Lena L. Tucker and Allen R. Benham's bibliography, 1928.

17 Poole, Reginald L. and Mary Bateson (eds.). *John Bale's Index of British and other writers* (Anecdota Oxoniensia; Medieval and Modern Series, Part 9). 1902. A careful catalogue compiled alphabetically in the mid-sixteenth century; overlaps (2413).

18 Taylor, John. *The use of medieval chronicles* (Historical Association, Helps for Students of History, no. 70). 1965. Handy guide to this sort of evidence, with (705) and pamphlet for Yorkshire, St Anthony's Hall Publication, no. 19, 1961.

19 Trautz, Fritz (ed.). 'Literaturbericht über die geschichte Englands im mittelalter. Veröffentlichungen 1945 bis 1962/63', *Historische Zeitschrift, sonderheft 2* (1965), 108—259. Thorough listing that parallels Hastings (11) and is exceedingly valuable.

20 Wells, John E. *A manual of writings in middle English 1050—1400.* New Haven, Conn., 1916—51, 9 vols. Exhaustively catalogued, indexed, and thus invaluable; for revisions and additions, see Jonathan B. Severs, 1967, and Albert Hartung; also (46, 54, 2403).

21 Wilkinson, Bertie. 'Fact and fancy in fifteenth-century English history', *Speculum*, XLII (1967), 673—92. Provides sound, general historiographical survey. See Guth (10), Hastings (11), and Trautz (19); also the introspective essay by Thomas F. Tout in *PBA*, VI, 1913—14, pp. 151—66. On legal history, see the dated but still useful essay by Joseph F. Francis, *Michigan Law Review*, XXVII, 1929, pp. 650—76.

22 *Writings on British history 1901—1933, I, Auxiliary sciences and general works* (ed. by H.H. Bellot and A. Taylor Milne), 1968; *II, The middle ages, 450—1485,* 1968. A third series, ed. by Milne, provides annual bibliographies, covering 1938 to 1945. Then see Kellaway (13) and Donald J. Munro's compilation for 1946—1948; and (39). There is *A handbook to county bibliography* by Arthur L. Humphreys, 1917, that is useful for pre-1914 scholarship, with (7, 39, 40).

II. CATALOGUES, GUIDES, AND HANDBOOKS

1 Basic reference

23 British Museum. *General catalogue of printed books.* 1960—66, 263 vols., [and] *Ten-year supplement, 1956—1965.* 1968, 50 vols. Quickest means of verifying existence and editions of published materials in the recently renamed British Library.

24 Cheney, Christopher R. *Handbook of dates for students of English history* (Royal Historical Society Guides and Handbooks, no. 4). 1961. Essential for calculating dates: with ecclesiastical, regnal, Roman, and legal systems. Provides list of Saints' days and the tables needed to determine days of the week and movable feast-days (1934); nature's calendar, as defined

poetically, has been studied by Rosemond Tuve, *Seasons and Months*, 1931 (reprinted 1974).
25　Cokayne, George E. *Complete peerage of England, Scotland, Ireland . . .* , ed. by Vicary Gibbs, H.A. Doubleday, G.H. White, and R.S. Lea. Rev. ed., 1910–59, 12 vols. Fundamental when searching for all titles of nobility and their possessors (163, 227, 1057).
26　Davies, Godfrey R.C. *Medieval cartularies of Great Britain: A short catalogue.* 1958. Includes published and unpublished items (152, 1149).
27　De Ricci, Seymour with W.J. Wilson. *Census of medieval and renaissance manuscripts in the United States and Canada.* New York, 1935–40, 3 vols. Also made a census of Caxton printings, for the Bibliographical Society, XV, 1909.
28　Emmison, Frederick G. *Guide to the Essex Record Office.* 2nd ed., rev., Chelmsford, 1969. A model guide to a county archive. Other counties usually publish ms. lists which too often are available only at their archives. The National Register of Archives, Quality Court, Chancery Lane, London, provides the central repository for such lists (33).
29　Hall, Hubert. *A formula book of English official historical documents.* Cambridge, 1908–9, 2 pts. Part I: Diplomatic documents. Part II: Ministerial and judicial records. See also his *Studies in English official historical documents*, Cambridge, 1908; and (66, 216, 227).
30　HMSO. *British national archives* (Sectional List No. 24). 1972. Regularly revised list of all government publications of materials in the PRO, plus the Rolls Series and Record Commission publications.
31　——— *Guide to the contents of the Public Record Office.* 1963, 2 vols. Replaces guide of Montague S. Giuseppi and provides most complete introduction to research in the PRO and its millions of royal, central government documents. Consult Vivian H. Galbraith's succinct introduction, Oxford, 1934, rev. ed., 1952. And see the particular, printed materials (145–9, 228–41).
32　——— *Publications of the royal commission on historical manuscripts* (Sectional List No. 17). 1970. Regularly revised list of vols reporting mss. owned by over 400 private individuals and over 200 corporations (towns, cathedrals, colleges, gilds). The necessary starting point for materials extant outside the PRO and British Library.
33　——— *Record repositories in Great Britain.* 4th ed., 1971. Provides names and addresses of archivists for all public archives and libraries in England and Wales.
34　Irwin, Raymond and Ronald Staveley (eds.). *The libraries of London* (Library Association of the United Kingdom). 2nd ed., rev., 1961. Good collection of essays introducing students to London's resources; also an earlier guide by R.A. Rye, 3rd ed., 1927. For London Corporation records see Philip E. Jones and Raymond Smith, 1951; also (130).
35　Ker, Neil R. (ed.). *Medieval libraries of Great Britain. A list of surviving books* (Royal Historical Society Guides and Handbooks, no. 3). 2nd ed., 1964. See (41, 2397, 2474).
36　——— *Medieval manuscripts in British libraries, I, London.* Oxford, 1969. First of projected three volumes listing all mss. in public and institutional libraries.
37　Kirby, John L. *A guide to historical periodicals in the English language* (Historical Association). 1970. Also edits the essential *Annual Bulletin of Historical Literature* for the Association, volume LVI current in 1973 providing reference for publications of 1970.
38　MacFarlane, Leslie J. 'The Vatican Archives, with special reference to sources for British medieval history', *Archives*, IV (1959–60), 29–44, 84–101. Lucidly detailed explication now enhanced by Leonard E. Boyle, *A survey of the Vatican Archives and of its medieval holdings*, Toronto, 1972.
39　Mullins, Edward L.C. *A guide to the historical and archaeological publications of societies in England and Wales, 1901–1933.* 1968. Essential reference list to the contents of numerous well known and obscure periodicals for the period, complementing (22).

40 ―――― *Texts and calendars: an analytical guide to serial publications* (Royal Historical Society Guides and Handbooks, no. 7). 1958. Excellent descriptive annotations for all royal, national, and local record society publications.

41 Pollard, Alfred W. and Gilbert R. Redgrave. *A short-title catalogue of books printed in England, Scotland & Ireland and of English books printed abroad 1475–1640.* 1926. Organized by author only but invaluable for identifying late-fifteenth-century printed materials (2397, 2456, 2474, 2475).

42 Powicke, Frederick M. and Edmund B. Fryde (eds.). *Handbook of British chronology* (Royal Historical Society Guides and Handbooks, no. 2). 1961. Essential reference for its lists of monarchs, diverse officers of state, archbishops and bishops, dukes, marquesses, and earls for England, Scotland, Wales, and Ireland. Also lists chronologically the meetings of parliaments and national ecclesiastical councils, to 1536.

43 Skeat, Theodore C. *British Museum: The catalogues of the manuscript collections.* Rev. ed., 1962. Succinct descriptions and lists of the mss. resources, such as Lansdowne, Harleian, Arundel. A more general and practical introduction to the BM is by Arundell Esdaile. More specifically, see the manuscript index by Henry J. Ellis and Francis B. Bickley.

44 Stephen, Leslie and Sidney Lee (eds.). *Dictionary of national biography.* 1885–1903, 63 vols. Basic biographical reference for the famous, infamous, established, but rarely the obscure persons in English history.

2 Dictionaries

45 Baudrillart, Henri M.A. . . . and R. Aubert (eds.). *Dictionnaire d'histoire et de géographie ecclésiastiques.* Paris, 1908–. Monumental enterprise, with its eighteenth volume published in 1971, through the letter F.

46 Bradley, Henry (ed.). *A middle-English dictionary . . . from the twelfth to the fifteenth century, by Francis Henry Stratmann.* Oxford, 1940. And see Tauno F. Mustanoja for important studies of syntax; similarly but more generally see monographs of Fredericus T. Visser and Karl Brunner; and esp. see Kurath (54) and Fernand Mossé, rev. ed., 1968; and (2404). There is a *Dictionary of early modern English pronunciation* in progress.

47 Cabrol, Fernand and Henri Leclerq (eds.). *Dictionnaire d'archéologie chrétienne et de liturgie.* Paris, 1903–53, 15 vols.

48 Du Boulay, Francis R.H. *Handlist of medieval ecclesiastical terms.* 1952. More generally for church references use Frank L. Cross's dictionary, 1957, or Sidney L. Ollard, 1912, or John S. Purvis, 1962; for a general guide, see *The materials, sources and methods of ecclesiastical history*, 1975, by Derek Baker, and (94, 1943).

49 Du Cange, Charles. *Glossarium mediae et infimae latinitatis*, ed. by L. Favre. Niort, 1883–7, 5 vols. in 10 pts. The basic and most exhaustive dictionary for Latin usages, otherwise use Latham (55).

50 Fisher, John L. *A medieval farming glossary of Latin and English words.* 1968. And (1114).

51 Godefroy, Frédéric. *Dictionnaire de l'ancienne langue française.* Paris, 1880–1902, 10 vols. Especially for the Lancastrian era and when studying diplomatic sources; also Robert Kelham's 1770 dictionary is usually reliable for the Norman French (56).

52 Gooder, Eileen A. *Latin for local history, an introduction.* 1961. Simple and straightforward guide for anyone whose knowledge or memory of Latin is shaky.

53 Jacob, Giles. *A new law dictionary.* (Various eighteenth-century eds.). Over two centuries later than the fifteenth, but a good starting point for the technical terminology of the law (280).

54 Kurath, Hans, Sherman Kuhn and John Reidy (eds.). *Middle English dictionary.* Ann Arbor, Michigan, 1952–. Monumental, exhaustive compilation now complete through the letter L and being published at a rate of 3 or 4 fascicles each year; also (20, 46, 2404).

55 Latham, Ronald E. *Revised medieval Latin word-list, from British and Irish sources.* 1965. Replaces and revises the edition of James H. Baxter and Charles Johnson, 1934; now the most accessible, useful, and accurate dictionary of the medieval meanings and usages of words; see Latham, *Bulletin du Cange*, XXVII, 1957, pp. 189–229, for his explanation of the method of compilation.

56 Maitland, Frederic W. (ed.). '[A Law-French grammar and glossary for the Year Book period]', *Selden Society*, XVII (1903), xxi–lxxxix. Handy reference for anyone using legal sources (53, 280).

57 Meyer, Otto and Renate Klauser (eds.). *Clavis mediævalis: kleines wörterbuch der mittelalterforschung.* Wiesbaden, 1962.

58 *Oxford English dictionary*, ed. by James A.H. Murray, Henry Bradley, W.A. Craigie, and C.T. Onions. Oxford, 1888–1933, 11 vols. in 18 pts. (1933, 13 vols., corrected re-issue). Magnificent etymological source, now being supplemented in three volumes, with vol. I, A–G, by R.W. Burchfield completed, Oxford, 1971.

59 Wright, Joseph (ed.). *The English dialect dictionary.* Oxford, 1923, 6 vols. (re-issue of 1896 original ed.).

60 Zupko, Ronald E. *A dictionary of English weights and measures; from Anglo-Saxon times to the nineteenth century.* Madison, Wisconsin, 1968. And see (1173, 1385).

3 Palaeography and abbreviations

61 Cappelli, Adriano. *Lexicon abbreviaturarum quae in lapidibus, codicibus et chartis praesertim medii-aevi occurrunt.* Milan, 1899, and 6th ed., 1961. Basic reference for elisions and abbreviations found in medieval mss., with Walther (72).

62 Chaplais, Pierre (ed.). *English royal documents: King John–Henry VI (1199–1461).* Oxford, 1971. Practical introduction to court handwriting, with plates and transcriptions; see also, Leonard C. Hector's general guide, 2nd ed., 1966, or the more detailed Johnson (66).

63 Giry, Arthur. *Manuel de diplomatique.* Paris, 1894.

64 Haselden, Reginald B. *Scientific aids for the study of manuscripts* (Bibliographical Society, Supp. 10). Oxford, 1935. Contains excellent bibliographies on palaeographical topics.

65 Hollaender, Albert E.J. (ed.). *Essays in memory of Sir [Charles] Hilary Jenkinson.* 1962. Major emphasis on archival and palaeographical sciences, not to be confused with the *festschrift* (798).

66 Johnson, Charles and Charles Hilary Jenkinson. *English court hand, A.D. 1066 to 1500, illustrated chiefly from the public records.* Oxford, 1915, 2 vols. For royal formulary, see also (29, 216, 227).

67 Mabillon, Jean. *De re diplomatica libri VI.* Paris, 1681–1704.

68 Martin, Charles T. *The record interpreter: a collection of abbreviations, Latin words, and names used in English historical manuscripts and records.* 1892, reissued 1949.

69 Newton, Kenneth C. *Medieval local records.* 1971. Handy guide for beginning readers of medieval, local records; similarly, see Hilda E.P. Grieve's practical examples, 1949, or Frederick G. Emmison, *Archives and local history*, 1974, rev. ed. (7).

70 Thompson, Edward M. *Handbook of Greek and Latin palaeography.* 1893. Also, the 1912 Oxford edition contains 250 plates, many relevant to later medieval handwriting, and was published under the title *An introduction to Greek and Latin palaeography.*

71 Thomson, Samuel H. *Latin bookhands of the later middle ages 1100–1500.* 1969. And see Malcolm B. Parkes, *English cursive book hands*, 1869.

72 Walther, Johann L. *Lexicon diplomaticum, abbreviationes syllabarum et vocum in diplomatibus et codicibus a seculo viii. ad xvi. usque occurrentes exponens.* Göttingen, 1745–7, 3 parts (Also, Ulm, 1756). The single most extensive list of abbreviations extant, with Cappelli (61).

73 Wright, Cyril E. *English vernacular hands from the twelfth to the fifteenth centuries*. Oxford, 1960.

4 Special reference

74 Beresford, Maurice W. *History on the ground: six studies in maps and landscapes*. 1971, rev. ed. Splendid methodological introduction to topographical reconstitution; also (78, 83, 1052).

75 ——, and J.K.S. St Joseph. *Medieval England: an aerial survey*. Cambridge, 1958. Especially for detecting fields, villages, towns, and industrial areas.

76 Britton, Charles E. *A meteorological chronology to A.D. 1450*. 1937. For the important topic of climatic history, see H.H. Lamb, 1972, and E.L. Ladurie, *Times of feast, times of famine*, 1971; generally, see *Scientific methods in medieval archaeology*, ed. by R. Berger, California, 1970, for new techniques in discovery, reconstitution and dating (840, 2288).

77 Cameron, Kenneth. *English place-names*. 1961. Scholarly summary of broad interest and usefulness, as is Gordon J. Copley's monograph, 1968. Regarding surnames (1049).

78 Darby, Henry C. (ed.). *An historical geography of England before 1800*. Cambridge, 1936. Or see his *New* version, 1973, and Hoskins (83); more specifically, read Michael Williams, *The draining of the Somerset Levels*, Cambridge, 1970, for an excellent model and valuable reconstruction (1422).

79 East, William G. (ed.). *Regions of the British Isles*. 1960–. Projected 14 volumes, and to date: A.E. Smailes, *North England* (1960); Alfred H. Shorter, W.L.D. Ravenhill, and K.J. Gregory, *Southwest England* (1969); G.H. Dury, *The east midlands and the Peak* (1963). Superb for topographical, geographical, climatic descriptions.

80 Ekwall, B.O. Eilert (ed.). *The concise Oxford dictionary of English place-names*. 4th ed., Oxford, 1960. Also his *English river-names*, 1968.

81 *English Place-Name Society*. Cambridge, 1924–, 43 vols.

82 Grierson, Philip. *Bibliographie numismatique*. Brussels, 1967. Also, G.C. Brooks, *English coins from the seventh century to the present day*, 3rd ed., 1952, describes the coinage. Consult B.A. Seaby's annual catalogue and literature from Baldwin's, or Spink, the three major numismatic dealers in London, for current information on fifteenth-century coins (312).

83 Hoskins, William G. *The making of the English landscape*. 1955. General but most informative synthesis, pre-Roman to the industrial revolution; also (74, 1052)

84 Lewis, Samuel. *A topographical dictionary of England*. 3rd ed., 1835, 5 vols. Also the important 3 vols. of William Upcott detailing the bibliography of diverse antiquarian studies, 1818; and Richard Gough's catalogue, 1814.

85 —— *A topographical dictionary of Wales*. 3rd ed., 1845, 2 vols. Most recently, use excellent atlas of William Rees, 2nd ed., 1959 (88), and generally (97); but best of all, see (1013, 2413).

86 Martin, Alexander F. and Robert W. Steel (eds.). *The Oxford region: a scientific and historical survey*. Oxford, 1954.

87 Raine, Angelo. *Medieval York: a topographical survey based on original sources*. 1955. An interesting and valuable model, as is Honeybourne for London (1483, 1484), and Walker for Nottingham (1493); more for York (153).

88 Steers, James A. *The coastline of England and Wales*. 2nd ed., Cambridge, 1964. Provides detailed geological descriptions, and see his 1960 ed. for photographs of same.

89 Wagner, Anthony R. *English genealogy*. 2nd ed., enlarged, Oxford, 1972. Broad chronological coverage but the single best guide to this popular topic, and absolutely essential for social history, esp. for heraldry (1045).

III. GENERAL SURVEYS

90   Bagley, John J. *Historical interpretation: sources of English medieval history, 1066–1540*. Baltimore, 1965. Collection of translated excerpts from well-known documents of general interest, available in paperback.

91   Chrimes, Stanley B. *Lancastrians, Yorkists and Henry VII*. 1964. Straight political history, allegedly for first-year undergraduates; sometimes unconvincing because of author's arbitrary judgements.

92   Curtis, Edmund. *A history of medieval Ireland, from 1086 to 1513*. New York, 1968. A revision of the 1938 edition, of solid merit, as is James Lydon's succinct 1973 survey, available in paperback, and see (108).

93   Du Boulay, Francis R.H. *An age of ambition: English society in the late middle ages*. 1970. Learned and well-written essays that raise stimulating themes without resolving them.

94   Elton, Geoffrey R. *England: 1200–1640* (Sources of History series). 1969. Comprehensive, excellent introduction to the variety and uses of extant sources, published and unpublished. Research students must begin here, then Baker (48) and (69, 97, 295).

95   Green, Vivian H.H. *The later Plantagenets: a survey of English history between 1307 and 1485*. 1955. See (710).

96   Holmes, George A. *The later middle ages, 1272–1485*. 1962. Well-written, comprehensive narrative of events with a wide range of social and institutional analyses, available in paperback; similarly, see Wilkinson (293).

97   Jack, R. Ian. *Medieval Wales* (Sources of History series). 1972. Fundamental, essential description of the evidence, following Elton (94); for Welsh history, read (1953) and see (3, 12, 85, 123, 139, 205, 240–2, 317, 321, 324, 340, 399, 605, 606, 634, 655, 660, 672, 716, 749, 754, 765, 766, 775, 780, 781, 793, 809, 851, 1093, 1098, 1165, 1186, 1195, 1196, 1213, 1297, 1321, 1351, 1424, 1728, 1786, 1901, 1927, 2044, 2172, 2282, 2283, 2322, 2465, 2484, 2486); and generally, Howell T. Evans, *Wales in the wars of the roses*, Cambridge, 1915.

98   Jacob, Ernest F. *The Oxford history of England. The fifteenth-century, 1399–1485*. Oxford, 1961. Disappointingly difficult but detailed prose, containing a thorough bibliography. Substantial criticism by Stanley B. Chrimes in *History*, XLVIII, 1963, pp. 18–27.

99   Keen, Maurice H. *England in the later middle ages*. 1973. Lively and first-rate survey based on latest scholarship.

100   Kingsford, Charles L. *English historical literature in the fifteenth-century*. Oxford, 1913 (repr. New York, 1963). Unique survey of the literary evidence, pioneering an historiographical perception of literature that too often remains unappreciated (1569, 2478, 2483); also, his important survey (1067).

101   Lander, Jack R. *Conflict and stability in fifteenth-century England*. 1969. Readable, intelligent survey for undergraduates.

102   —— *The wars of the roses*. 1965. Somewhat turgid narrative sandwiched amongst lengthy quotes from the major literary sources; a straight, well-illustrated description of these events has been published by Hubert Cole, 1974, or preferably the well produced study by Charles D. Ross, 1976.

103   McFarlane, Kenneth B. 'England: The Lancastrian kings, 1399–1461', and Charles H. Williams, 'England: The Yorkist kings, 1461–1485', in Charles W. Previté-Orton and Z.N. Brooke (eds.), *The Cambridge medieval history*, VIII, *The close of the middle ages*. Cambridge, 1936, pp. 362–449. The McFarlane chapter is assuredly fundamental, with a sound bibliography (701).

104   McKisack, May. *The Oxford history of England. The fourteenth-century, 1307–1399*. Oxford, 1959. Vigorous, scholarly, well-written narrative of events and major institutions.

105   Myers, Alec R. *England in the late middle ages*. 2nd ed., 1963. Careful, detailed, and considered judgements make this a reliable paperback survey.

106   —— (ed.). *English historical documents*, IV, *1327–1485*. 1969. Superb
       collection of sources, organized and introduced in a judicious, compre-
       hensible manner, exemplifying political and cultural life, with helpful
       bibliographies.
107   Nicholson, Ranald. *Scotland: the later middle ages*. Edinburgh, 1974.
       Thorough, immensely learned, and readable, with good bibliography (629,
       1520).
108   Otway-Ruthven, Annette J. *A history of medieval Ireland*. 1968. An erudite
       and important synthesis, but crippled by its prose; so see (92).
109   Poole, Austin L. (ed.). *Medieval England*, 1958, 2 vols. Collection of nineteen
       essays on recreation, education, costumes, religion, and diverse other
       topics (1062).
110   Powicke, Frederick M. *Medieval England, 1066–1485*. 1931.
111   —— *Modern historians and the study of history*. 1955. Historiographical
       essays and biographies of Tait, Tout, Willard, Haskins, and other scholars
       of the period.
112   Powicke, Michael R. *The community of the realm [1154–1485]*. New York,
       1973.
113   Smith, Lacey B. *This realm of England 1399–1688*. Boston, 1966. General,
       usually reliable relation of events in a jaunty prose.
114   *Victoria history of the counties of England*. (Many volumes still in progress,
       ed. by William Page, Ralph B. Pugh *et alii*.) See R.B. Pugh, *Victoria His-
       tory of the Counties of England: General Introduction*. 1970. Consult
       appropriate volume for each county on a wide variety of topics, especially
       for references to local evidence.

IV. CONSTITUTIONAL AND ADMINISTRATIVE HISTORY

1 Printed sources

115   Abram, William A. (ed.). *The rolls of burgesses at the guilds merchant of the
       borough of Preston, 1397–1682* (Record Society for Lancashire and
       Cheshire, IX). 1884.
116   Amphlett, John (ed.). *Lay subsidy rolls, 6 and 7 Henry VI, 1427–9, for the
       county of Worcester*. 1902. Further material on royal taxation (119, 126,
       135, 140, 156, 172, 195, 212, 214, 221, 252, 262, 275, 356, 413, 460,
       485, 514, 515, 539, 952, 956, 957, 1161, 1172, 1632, 1733, 2018).
117   Anderson, Roger C. (ed.). *Letters of the fifteenth and sixteenth centuries,
       from the archives of Southampton* (Southampton Record Society, XXII).
       1921. Further material for city and town government (115, 118, 130–2,
       134, 150, 153, 154, 162, 169, 180–4, 190, 197, 210, 222, 245, 249, 251,
       254, 256, 258, 266, 269, 294, 314, 325, 331, 333, 353, 1061).
118   —— (ed.). *The assize of bread book 1477–1517* (Southampton Record
       Society, XXIII). 1923. More for Southampton in (117, 150, 180–3,
       1153, 1156, 1157, 1169, 1170, 1211, 1226, 1227, 1274, 1284).
119   Anon. (ed.). 'Assessment roll of the poll-tax for Howdenshire, etc., 1379',
       Yorks J, IX (1886), 129–162. And see (116), also (126, 212).
120   —— *Court rolls of the manor of Carshalton, [Edward III–Henry VII]*
       (Surrey Record Society, II, no. 8). 1916. More material on manor courts
       (138, 141, 175, 185, 192, 229, 296, 330, 360, 370, 402, 421, 431, 446,
       532, 1160, 1162, 1168, 1175, 1180, 1182, 1183, 1196, 1199, 1218,
       1228, 1230, 1246, 1360).
121   —— *Natura brevim, or la vieux natura brevium*. 1510, 1516, 1528, etc.
       Probably compiled temp. Edward III for original and judicial writs; then
       Anthony Fitzherbert (171) compiled temp. Henry VIII. See *Registrum*
       (125), Maitland (285, 462), and (144, 170, 280).
122   —— *Original documents: I, Add. Roll 26596, Brit. Mus. . . . ; II, Add.*

Charters 7198 ... ; III, *Add. Roll 26595* (Supp. to *Arch Camb*). 1913–15.

123 —— 'Proceedings before the commissioners appointed by the lords of the lordship of Bromfield and Yale, and statutes made at the great court of that lordship, holden at Castle Leon, Anno 7° Edw. IV, A.D. 1467', *Arch Camb*, II (1847), 147–52, 210–15, 335–8; III (1848), 66–8, 107–10. See (97, 139, 242).

124 —— *The records of the honourable society of Lincoln's Inn: admissions, 1420–1893, and chapel registers*, 1896, 2 vols; [and] ... *the black books [1422–1485]*, 1897–1902, 4 vols. Materials on the legal profession (136, 267, 271, 318), and generally (280).

125 —— *Registrum omnium brevium tam originalium quam judicialium*. 1531. See (121).

126 —— 'Rolls of the collectors in the West-Riding of the lay subsidy of (poll-tax) 2 Richard II', *Yorks J*, V (1879), 1–51, 241–66, 417–32; VI (1880), 1–44, 129–71, 287–342; VII (1882), 6–31, 145–93. See (116).

127 Baildon, William P. (ed.). *Select cases in chancery, A.D. 1364–1471* (Selden Society, X). 1896. Inadequate selection of documents and introduction must be used with care; other materials on chancery are in (145–9, 228, 231–3, 272, 278, 324, 361, 362, 365, 394, 420, 429, 490, 501, 529, 541, 548, 2280, 2296).

128 Bateson, Mary (ed.). *Borough customs* (Selden Society, XVIII, XXI). 1904–6, 2 vols. Extensive coverage, organized topically, from twelfth through fifteenth centuries; more materials for borough government and courts leet (129, 143, 159, 160, 166, 203, 250, 264, 274, 303, 340, 369, 395, 487, 517, 540, 543, 544).

129 —— (ed.). *Records of the borough of Leicester* ... , II, *1327–1509*. Cambridge, 1901. Also ed. of *Cambridge gild records*, esp. for 1378–86, and use Charles H. Cooper's 1842 ed. of diverse town and university annals.

130 Beaven, Alfred B. *The aldermen of the city of London, temp. Henry III–1908*. 1908–13, 2 vols. Complete lists, ward by ward, with full notes; further materials for London (34, 156, 249, 258, 262, 266, 294, 304, 312, 331, 384, 504, 583, 588, 598, 626, 647, 674, 733, 734, 785, 1158, 1188, 1198, 1223, 1263, 1293, 1303, 1309, 1330, 1355, 2337).

131 Benham, William G. (ed.). *The red paper book of Colchester*. Colchester, 1902. Diary of a fifteenth-century town; also ed. of *The oath book or red parchment book*, 1907.

132 Bennett, John H.E. (ed.). *The rolls of the freemen of the city of Chester 1392–1700* (Record Society for Lancashire and Cheshire, LI). 1906. Contains records for the twenty-two years preceding 1485.

133 Berry, Henry F. (ed.). *Statutes and ordinances and acts of parliament of Ireland, John to* ... *[1472]*. Dublin, 1907–14, 3 vols. Two continuing volumes ed. by James F. Morrissey, Dublin, 1934–41; and see Graves (186), Hunter (201); on the Irish parliamentary rolls read Henry G. Richardson, *EHR*, LVII, 1943, pp. 448–61; and see (1, 142, 313, 409, 678, 877).

134 Bickley, Francis B. (ed.). *The little red book of Bristol*. 1900, 2 vols. Especially for diverse fifteenth-century town and guild ordinances; also, Henry Bush's ed. of town documents, 1828; see (154, 269, 664, 1154, 1243, 1290) on Bristol, or generally (117).

135 Blaauw, William H. (ed.). 'Subsidy collected from the clergy of Sussex, 3 Richard II, 1380', *SussexS*, V (1852), 229–43. See (116).

136 Bland, Desmond S. (ed.). *Early records of Furnival's Inn*. Newcastle-upon-Tyne, 1957. Various accounts, fifteenth through seventeenth centuries (124).

137 Bond, Maurice F. *Guide to the records of parliament*. 1971. Further materials for parliament generally (163, 227, 248, 253, 257, 261, 263, 273, 288, 308, 316, 319, 320, 336, 338, 341, 344, 345, 348, 379, 382, 387, 388, 396, 405, 407, 408, 426, 480, 482, 483, 498, 508, 512, 524, 525, 561).

9

138 ——— (ed.). 'A Farnborough [Kent] court roll of 1408', *Arch Cant*, LVII (1944), 21–5. See (120).

139 Bowen, Ivor (ed.). *The statutes of Wales [1215–1902]*. London, 1908. For Welsh law generally, see (167, 240, 242, 250, 260, 317, 321); and (97, 1953, 2283).

140 Boyd, William K. (ed.). 'Poll-tax of A.D. 1379–81 for the hundreds of Offlow and Cuttlestone', *SaltS*, XVII (1896), 153–205. See (116).

141 Bradbrook, William (ed.). 'Manor court rolls of Fenny Stratford and Etone (Bletchley)', *Records of Buckinghamshire*, XI (1924), 289–314. Thoroughly abstracted for 1373–95 (120).

142 Brewer, John S., and William Bullen (eds.). *Calendar of the Carew manuscripts, preserved in the archiepiscopal library at Lambeth*, V: *Book of Howth and miscellaneous papers*. 1871. Important for administration of Ireland (133).

143 Briers, Phyllis M. (ed.). *Henley borough records; assembly books i–iv, 1395–1543* (Oxfordshire Record Society, XLI). 1960. See (128).

144 Brooke, Robert. *La graunde abridgement*. 1568. Revisions and additions to original compilation of Anthony Fitzherbert (170), organized by topics.

145 *Calendar of charter rolls; Vols. V and VI, [1341–1516]*, ed. by Henry C. Maxwell Lyte *et al.* 1916–27, 2 vols. Recording royal grants, or confirmations of existing grants, of land, peerage, or privilege to numerous subjects and of a more private nature. See particular lists (228–41).

146 *Calendar of close rolls [1377–1485]*, ed. by Henry C. Maxwell Lyte *et al.* 1914–54, 22 vols. Recording royal administrative and executive orders, writs of summons to parliament, and endorsements with private deeds and titles to land.

147 *Calendar of fine rolls [1377–1485]*, ed. by Henry C. Maxwell Lyte *et al.* 1926–61, 13 vols. Recording royal receipt of money for charters, licenses, naturalizations, pardons, livery of lands, etc. Also records appointments of sheriffs, customers, and diverse other royal officers.

148 *Calendar of miscellaneous inquisitions [1377–1422]*. 1957–69, 4 vols. Includes diverse royal attempts to obtain information, for example, regarding rebels or persons possessing liberties, in order to protect royal interest.

149 *Calendar of patent rolls [1377–1485]*, ed. by Henry C. Maxwell Lyte *et al.*, 1895–1911, 21 vols. Distinct from the Close Rolls (146), recording royal letters of a public nature that grant and authenticate various gifts of office, privilege, or delegated prerogative.

150 Chapman, Annie B.W. (ed.). *The black book of Southampton [1388–1503]* (Southampton Record Society, XIII–XIV). 1912, 2 vols. Includes town regulations and diverse legal memoranda (117, 118).

151 Chrimes, Stanley B. (ed.). 'Some letters of John of Lancaster as warden of the east marches toward Scotland [1399–1412]', *Speculum*, XIV (1939), 3–27. See (510, 556, 1513).

152 Clough, Marie (ed.). 'The book of Bartholomew Bolney', *Sussex Record Society*, LXIII (1964), 1–83. Extent book for legal titles in land, Bolney died 1477; for other cartulary and family muniments (26, 154, 155, 181, 249, 259, 274, 1149).

153 Collins, Francis (ed.). *Register of the freemen of the city of York, 1272–1558* (Surtees Society, XCVI). 1897. Other York materials are available in C. Caine's ed. of Thomas Widdrington, *Analecta Eboracensia* and in Francis Drake, *Eboracum*, 1736; for all of this see Dobson (1320). There is a general monograph on fifteenth-century York by Edwin Benson, 1920; other materials on York (87, 245, 246, 256, 735, 1096, 1187, 1220, 1301, 2257).

154 Cronne, Henry A. (ed.). *Bristol charters 1378–1499* (Bristol Record Society, XI). 1946. See (26, 134, 117).

155 Davies, John S. (ed.). *The Tropenell cartulary*, 1908, 2 vols. Transcripts of wide variety of Wiltshire family muniments, compiled 1464–88.

156 Davis, Eliza J. and Margaret I. Peake (eds.). 'Loans from the city of London to Henry VI, 1431–1449', *BIHR*, IV (1927), 165–72. See (116, 130).

157 Deiser, George F. (ed.). *Year books of Richard II. 12 Richard II. A.D. 1388–*

1389. Cambridge, Mass., 1914. Others edited by Neilson (217), Plucknett (226), Thornley (268), and Williams (276); generally (280).

158   Devon, Frederick (ed.). *Issues of the Exchequer, Henry III — Henry VI, from the Pell Records* (Record Commission). 1835. Translated extracts of royal payments, to 1461; on the legal side, some Exchequer plea rolls are described by DeLloyd J. Guth, in Arthur J. Slavin (ed.), *Tudor men and institutions,* Baton Rouge, Louisiana, 1972, pp. 101—22; further materials for the exchequer in (193, 194, 224, 228, 231, 234, 235, 237, 238, 350, 422, 423, 443, 444, 465, 528, 2280).

159   Dilks, Thomas B. (ed.). *Bridgwater borough archives [1377—1468]* (Somerset Record Society, LIII, LVIII, LX). 1938—48, 3 vols. See also, *HMC*, 1st and 3rd Reports, 1870—2; for the period 1468—85, see Dunning and Tremlett (166); generally (128).

160   ——— (ed.). 'A calendar of some medieval MSS in the custody of the Bridgwater Corporation. Brymore and Steyning MSS. [1200-1484]', *Collectanea II* (Somerset Record Society, LVII). 1942, pp. 25—50.

161   ——— (ed.). 'A summons of the green wax to the sheriff of Somerset and Dorset', *Collectanea I* (Somerset Record Society, XXXIX). 1924, pp. 175—206. Bridgwater borough muniment no. 187, dated 1465—8.

162   Drinkwater, Charles H. (ed.). 'Burgess roll of Shrewsbury, 1416—17', *ShropsT*, 3rd ser., V (1905), 188—90. See also, *HMC*, 15th Report, series 47, 1899; more material for Shrewsbury in (172, 173, 195, 196, 208, 630, 1164, 1194, 1215, 1322, 1507); and (117).

163   Dugdale, William (ed.). *A perfect copy of all summons of the nobility to the great councils and parliaments of this realm from XLIX of King Henry III* . . . . 1685. Along with Prynne (227), still useful, as is (25, 44, 137, 1057).

164   Dunham, William H., Jr. (ed.). *The Fane fragment of the 1461 lords' journal* (Yale University Historical Publications, XIV). New Haven, Conn., 1935. For these records generally, see Geoffrey R. Elton, *EHR*, LXXXIX, 1974, pp. 481—512; and (176, 553).

165   Dunning, Robert W. (ed.). 'Thomas, Lord Dacre and the west march towards Scotland ? 1435', *BIHR*, XLI (1968), 95—9. Bid for office to Henry VI regarding financial accounts.

166   ——— and T.D. Tremlett (eds.). *Bridgwater borough archives V, 1468—1485* (Somerset Record Society, LXX). 1971. See Dilks (159), and (128, 1319).

167   Edwards, John G. (ed.). *Calendar of ancient correspondence concerning Wales* (University of Wales, History and Law Series, II). Cardiff, 1935. See (97, 139).

168   Ellis, Henry (ed.). 'Regulations framed in the reign of Richard II. for the government of the Tower of London', *Arch*, XVIII (1817), 275—80.

169   Elton, John (ed.). 'Early recorded mayors of Liverpool [1351—1481]: an original list with documentary authorities', *Lancs Historic*, LIV (1902), 119—30. See (117, 130).

170   Fitzherbert, Anthony. *La graunde abridgement.* 1514. Digests the Year Books under specific topics, cases cited chronologically, and revised later by Brooke under same title (144); see Winfield's general discussion (560).

171   ——— *La novelle brevium.* 1534. See (121, 125), all necessary when studying the various writs at common law.

172   Fletcher, William G.D. (ed.). 'The poll-tax for the town and liberties of Shrewsbury, 1380', *ShropsT*, 2nd ser., II (1890), 17—28. See (116, 162).

173   ——— (ed.). 'Some proceedings at the Shropshire assizes, 1414', *ShropsT*, 3rd ser., VII (1907), 390—6. See (208, 255).

174   Flower, Cyril T. (ed.). *Public works in mediaeval law* (Selden Society, XXXII, XL). 1915—23, 2 vols. Some fifteenth century materials but mainly earlier.

175   France, Reginald S. (ed.). 'Two custumals of the manor of Cockerham, 1326 and 1483', *Lancs Antiq*, LXIV (1954), 38—54. See (120).

176   Fraser, Constance M. (ed.). 'Some Durham documents relating to the Hilary Parliament of 1404', *BIHR*, XXXIV (1961), 192—9. Further materials for specific parliaments in (164, 346, 403, 418, 451, 452, 481, 498, 509, 511, 515, 531, 547, 552, 553, 843).

177   Furber, Elizabeth C. (ed.). *Essex sessions of the peace: 1351, 1377—1379*

(Essex Archaeological Society, Occasional Publications, no. 3). 1953. See (206–9, 255).

178   Furley, John S. (ed.). *The city government of Winchester from the records of the 14th and 15th Centuries*. Oxford, 1923. See also, *HMC*, 6th Report, 1877–8; also (117).

179   Gairdner, James (ed.). 'Ralph Lord Cromwell', *AJ*, XXX (1873), 75–89. Two letters: (1) states conditions under which he will become Lord Treasurer, 1432–3, and (2) enrolls patent 1452–3 of his exculpatory plea to Henry VI against Suffolk. See also (762).

180   Gidden, Harry W. (ed.). *The book of remembrance of Southampton 1440–1620 [and] 1303–1518* (Southampton Record Society, XXVII–XXVIII). 1927–8, 2 vols. See (117, 118).

181   —— (ed.). *The charters of the borough of Southampton* (Southampton Record Society, VII, IX). 1909–10, 2 vols.

182   —— (ed.). *The letters patent of Southampton 1415–1612* (Southampton Record Society, XX). 1919.

183   —— (ed.). *The sign manuals, and the letters patent of Southampton to 1422* (Southampton Record Society, XVIII). 1916.

184   Giraud, Francis F. (ed.). 'Faversham: regulations for the town porters, 1448', *Arch Cant*, XX (1893), 219–21.

185   Gomme, George L. (ed.). *Court rolls of Tooting Beck manor . . . 1394–1422.* 1909. See (120).

186   Graves, James (ed.). *A roll of the proceedings of the king's council in Ireland, (1392–93)* (Rolls Series, LXIX). 1877. See (133).

187   Gross, Charles (ed.). *Select cases from the coroners' rolls, A.D. 1265–1413, with a brief account of the history of the office of coroner* (Selden Society, IX). 1896. See Hunnisett (329), and generally (255).

188   —— (ed.). *Select cases concerning the law merchant A.D. 1270–1638*, I, *Local courts* (Selden Society, XXIII). 1908. Especially the Piepowder and the Fair Courts (373, 128).

189   Hall, Hubert (ed.). *Select cases concerning the law merchant A.D. 1239–1633*, II and III, *Central Courts* (Selden Society, XLVI, XLIX). 1929–32, 2 vols.

190   Harris, Mary D. (ed.). *The Coventry leet book, or mayor's register . . . [1420–1555]* (EETS, CXXXIV, CXXXV, CXXXVIII, CXLVI). 1907–13, 4 vols. See also, *HMC*, 15th Report, Series 47, 1899; also (412, 1151, 1229, 1331) and generally (117).

191   Harrod, Henry D. (ed.). 'A defence of the liberties of Chester, 1450', *Arch*, LVII (1900), 71–86. Against the Abbot and the crown.

192   Harvey, Barbara (ed.). 'Custumal [1391] and bye-laws [1386–1540] of the manor of Islip', *Oxfordshire Record Society*, XL (1959), 80–119. See (120).

193   Haskins, Charles H. and Mary D. George (eds.). 'Verses on the exchequer in the fifteenth-century', *EHR*, XXXVI (1921), 58–67. Written between 1398 and 1410, describing all stages of foreign accounts and who must be given fees and gifts (158).

194   Hemmant, Mary (ed.). *Select cases in the exchequer chamber before all the justices of England, 1377–1461 [and] 1461–1509* (Selden Society, LI, LXIV). 1933–45, 2 vols. See (158).

195   Hobbs, John L. (ed.). 'A Shrewsbury subsidy roll, 1445–46', *ShropsT*, LIII (1949–50), 68–75. See (116, 162).

196   Houghton, Kathleen N. (ed.). 'A document concerning the parliamentary election at Shrewsbury in 1478', *ShropsT*, LVII (1961–4), 162–5. Details the procedures followed; further materials for parliamentary elections in (273, 299, 328, 341, 347, 383, 384, 406, 430, 436, 453, 456, 471–3, 488, 509, 510, 519, 520, 523, 550, 554, 556, 557, 559).

197   Howlett, Richard (ed.). 'A fabric roll of the Norwich guildhall, A.D. 1410–1411', *NA*, XV (1904), 164–89. See (117).

198   Hull, Felix (ed.). *A calendar of the white and black books of the cinque ports, 1432–1955* (HMC and Kent Archaeological Society, Record Series, XIX). 1966. Previously only indexed by Henry B. Walker, 1905.

199 —— and Rosemary A. Keen (eds.). 'English politics and the sheriff of Kent, 1378', *Arch Cant*, LXXI (1957), 206–13. An indenture for transfer of twenty-three prisoners.

200 Hunnisett, Roy F. (ed.). 'Sussex coroners in the middle ages', *SussexS*, XCV (1957), 42–58; XCVI (1958), 17–34; XCVIII (1960), 44–70. See (329, 255).

201 Hunter, Joseph (ed.). *Rotuli selecti ad res Anglicas et Hibernicas spectantes* (Record Commission). 1834. Copies of grants from Irish Exchequer Memoranda Rolls, Henry V and Henry VI (133).

202 Jackson, John E. (ed.). 'Sheriff's turn, co. Wilts., A.D. 1439', *WiltsMag*, XIII (1872), 105–18.

203 Jeayes, Isaac H. (ed.). 'Court rolls of the borough of Colchester [1405–6]', *EssexT*, n.s., XIV (1918), 81–9. See (128).

204 Jenkins, John G. (ed.). 'An early coroner's roll for Buckinghamshire [1377–90]', *Records of Buckinghamshire*, XIII (1936), 163–85. See (329, 255).

205 Jones, Gwilym P. and Hugh Owen (eds.). *Caernarvon court rolls 1361–1402* (Caernarvonshire Historical Society, Record Series, I). 1951. See (97, 1165, 1437).

206 Kimball, Elisabeth G. (ed.). *Records of some sessions of the peace in Lincolnshire 1381–1396* (Lincolnshire Record Society, XLIX, LVI). 1955–62, 2 vols. See (247, 255).

207 —— (ed.). *Rolls of the Warwickshire and Coventry sessions of the peace, 1377–1397* (Dugdale Society, XVI). 1939. Also her important bibliographical essay in *University of Toronto Law Journal*, VI, 1945–6, pp. 401–13. Cautionary, contextual remarks about these peace rolls are in John B. Post's article, *Journal of the Society of Archivists*, IV, 1973, pp. 633–9.

208 —— (ed.). *The Shropshire peace roll, 1400–1414*. Shrewsbury, 1959. Indictments taken before JP's compiled for King's Bench justices' visit in 1414, with good introductory explanations; and (162, 173).

209 —— (ed.). 'Rolls of the Gloucestershire sessions of the peace, 1361–1398', *Bristol-Gloucs*, LXII (1940), 5–186. See (255).

210 Leach, Arthur F. (ed.). *Beverley town documents* (Selden Society, XIV). 1900. See also, *HMC*, Series 54, 1900; and (117).

211 Leadam, Isaac S. and James F. Baldwin (eds.). *Select cases before the king's council, 1243–1482* (Selden Society, XXXV). 1918. And Leadam's ed. regarding the Star Chamber jurisdiction *post* 1477, in Selden Society, XVI, 1902.

212 Lloyd, Eleanor (ed.). 'Poll-tax returns for the east riding, 4 Ric. II', *Yorks J*, XX (1909), 318–52. See (116, 119).

213 Lysons, Samuel (ed.). 'Copies of three remarkable petitions to king Henry the sixth . . . ', *Arch*, XVI (1812), 3–8.

214 Maclean, John (ed.). 'Knights' fees in Gloucestershire, 3 Henry IV', *Bristol-Gloucs*, XI (1887), 312–30. Levy of marriage aid by the King.

215 MacKenzie, William (ed.). *Legislation by three of the thirteen Stanleys, kings of Man. Acts of Sir John Stanley, A.D. 1417–1430* . . . (Manx Society, III). 1860.

216 Madox, Thomas. *Formulare Anglicanum: a collection of antient charters and instruments of diverse kinds . . . from the Norman conquest to the end of the reign of Henry VIII*. 1702. Still a good introduction to the models and formulae of royal records (29).

217 Neilson, Nellie (ed.). *Year books of Edward IV: 10 Edward IV and 49 Henry VI, A.D. 1470* (Selden Society, XLVII). 1931. See (157).

218 Nichols, John G. (ed.). *Grants, etc., from the crown during the reign of Edward V., from the original docket book, MS. Harl. 433* (Camden Society, LX). 1854.

219 —— (ed.). 'An original appointment of Sir John Fastolfe to be keeper of the Bastille of St Anthony, at Paris, in 1421', *Arch*, XLIV (1873), 113–23.

220 Nicolas, Nicholas H. (ed.). *Proceedings and ordinances of the privy council of England, 1386–1542* (Record Commission). 1834–7, 7 vols. Essential for understanding royal government, especially for transcriptions for 1386–1461, and the first register for 1540–2 in the final volume; see (298, 380).

221 Noyes, Thomas H. (ed.). 'Roll of a subsidy levied 13 Henry IV., 1411—12, so far as relates to Sussex', *SussexS*, (1858), 129—46. See (116), also (135).

222 Ogle, Octavius (ed.). *Royal letters addressed to Oxford and now existing in the city archives [1136—1684]*. Oxford, 1892. See (117, 254).

223 *Old tenures*. 1567. Fourteenth century treatise, pre-Littleton, published by Richard Tottel; see Coke (309).

224 Palgrave, Francis [Francis Cohen] (ed.). *The antient kalendars and inventories of the treasury of his majesty's exchequer* (Record Commission). 1836, 3 vols. See (158).

225 Parker, John W.R. (ed.). *Plea rolls of the county palatine of Lancaster, roll I [1401]* (Chetham Society, n.s., LXXXVII). 1928. See (255).

226 Plucknett, Theodore F.T. (ed.). *Year books of Richard II. 13 Richard II. 1389—1390*. 1929. See (157, 280).

227 Prynne, William (ed.). *A brief register, kalender, and survey of the several kinds of all parliamentary writs [1203—1483]*. 1659—64, 4 pts. See (137, 163).

228 Public Record Office. *Index of ancient petitions of the chancery and of the exchequer*. Rev. ed., 1966 (orig. ed., 1892), no. 1. See (127, 158, 231—3). For fuller meaning to the following entries consult HMSO (31), *Guide* under the appropriate institutional heading.

229 —— *List and index of court rolls*. 1896, No. 6. That is, of manorial court records now preserved in the PRO (120, 1179).

230 —— *List and index of warrants for issues, 1399—1485; with an appendix: indentures of war, 1297—1527*. 1964, Supp. Series No. 9, II.

231 —— *List of ancient correspondence of the chancery and the exchequer*. Rev. ed., 1970 (orig. ed., 1902), No. 15. And use *Index* to the same, 1969, 2 vols., Supp. Series No. 15.

232 —— *List of chancery rolls, 1199—1903*. 1908, No. 27. That is, the patent, close, charter, fine, liberate, and other rolls; see calendars (145—9).

233 —— *List of early chancery proceedings [1377—1485]*. 1901—3, 2 vols, nos. 12 and 16. Litigation before the lord chancellor, sitting at equity in civil pleadings; and use Walmisley's index (272).

234 —— *List of exchequer accounts, various. Henry III to George III*. 1912—69, 2 vols; no. 35 and no. 9 in Supp. Series, I. See (158).

235 —— *List of foreign accounts enrolled on the great rolls of the exchequer. Henry III to Richard III*. 1900, no. 11.

236 —— *List of inquisitions ad quod damnum. 19 Edward III — 2 Richard III*. 1906, no. 22.

237 —— *List of ministers' accounts*. 1894—97, 2 vols, nos. 5 and 8.

238 —— *List of plea rolls of various courts*. 1910, no. 4. That is, records of the formal enrollments of annual litigation before the justices in king's bench, common pleas, and elsewhere (255, 323).

239 —— *List of records of the duchy of Lancaster*. 1901, no. 14. Then see Somerville (349).

240 —— *List of records of the palatinates of Chester, Durham, and Lancaster, honour of Peveril, and principality of Wales*. 1914, no. 40. For Wales (97, 139).

241 —— *List of sheriffs for England and Wales from the earliest times to A.D. 1831*. 1898, no. 9.

242 Pugh, Thomas B. (ed.). *The marcher lordships of south Wales, 1415—1536*. Cardiff, 1963. Selection of documents with scholarly introductions (97, 123, 139).

243 Putnam, Bertha H. (ed.). *Early treatises on the practice of the justices of the peace in the fifteenth and sixteenth centuries*. (Oxford Studies in Social and Legal History, VII). Oxford, 1924. With the following item, the best introduction to royal judicial activities at the county level (280).

244 —— (ed.). *Proceedings before the justices of the peace in the fourteenth and fifteenth centuries: Edward III to Richard III*. 1938.

245 Raine, Angelo (ed.). *York civic records [The house books I—IV: 1474—1487]* (YorksRS, XCVIII). 1938. And see (117, 153).

246 Raine, James [the younger] (ed.). 'An account of the proceedings in a

14

remarkable case of adulteration at York (Reg. Civ. Ebor. A.Y. 255)', *English Miscellanies* (Surtees Society, LXXXV). 1890, pp. 1–10, 11–22. 22–34. The latter two articles pertain to presentments made in the 1470s in courts of the abbot of Selby and to diverse verdicts against violators of York's economic rules (153).

247　Redstone, Lilian J. (ed.). 'Norfolk sessions of the peace. Roll of mainpernors and pledges, 1394–1397', *Norfolk Record Society Publications*, VIII (1936), 1–14. See (206–9).

248　*Register of the ministers and of the members of both houses, 1439–1509. Issued by the committee of both houses charged with the production of the history.* 1938. See (137, 176, 196, 273).

249　Riley, Henry T. (ed.). *Munimenta gildhallae Londoniensis; liber albus, liber custumarum, et liber horn [to 1419]* (Rolls Series, XII). 1859–62, 3 vols. in 4 parts. The third volume is his translation of *Liber Albus* separately, 1862; see his *Memorials* (1032).

250　Robinson, W.R.B. (ed.). 'An analysis of a minister's account for the borough of Swansea for 1449', *BBCS*, XXII (1967), 169–98. See (128).

251　Rogers, James E. Thorold (ed.). 'Miscellaneous', in *Oxford City Documents, Financial and Judicial 1268–1665* (Oxford Historical Society, XVIII). 1891, pp. 301–37. Merton College accounts 1448–50 and rental for Oxford town 1379 (254).

252　—— (ed.). 'Poll-tax and civil population of Oxford, 1380–1', in *Oxford City Documents, Financial and Judicial 1268–1665* (Oxford Historical Society, XVIII). 1891, pp. 1–75. See (116, 254).

253　*Rotuli parliamentorum; ut et petitiones et placita in parliamento [1278–1504].* 1832, 6 vols. Volumes III–VI cover 1377 through 1504, complemented by (263); see (137).

254　Salter, Herbert E. (ed.). *Munimenta civitatis Oxonie* (Oxford Historical Society, LXXI). 1917. See (222, 251, 252, 261, 1077).

255　Sayles, George O. (ed.). *Select cases in the court of king's bench under Richard II, Henry IV and Henry V; Vol. VII* (Selden Society, LXXXVIII). 1971. Further materials for king's bench and the criminal jurisdiction (173, 177, 187, 200, 204–9, 225, 238, 247, 265, 270, 279, 302, 329, 339, 370, 377, 415–17, 419, 432, 439, 500, 502, 2280).

256　Sellers, Maud (ed.). *York memorandum book (1376–1419) ... (1388–1493)* (Surtees Society, CXX, CXXV). 1912–15, 2 vols. Contains records of elections, ordinances and accounts (153, 117).

257　Shadwell, Lionel L. (ed.). *Enactments in parliament specially concerning the universities of Oxford and Cambridge, the colleges and halls therein and the colleges of Winchester, Eton, and Westminster, Volume I, 37 Edward III–13 Anne* (Oxford Historical Society, LVIII). 1911.

258　Sharpe, Reginald R. (ed.). *Calendar of letter-books preserved among the archives of the corporation of the city of London [to 1497].* 1899–1912, 11 vols. See Thomas (266), and generally (130, 117).

259　Shickle, Charles W. (ed. and trans.). *Ancient deeds belonging to the corporation of Bath* (Bath Record Society, I). 1921. See (264, 1172).

260　Smith, J. Beverley (ed.). 'The regulation of the frontier of Meirionnydd in the fifteenth-century', *Journal of the Merioneth Historical and Record Society*, V (1966), 105–11. See his article in Welsh on bonds and agreements, *BBCS*, XXI, 1966, pp. 309–24.

261　Smith, Lucy T. (ed.). 'Parliamentary petitions [1279–1496] relating to Oxford', *Collectanea III* (Oxford Historical Society, XXXII). 1896, pp. 77–161. See (137, 176, 196).

262　Stahlschmidt, J.C.L. (ed.). 'Lay subsidy, temp. Henry IV [London, 1411–12]', *AJ*, XLIV (1887), 56–82. See (116, 130).

263　*Statutes of the realm [1235–1713]*, ed. Alexander Luders, T.E. Tomlins, et al. (Record Commission). 1810–28, 11 vols. Particularly vol. II covering 1377 through 1504, and see (253).

264　Stevenson, William H. (ed.). *Records of the borough of Nottingham: extracts from the archives of the corporation [1155–1702].* 1882–1900, 5 vols. See also *HMC*, 1st Report, 1870; similarly, for Northampton borough, see

Christopher A. Markham and John C. Cox, 1898, 2 vols.; Stevenson cal-
endared relevant Gloucester corporation records, 1893; for Bath, see
Austin J. King and B.H. Watts, 1885; for Norwich, William Hudson and
John C. Tingey, 1906–10, 2 vols.; for King's Lynn, Henry D. Harrod,
1874; for Reading corporation, John M. Guilding, 1892–96, 4 vols.;
Henry Wood for Tamworth, 1952; generally (128).

265 Taylor, Mary M. (ed.). 'Some sessions of the peace in Cambridgeshire in the
fourteenth-century, 1340, 1380–83', *Cambridge Antiquarian Society*,
LV (1942), 1–66. See (255, 206–9).

266 Thomas, Arthur H. (ed.). *Calendar of select pleas and memoranda of the city
of London preserved . . . at Guildhall, A.D. 1381–1412* [and] . . . *1413–
1437*, Cambridge, 1932–43, 2 vols. And Philip E. Jones' continuation for
1458–82, publ. 1961; also (258, 130), and generally (117).

267 Thorne, Samuel E. (ed.). *Readings and moots at the Inns of Court in the
fifteenth-century* (Selden Society, LXXI). 1954. Essential for understanding legal training (280); specifically (124, 433, 537).

268 Thornley, Isobel D. (ed.). *Year books of Richard II. 11 Richard II. 1387–
1388.* 1937. See (157).

269 Veale, Edward W.W. (ed.). *The great red book of Bristol* (Bristol Record
Society, II, IV, VIII, XVI, XVIII). 1931–53, 5 vols. Contains deeds, wills,
safeconducts, trade licenses, and ordinances from fourteenth through sixteenth centuries; see Bickley (134).

270 Virgoe, Roger (ed.). 'Some ancient indictments in the king's bench referring
to Kent, 1450–1452', in Francis R.H. Du Boulay (ed.), *Kent records:
documents illustrative of medieval Kentish society*. Ashford, 1964, pp.
214–65. Regarding Cade's rebellion; generally (255, 290).

271 Walker, James D. and William P. Baildon (eds.). *The records of the honourable society of Lincoln's Inn. The black books*, I, *from A.D. 1422 to A.D.
1586*. 1897. See (124).

272 Walmisley, Claude A. (ed.). *An index of persons named in early chancery proceedings, Rich. II (1385) to Edward IV (1467), preserved in the Public
Record Office, London* (Harleian Society, LXXVIII–LXXIX). 1927–28,
2 vols. See (127, 233).

273 Wedgwood, Josiah C. [with Anne D. Holt]. *History of parliament. Biographies of the members of the Commons House, 1439–1509*. 1936, 2 vols.
In serious need of correction and revision, remains the valuable compilation of names (248); and generally (137, 176, 196). The 'History of
Parliament' project is currently at work in the pre-1439 era, under the
direction of John S. Roskell.

274 Weinbaum, Martin. *British borough charters, 1307–1660*. Cambridge, 1943.
See (128, 1149).

275 Willard, James F. and Harold C. Johnson (eds.). *Surrey taxation returns,
fifteenths and tenths; being the 1332 assessment and subsequent assessments to 1623* (Surrey Record Society, XI). 1932. Important introduction
on the royal tax structure (116).

276 Williams, Charles H. (ed.). *Year books of Henry VI: 1 Henry VI, A.D. 1422*
(Selden Society, L). 1933. See (157, 280).

277 Williams, George (ed.). *Official correspondence of Thomas Bekynton, secretary to Henry VI, and bishop of Bath and Wells* (Rolls Series, LVI).
1872, 2 vols. See (808, 896).

278 Wrottesley, George (ed.). 'Early chancery proceedings, Richard II to Henry
VII', *SaltS*, n.s., VII (1904), 239–93. See (127).

279 ——— (ed.). 'Extracts from plea rolls [1360–1485]', *SaltS*, 1st ser., XIII
(1892), 1–204; XIV (1893), 1–162; XV (1894), 1–126; XVI (1895),
1–93; XVII (1896), 1–153; n.s., III (1900), 121–229; IV (1901), 95–
212; VI (1903), 89–164. And generally (255).

2 Surveys

280 Beale, Joseph H. *A bibliography of early English law books*. Cambridge,
Mass., 1926. Also, *A supplement . . .* by Robert B. Anderson, 1943;

further materials in legal literature, including the year-books (6, 53, 56, 157, 226, 243, 267, 268, 276, 287, 295, 305, 309, 326, 327, 2315).

281 Chrimes, Stanley B. and Alfred L. Brown. *Select documents of English constitutional history, 1307–1485*. 1961.

282 Jolliffe, John E.A. *The constitutional history of medieval England, from the English settlement to 1485*. 1937; 4th ed., 1961 [1962]. Like Thomas P. Taswell-Langmead's survey, use only if Lyon (284) or Wilkinson (292) are unavailable.

283 Lodge, Eleanor C. and Gladys A. Thornton. *English constitutional documents, 1307–1485*. Cambridge, 1935.

284 Lyon, Bryce D. *A constitutional and legal history of medieval England*. New York, 1960. Excellent basic reference for students (286).

285 Maitland, Frederic W. *The collected papers of Frederic William Maitland*, ed. by Herbert A.L. Fisher. Cambridge, 1911. 3 vols. Provides enormous range of sensible and sensitive insights; also, use his published lectures on *Equity [and] Forms of Action at Common Law*, Cambridge, 1909, and *Constitutional History*. Although considerably earlier in time, his *History of English law*, written with Frederick Pollock, is the basic reference that you ignore at your peril.

286 Milsom, Stroud F.C. *Historical foundations of the common law*. 1969. Most important survey for English legal history: clear, complex, trenchant. Further materials on the common law, generally (284, 285, 289, 323, 326, 327, 351, 366, 458, 477, 484, 494).

287 Nicholson, Jennifer. *Register of manuscripts of year books extant* (Preliminary edition). 1956. A useful essay by William S. Holdsworth is in *LQR*, XXII, 1906; and see Charles C. Soule's *Year book bibliography*, Cambridge, Mass., 1900, with addenda in *Harvard Law Review*, XIV, 1900, pp. 557–87; also (305).

288 Pike, Luke O. *A constitutional history of the House of Lords, from original sources*. 1894. Or the survey by Powell and Wallis (338); generally (137, 176, 196).

289 Plucknett, Theodore F.T. *A concise history of the common law*. 5th ed., 1956.

290 Storey, Robin L. *The end of the house of Lancaster*. 1966. Interesting analysis, particularly in his use of King's Bench manuscripts, but occasionally uneven and uncritical.

291 Stubbs, William. *The constitutional history of England*. Oxford, 1874–8, 3 vols. Remains the great, old survey despite criticisms of Richardson and Sayles, but now outdated in method and conclusions.

292 Wilkinson, Bertie. *Constitutional history of England in the fifteenth-century, 1399–1485*. 1964. Also, see his three volumes for period before 1399.

293 ——— *The later middle ages in England 1216–1485*. 1969.

294 Williams, Gwyn A. *Medieval London: from commune to capital*. 1963. Generally, see (130); and Caroline M. Barron, *The medieval Guildhall of London*, 1974.

295 Winfield, Percy H. *The chief sources of English legal history*. Cambridge, Mass., 1925.

3 Monographs

296 Ault, Warren O. *Open-field husbandry and the village community: a study of agrarian by-laws in medieval England* (Transactions of the American Philosophical Society, n.s., LV, pt. 7). 1965. See (120, 360, 1417, 1426).

297 Baldwin, Frances E. *Sumptuary legislation and personal regulation in England* (Johns Hopkins University Studies in History and Political Science 44, i). Baltimore, Md., 1926. Mainly sixteenth century but still of interest.

298 Baldwin, James F. *The king's council in England during the middle ages*. Oxford, 1913. Good discussion of the institution and its records, including an edition of extant council register 1392–3 (220), and generally (380).

299 Bassett, Margery. *Knights of the shire for Bedfordshire during the middle ages* (Bedfordshire Historical Record Society, XXIX). Streatley, 1949. And generally (137, 176, 196).

300 Bean, John M.W. *Decline of English feudalism, 1215–1540*. Manchester, 1968. Emphasizes alienation of land and the employment of *cestui que use*, presenting a most important discussion about administration.

301 Bellamy, John G. *The law of treason in England in the later middle ages*. (Cambridge studies in English Legal History). 1970. Stresses growth of royal interest and pre-emption of more popular styles of offences against the nobility and crown; and see (493, 496–7, 518, 527), plus some literary evidence (445) and the Rezneck (507) – Thornley (546) debate. Other materials on treason (392, 441, 447, 450, 508, 1979).

302 —— *Crime and public order in England and the later middle ages*. 1972. Detailed survey from published and unpublished cases with numerous anecdotes and generalizations but little quantitative analysis or careful definition (371); generally (255).

303 Beresford, Maurice W. and Herbert P.R. Finberg. *English medieval boroughs: a handlist*. Newton Abbot, 1973. See (128, 274).

304 Bird, Ruth. *The turbulent London of Richard II*. 1949. To be read with Barron (733); generally (130).

305 Bolland, William C. *A manual of year book studies*. Cambridge, 1925. Remains useful introduction and reference for legal sources (287).

306 Chrimes, Stanley B. *English constitutional ideas in the fifteenth century*. Cambridge, 1936. Basic study, despite Kenneth B. McFarlane's devastating review in *EHR*, LIII, 1938, pp. 707–10; Chrimes synthesized vital themes, mainly from the Year Books.

307 —— *An introduction to the administrative history of medieval England* (Studies in Medieval History, VII). Oxford, 1952. Excellent reference to sources for royal government, with unusually clear descriptions; and see Jewell (330) for local government.

308 Clarke, Maude V. *Medieval representation and consent. A study of early parliaments in England and Ireland*. 1936. See (137, 176, 196).

309 Coke, Edward. *The first part of the Institutes of the lawes of England; or, A commentarie on Littleton*. 1628. See (223).

310 Cox, John C. *The royal forests of England*. 1905.

311 —— *Sanctuaries and sanctuary seekers of medieval England*. 1911.

312 Craig, John H.M. *The mint: a history of the London mint from A.D. 282 to 1948*. Cambridge, 1953. And see Albert E. Feavearyear on the pound sterling, 1931; also (82, 130, 504).

313 Curtis, Edmund. *Richard II in Ireland 1394–5 and submissions of the Irish chiefs*. Oxford, 1927. See (133).

314 Curtis, Muriel E.H. *Some disputes between the city and the cathedral authorities of Exeter* (History of Exeter Research Group, V). Manchester, 1932. Mainly 1409 to 1449 (117, 1241); also, see the brief study of *The mediaeval council of Exeter*, Manchester, 1931, by Bertie Wilkinson (1395, 1412, 1618).

315 Du Boulay, Francis R.H. and Caroline M. Barron (eds.). *The reign of Richard II: essays in honour of May McKisack*. 1971. Superb collection of papers relating mainly to royal administration (692, 706).

316 Edwards, John G. *The commons in medieval parliaments*. 1958. Brief but learned synthesis for the fifteenth century (137, 176, 196, 348).

317 Ellis, Thomas P. *Welsh tribal law and custom in the middle ages*. Oxford, 1926, 2 vols. Fundamental, exhaustive work on the subject, now supplemented by (399); and generally (97).

318 Foss, Edward. *The judges of England, with sketches of their lives and miscellaneous notices connected with the courts at Westminster, from the time of the conquest*. 1848–64, 9 vols. There is a one volume abridgement, entitled *Biographia juridica*, 1870; and see his *Tabulae curiales*, 1865, for alphabetical lists of judges and attorneys-general.

319 Fryde, Edmund B. and Edward Miller (eds.). *Historical Studies of the English*

parliament. Cambridge, 1970, 2 vols. Valuable collection of recent, authoritative articles on parliament before 1603; and see Sayles (348); generally (137, 176, 196).

320 Gray, Howard L. *The influence of the commons on early legislation: a study of the fourteenth and fifteenth centuries*. Cambridge, Mass., 1932. For 'The first benevolence' in 1472–5, see *Facts and factors in economic history*, ed. by Norman S.B. Gras *et al.*, Cambridge, Mass., 1932, pp. 90–113.

321 Griffiths, Ralph A. *The principality of Wales in the later middle ages: the structure and personnel of its government*; I, *South Wales 1277–1538*. 1972. A biographical dictionary of local and royal officials (97, 139, 240–2).

322 Harcourt, Leveson W.V. *His grace the steward and trial of peers*. 1907.

323 Hastings, Margaret. *The court of common pleas in fifteenth-century England*. Ithaca, New York, 1947. Excellent institutional reconstruction by a careful, learned scholar, and a good introduction to the common law in execution.

324 Hearder, B.H. and H.R. Loyn (eds.). *British government and administration*. Cardiff, 1974. This *Festschrift* to S.B. Chrimes contains excellent articles: on Welsh political patronage, by Ralph A Griffiths; on north-eastern Welsh government by J. Gwynfor Jones; on the Chancery's personnel and jurisdiction, by Nicholas Pronay (127)'s reign, by Anthony B. Steel (1065); and on the campaign into Scotland in 1400, by A.L. Brown.

325 Hill, James W.F. *Medieval Lincoln*. Cambridge, 1948. And see the less impressive study of Leicester by Charles J. Billson (117).

326 Holdsworth, William S. *A history of English law*. 6th ed., rev., 1938. Particularly vols. I (use 1956 rev. ed.) and III, to be used with care and for general information only (286).

327 —— *Sources and literature of English law*. Oxford, 1925. See (280).

328 Hornyold-Strickland, Henry. *Biographical sketches of the members of parliament of Lancashire (1290–1550)* (Chetham Society, n.s., XCIII). 1935. And generally (137, 176, 196).

329 Hunnisett, Roy F. *The medieval coroner*. Cambridge, 1961. Essential in understanding criminal law enforcement; see also (187, 200, 204, 255).

330 Jewell, Helen M. *English local administration in the middle ages*. Newton Abbot, 1972. Useful as general introduction to institutional terms, structures, and sources, complementing Chrimes (307); and see (120).

331 Johnson, David J. *Southwark and the city*. 1969. Especially parts I and III; for London (130), and generally (117).

332 Legg, Leopold G.W. *English coronation records*. 1901. More on this topic (571).

333 Lobel, Mary D. *The borough of Bury St Edmunds. A study in the government and development of a monastic town*. Oxford, 1935.

334 Lyon, Bryce D. *From fief to indenture: the transition from feudal to nonfeudal contract in western Europe*. Cambridge, Mass., 1957. Fundamental study comparing military and social relationships defined in law and practice in England, France, and the Low Countries.

335 Lyte, Henry C. Maxwell. *Historical notes on the use of the great seal of England*. 1926. Still a good guide in royal Chancery procedure, along with Eugène Déprez's *Études*, Paris, 1908; for sigillography (337, 437, 564, 1986, 2262, 2277, 2338, 2339), and esp. the first 3 vols. by Walter de Gray Birch, *Catalogue of seals in the department of manuscripts in the British Museum*, 1887–1900, 6 vols.

336 McKisack, May. *The parliamentary representation of the English boroughs during the middle ages*. Oxford, 1932. Standard study, brief but thorough (137, 176, 196, 308).

337 Otway-Ruthven, Annette J. *The king's secretary and the signet office of the XV century*. Cambridge, 1939. For the work of royal clerks (277, 335, 381, 427, 486, 951).

338 Powell, J. Enoch and Keith Wallis. *The House of Lords in the middle ages*. 1968. Important but not especially profound, see Pike (288).

339   Pugh, Ralph B. *Imprisonment in medieval England*. 1968. Exhaustive
       catalogue-in-prose of data drawn from the Conquest to Elizabeth I, but
       weak on synthesis and institutional evolution; generally (255).

340   Pugh, Thomas B. (ed.). *Glamorgan county history*, III *The middle ages*.
       Cardiff, 1971. Extraordinarily valuable collection of careful, thorough
       articles on government in the lordships and boroughs (97, 128) by Pugh,
       Ralph A. Griffiths, and W.R.B. Robinson.

341   Reich, Aloyse M. *The parliamentary abbots to 1470. A study in English con-
       stitutional history* (University of California Publications in History, XVII).
       Berkeley, Calif., 1941. And (137, 176, 196).

342   Reid, Rachel R. *The king's council in the north*. 1921. Mainly Tudor.

343   *Reports from the Lords committees touching the dignity of a peer of the
       realm [to 1483]*. 1829, 5 vols.

344   Riess, Ludwig. *The history of the English electoral law in the middle ages*,
       trans. by Kathleen L. Wood-Legh. Cambridge, 1940. Actually revises the
       original 1885, German edition, relying upon *Rotuli parliamentorum* (253),
       and still valuable for reforms.

345   Roskell, John S. *The commons and their speakers in English parliaments
       1376–1523*. Manchester, 1965. Solid institutional analysis, with a lengthy
       description of parliamentary history from the Speakers' biographical per-
       spectives. Roskell has published at least 16 separate articles on individual
       speakers in diverse county historical periodicals.

346   —— *The commons in the parliament of 1422*. Manchester, 1954. Structural
       analysis, essential for understanding late-medieval parliaments, with em-
       phasis on reconstructing social composition and parliamentary process
       (176, 196, 137).

347   —— *The knights of the shire for the county palatine of Lancaster, 1377–
       1460* (Chetham Society, n.s., XCVI). 1937. And for Yorkshire's parlia-
       mentary representatives see [Eileen] A. Gooder in *YorksRS*, XCI, 1935;
       and generally (137, 176, 196).

348   Sayles, George O. *The king's parliament of England*. 1975.

349   Somerville, Robert. *History of the duchy of Lancaster*, I, *1265–1603*. 1953.

350   Steel, Anthony B. *The receipt of the exchequer 1377–1485*. Cambridge,
       1954. Uncritical but important starting point when attempting to under-
       stand the exchequer; this book incorporates at least seven of his earlier
       articles on the topic. See (422, 423, 443), for important addenda to Steel;
       on the Exchequer (158).

351   Sutherland, Donald W. *The assize of novel disseisin*. 1973. Definitive for law
       of property.

352   Tout, Thomas F. *Chapters in the administrative history of mediaeval England:
       the wardrobe, the chamber, and the small seals*. Manchester, 1920–33, 6
       vols. See interesting review by Charles Petit-Dutaillis, *Journal des Savants*,
       1929.

353   Winston, James E. *English towns in the wars of the roses*. Princeton, N.J.,
       1921. For towns, see Green (1061).

354   Wolffe, Bertram P. *The crown lands, 1461 to 1536: an aspect of Yorkist and
       early Tudor government*. New York, 1970. Careful introduction to a com-
       plicated subject, with superbly illustrative documentary examples; basic
       thesis challenged by Charles Ross (691). See Wolffe's useful Historical
       Ass'n., Aid for Teachers No. 12, 1966.

355   —— *The royal demesne in English history: the crown estate in the govern-
       ance of the realm from the conquest to 1509*. 1971. Fresh and fundamen-
       tal reappraisal of the limited role of land revenue in royal administration
       and the changes occurring in the fifteenth century.

4 Articles

356   Abbott, Isabel R. 'Taxation of personal property and of clerical incomes,
       1399 to 1402', *Speculum*, XVII (1942), 471–98. See (116).

357   Adams, Norma. 'The judicial conflict over tithes', *EHR*, LII (1937), 1–22.

Traces expansion of common law of property, through patronage and declaration that tithe questions are secular matters: more materials for the common law competition with the church (385, 397, 409, 440, 459, 461, 541, 555, 563, 1082, 1922, 2039, 2104, 2111, and especially (1756).

358 —— '*Nullius filius*: a study of the exception of bastardy in the law courts of medieval England', *University of Toronto Law Journal*, VI (1945–6), 361–84. Covering the thirteenth through the fifteenth centuries.

359 Allmand, Christopher T. 'Alan Kirketon: a clerical royal councillor in Normandy during the English occupation in the fifteenth-century', *JEH*, XV (1964), 33–9.

360 Ault, Warren O. 'Manor court and parish church in fifteenth-century England: a study of village by-laws', *Speculum*, XLII (1967), 53–67. See (120, 296, 1417).

361 Avery, Margaret E. 'An evaluation of the effectiveness of the court of chancery under the Lancastrian kings', *LQR*, LXXXVI (1970), 84–97.

362 —— 'The history of the equitable jurisdiction of chancery before 1460', *BIHR*, XLII (1969), 129–44. Both articles are sketchy and must be read with Nicholas Pronay's article (324), and see (127).

363 Bailey, Stanley J. 'Assignment of debts in England from the twelfth to the twentieth century', *LQR*, XLVII (1931), 516–35; XLVIII (1932), 248–71, 547–82. Especially Part II, but also see (476, 478, 549).

364 Barbour, Willard T. 'The history of contract in early English equity' in Paul Vinogradoff (ed.), *Oxford studies in social and legal history*, IV, pt. 1. Oxford, 1914, pp. 1–237. See (467–70, 478).

365 —— 'Some aspects of fifteenth-century chancery', *Harvard Law Review*, XXXI (1918), 834–59. See (127).

366 Barraclough, Geoffrey. 'Law and legislation in medieval England', *LQR*, LVI (1940), 75–92. Emphasizes revolution to modernity in 1399 (286).

367 Barton, John L. 'The medieval use', *LQR*, LXXXI (1965), 562–77.

368 Bassett, Margery. 'The Fleet Prison in the middle ages', *University of Toronto Law Journal*, V (1943–4), 383–402; *Speculum*, XVIII (1943), 233–46. Detailed description based on fifteenth century evidence, the second article focussing on Newgate (339); and (1484, 2074).

369 Bateson, Mary. 'The English and the Latin versions of a Peterborough court leet, 1461', *EHR*, XIX (1904), 526–8. And see (128).

370 Beckermann, John S. 'The articles of presentment of a court leet and court baron, in English, *c.* 1400', *BIHR*, XLVII (1974), 230–4. And see (120, 255).

371 Bellamy, John G. 'Justice under the Yorkist kings', *AJLH*, IX (1965), 135–55. Generalizes from several select legal actions, with more of the same in (302).

372 Belsheim, Edmund O. 'The old action of account', *Harvard Law Review*, XLV (1931–2), 466–500. Good for history and procedure, particularly for fifteenth century.

373 Benham, William G. 'Piepowder courts in Colchester [1443–62]' *Essex Review*, XLVI (1937), 204–9. See (128, 188).

374 Bennett, Josephine W. 'The mediaeval loveday', *Speculum*, XXXIII (1958), 351–70.

375 Betts, Arthur. 'The sorrows of a sheriff in the fifteenth-century', *Juridical Review*, XXII (1911), 305–15. John Paston, and the distinction between a fine and an amercement; for the Pastons (1011).

376 Blatcher, Marjorie. 'Distress infinite and the contumacious sheriff', *BIHR*, XIII (1936), 146–50.

377 —— 'The working of the court of king's bench in the fifteenth century', *BIHR*, XIV (1937), 196–9. Unfortunately the thesis remains unpublished; for common pleas, see Hastings (323); and Charles H. Williams, *BIHR*, I, 1925, pp. 69–72, offers a morsel of information (255).

378 Brown, Alfred L. 'The authorization of letters under the great seal', *BIHR*, XXXVII (1964), 125–56. Particularly for 6 Henry IV, of fundamental significance; generally (335).

379 —— 'The commons and the council in the reign of Henry IV', *EHR*, LXXIX (1964), 1–30. And generally (137, 176, 196).

380 —— 'The king's councillors in fifteenth-century England', *TRHS*, 5th ser., XIX (1969), 95–118. Through the 1420s, then see Virgoe (551), Kirby (442), Lander (448–9); and more generally (495), and for Richard II (455, 298).

381 —— 'The privy seal clerks in the early fifteenth-century', in Donald A. Bullough and Robin L. Storey (eds.), *The study of medieval records: essays in honour of Kathleen Major*. Oxford, 1971, pp. 260–81. See (337).

382 Cam, Helen M. 'The legislators of medieval England', *PBA*, XXXI (1947), 127–50. Major significance in tracing evolution of legislative motivations in pre-Tudor parliaments, published also in her *Law-finders and law-makers in medieval England*, 1962, pp. 132–58; and see (137, 176, 196, 387).

383 —— 'The relation of English members of parliament to their constituencies in the fourteenth century; a neglected text', *Liberties and communities in medieval England*. Cambridge, 1944, pp. 223–35.

384 —— 'Representation in the city of London in the later middle ages', *Album E. Lousee III* (1963), pp. 109–23. See (130, 176, 196).

385 Cheyette, Frederic. 'Kings, courts, cures, and sinecure: The statute of provisors and the common law', *Traditio*, XIX (1963), 295–349. Of fundamental importance for kingship and legal jurisdictions.

386 Chope, Richard P. 'The aulnager in Devon', *DevonA*, XLIV (1912), 568–96. From 1394 to 1478, but see (1242), esp. chapter 8.

387 Chrimes, Stanley B. ' "House of Lords" and "House of Commons" in the fifteenth-century', *EHR*, XLIX (1934), 494–7. And generally (137, 176, 196).

388 —— 'The liability of lords for payment of wages of knights of the shire', *EHR*, XLIX (1934), 306–8. See (453).

389 —— 'Recent contributions to the study of the administrative history of medieval England', *Annali della Fondazione Italiana per la Storia Amministrativa*, I (1964), 431–6.

390 —— 'Richard II's questions to the judges, 1387', *LQR*, LXXII (1956), 365–90. See (393).

391 Clark, Andrew. 'Maldon civil courts, 1402', *Essex Review*, XVI (1907), 126–33. Held by bailiffs in mote-hall each Monday, records fairly complete 1402–1504.

392 Clarke, Maude V. 'Forfeitures and treason in 1388', *TRHS*, 4th ser., XIV (1931), 65–94. Now see Rogers (518), and (527) for rigorous criticisms; also (301, 843).

393 Clementi, Dione. 'Richard II's ninth question to the judges', *EHR*, LXXXVI (1971), 96–113.

394 Coing, Helmut. 'English equity and the *Denunciatio Evangelica* of the canon law', *LQR*, LXXI (1955), 223–41. Argues fifteenth century similarities as cause for Chancery's expanding jurisdiction (127).

395 Cole, Sanford D. 'English borough courts', *LQR*, XVIII (1902), 376–87. See (128).

396 Cooper, Ivy M. 'The meeting-places of parliament in the ancient palace of Westminster', *JBAA*, 3rd ser., III (1938), 97–138. And generally (137, 176, 196), also (2279).

397 Dahmus, Joseph H. 'John Wyclif and the English government', *Speculum*, XXXV (1960), 51–68. See (1750, 2107).

398 Davies, James C. 'The records of the royal court [of Guernsey] ', *Reports and Transactions of La Société Guernesiaise*, XVI (1959), 404–14.

399 Davies, R.R. 'The twilight of Welsh law, 1284–1536', *History*, LI (1966), 143–64; *WHR*, V (1970), 1–30; *Past and Present*, LXV (1974), 3–23. See (97, 139).

400 Deiser, George F. 'The origin of assumpsit', *Harvard Law Review*, XXV (1911–12), 428–42.

401 Dix, Elizabeth J. 'The origins of the action of trespass on the case', *Yale Law*

Journal, XLVI (1936–7), 1142–76. Argues against Plucknett and Holdsworth for their emphasis on Statute Westm. II, and sees origins in fourteenth and fifteenth centuries' action of trespass *vi et armis*.

402 Du Boulay, Francis R.H. 'The Pagham estates of the archbishops of Canterbury during the fifteenth-century', *History*, XXXVIII (1953), 201–18. Especially valuable for description of enforcement of manorial customs (120, 1249).

403 Dunham, William H., Jr. 'Notes from the parliament at Winchester, 1449', *Speculum*, XVII (1942), 402–15. See (176, 196).

404 Dupont, André. 'Pour ou contre Le Roi D'Angleterre (Les titulaires de fiefs à la date du 2 avril 1426 . . .)', *Bulletin de la Société des Antiquaires de Normandie*, LIV (1957–8), 147–69. See (799, 944).

405 Edwards, John G. 'The emergence of the majority rule in English parliamentary elections', *TRHS*, 5th ser., XIV (1964), 175–96. See (137, 176, 196).

406 —— 'The Huntingdonshire parliamentary election of 1450', in T.A. Sandquist and Michael R. Powicke (eds.), *Essays in medieval history presented to Bertie Wilkinson*. Toronto, 1969, pp. 383–95. See (196).

407 —— 'The parliamentary committee of 1398', *EHR*, XL (1925), 321–33.

408 —— (ed.). 'Some common petitions in Richard II's first parliament', *BIHR*, XXVI (1953), 200–13.

409 Edwards, Robert D. 'The kings of England and papal provisions in fifteenth-century Ireland', in John A. Watt, John B. Morrall, and Francis X. Martin (eds.), *Medieval studies presented to Aubrey Gwynn, S.J.* Dublin, 1961, pp. 265–80. See (133, 357).

410 Ehrlich, Ludwik, 'Petitions of right', *LQR*, XLV (1929), 60–85.

411 Fowler, Robert C. and M.T. Martin. 'Legal proofs of age', *EHR*, XXII (1907), 101–3, 526–7; XXIX (1914), 323–4. The last is an addendum by Alfred E. Stamp (1000, 1016).

412 Fox, Levi (ed.). 'The administration of gild property in Coventry in the fifteenth-century', *EHR*, LV (1940), 634–47. See (190).

413 French, John. 'Collecting the poll tax at Felstead in 1381', *EssexT*, n.s., XIV (1918), 209–17. See (116).

414 Gilson, Julius P. 'A defence of the proscription of the Yorkists in 1459', *EHR*, XXVI (1911), 512–25.

415 Gollancz, Marguerite E.H.J. 'The system of gaol delivery as illustrated in the extant gaol delivery rolls of the fifteenth-century', *BIHR*, XVI (1939), 191–3. Also, London M.Litt. thesis by Judith Avrutick, 1967, on *oyer et terminer* commissions; and see Sillem (533), and generally (255).

416 Green, Thomas A. 'Societal concepts of criminal liability for homicide in mediaeval England', *Speculum*, XLVII (1972), 669–94. Distinguishes murder and homicide, based on reluctance of trial juries to convict, and corrects Kaye (439).

417 Hamil, Frederick C. 'The king's approvers: a chapter in the history of English criminal law', *Speculum*, XI (1936), 238–58.

418 Hanbury, Harold G. 'The legislation of Richard III', *AJLH*, VI (1962), 95–113. Describes so-called 'public' statutes in a superficial manner (176).

419 Harcourt, Leveson W.V. 'The baga de secretis', *EHR*, XXIII (1908), 508–29. And generally (255).

420 Hargreaves, Anthony D. 'Equity and the latin side of chancery', *LQR*, LXVIII (1952), 481–99. See (127).

421 Harrison, Edward. 'The court rolls and other records of the manor of Ightham as a contribution to local history', *ArchCant*, XLVII (1936), 169–218; XLIX (1937), 1–95. Provides a thorough analysis of manorial society, to 1509 (120).

422 Harriss, Gerald L. 'Fictitious loans', *EcHR*, 2nd ser., VII (1955), 187–99. To be read alongside Steel (350).

423 —— 'Preference at the medieval exchequer', *BIHR*, XXX (1957), 17–40. See (158–350).

424 —— 'The struggle for Calais: an aspect of the rivalry between Lancaster and York', *EHR*, LXXV (1960), 30–53. See (920, 956).

23

425 Harvey, Barbara. 'Draft letters patent of manumission and pardon for the men of Somerset in 1381', *EHR*, LXXX (1965), 89—91.

426 Haskins, George L. 'Parliament in the later middle ages', *AHR*, LII (1947), 667—83. Argues that the Commons before the sixteenth century are merely servants and petitioners to the royal prerogative in council; see (348), and generally (137, 176, 196).

427 Higham, Florence M.G. 'A note on the pre-Tudor secretary', in Andrew G. Little and Frederick M. Powicke (eds.), *Essays in medieval history presented to Thomas F. Tout*. Manchester, 1925, pp. 361—6. See (337).

428 Holdsworth, William S. 'The legal profession in the fourteenth and fifteenth centuries', *LQR*, XXIII (1907), 448—60; XXIV (1908), 172—83. To be read with Ives (433).

429 Holmes, Oliver Wendell, Jr. 'Early English equity', *LQR*, I (1885), 162—74. Emphasizes activity in the law of contract and uses (127).

430 Houghton, Kathleen N. 'Theory and practice in borough elections to parliament during the later fifteenth-century', *BIHR*, XXXIX (1966), 130—40. See (137, 176, 196, 336).

431 Hull, Felix. 'Court rolls of the manor of Great Dunmow, 1382—1507', *Essex Review*, XLIX (1940), 152—7. See (120).

432 Hunnisett, Roy F. 'The medieval coroners' rolls', *AJLH*, III (1959), 95—124, 205—21, 324—59, 383. Includes a list of rolls extant before 1422 (329, 255).

433 Ives, Eric W. 'Promotion in the legal profession of Yorkist and early Tudor England', *LQR*, LXXV (1959), 348—63. Premier scholar on the English legal profession, its social composition, training, and political influence. See his study of Sir Thomas Keble and numerous articles relating to the early Tudor era; and Simpson (537).

434 —— 'The reputation of the common lawyer in English society 1450—1550', *UBHJ*, VII (1959—60), 130—61.

435 Jack, R. Ian. 'Entail and descent: the Hastings inheritance, 1370 to 1436', *BIHR*, XXXVIII (1965), 1—19.

436 Jalland, Patricia. 'The influence of the aristocracy on shire elections in the north of England, 1450—1470', *Speculum*, XLVII (1972), 483—507. Identifies MP's with York or Lancaster, assuming cause and effect without convincing local evidence (196), but plausibly criticizes McFarlane and Roskell about such elections.

437 Jenkinson, [Charles] Hilary. 'The study of English seals: illustrated chiefly from examples in the Public Record Office', *JBAA*, 3rd ser., I (1937), 93—127. Clear description of the mechanics of sealing and writing letters (335).

438 Jenks, Edward. 'The story of the habeas corpus', *LQR*, XVIII (1902), 64—77. Fifteenth-century developments in this writ and in certiorari and privilege.

439 Kaye, J.M. 'The early history of murder and manslaughter', *LQR*, LXXXIII (1967), 365—95, 569—601. Modified by Green (416).

440 Ke Chin Wang, H. 'The corporate entity concept (or fiction theory) in the year book period', *LQR*, LVIII (1942), 498—511; LIX (1943), 72—86. Rejects Maitland's arguments (461), that corporations are fictitious, unitary entities possessing legal personalities; also (459).

441 Keen, Maurice H. 'Treason trials under the law of arms', *TRHS*, 5th ser., XII (1962), 85—103. Part of his major study (1535); and now see Bellamy (301), and (445).

442 Kirby, John L. 'Councils and councillors of Henry IV, 1399—1413', *TRHS*, 5th ser., XIV (1964), 35—65.

443 —— 'The issues of the Lancastrian exchequer and Lord Cromwell's estimates of 1433', *BIHR*, XXIV (1951), 121—51. See (158, 350).

444 —— 'The rise of the under-treasurer of the exchequer [1412—83]', *EHR*, LXXII (1957), 666—7.

445 Kratins, Ojars. 'Treason in middle English metrical romances', *Philological Quarterly*, XLV (1966), 668—87. Compares literary evidence to the law (301).

446 Lambert, Henry C.M. 'The Banstead court roll in the reigns of Richard II

... [to Henry VI]', *Surrey Archaeological Collections*, XXXVII (1926), 164–79; XXXVIII (1930), 18–33. See (120).

447 Lander, Jack R. 'Attainder and forfeiture, 1453 to 1509', *HJ*, IV (1961), 119–51. See Ross (527) and Bellamy (301).

448 —— 'Council, administration and councillors, 1461 to 1485', *BIHR*, XXXII (1959), 138–80. See (380).

449 —— 'The Yorkist council and administration', *EHR*, LXXIII (1958), 27–46. Lander has collected these articles in *Crown and nobility, 1450–1509*, 1976.

450 —— 'The treason and death of the Duke of Clarence: a re-interpretation', *Canadian Journal of History*, II (1967), 1–28. See Levine (791).

451 Lapsley, Gaillard T. 'The parliamentary title of Henry IV', *EHR*, XLIX (1934), 423–49, 577–606.

452 —— 'Richard II's "last parliament"', *EHR*, LIII (1938), 53–78. See (176).

453 Latham, Lucy C. 'Collection of the wages of the knights of the shire in the fourteenth and fifteenth centuries', *EHR*, XLVIII (1933), 455–64. See (388).

454 Lewis, Norman B. 'Article VII of the impeachment of Michael de la Pole in 1386', *EHR*, XLII (1927), 402–7. See Palmer (489).

455 —— 'The "continual council" in the early years of Richard II, 1377–80', *EHR*, XLI (1926), 246–51. See (380).

456 —— 'Re-election to parliament in the reign of Richard II', *EHR*, XLVIII (1933), 364–94. And generally (137, 176, 196).

457 Lewis, Peter S. 'Sir John Fastolf's lawsuit over Titchwell 1448–1455', *HJ*, I (1958), 1–20.

458 Lewis, Tom E. 'The history of judicial precedent', *LQR*, XLVI (1930), 207–24, 341–60; XLVII (1931), 411–27. Evidence drawn mainly and thoroughly from the year-books (280, 286).

459 Lubasz, Heinz. 'The corporate borough in the common law of the late year-book period', *LQR*, LXXX (1964), 228–43. Analyzes the Abbot of Hulme case 1482 to define the status of a borough corporation, thereby challenging Ke Chin Wang (440); see (461, 563).

460 Madge, Sidney J. 'The Middlesex poll-tax of 1380–81', *LondonMidd*, n.s., IV (1921), 313–22. See (116, 130).

461 Maitland, Frederic W. 'The corporation sole', *LQR*, XVI (1900), 335–54. Using the fifteenth-century year books, disputed by Ke Chin Wang (440).

462 —— 'The history of the register of original writs', *Harvard Law Review*, III (1889–1890), 97–115, 167–79, 212–25. Important for forms of civil actions before Henry VIII; and see (121, 125, 171, 285).

463 —— 'The seisin of chattels', *LQR*, I (1885), 324–41.

464 McFarlane, Kenneth B. 'At the death-bed of Cardinal Beaufort', in Richard W. Hunt, William A. Pantin, and Richard W. Southern (eds.), *Studies in medieval history presented to Frederick M. Powicke*. Oxford, 1948, pp. 405–28. See (796).

465 —— 'Loans to the Lancastrian kings: the problem of inducement', *CHJ*, IX (1947), 51–68. See (158).

466 —— 'Parliament and "bastard feudalism"', *TRHS*, 4th ser., XXVI (1944), 53–79. Similarly, his development of the cliché in *BIHR*, XX, 1943–45, pp. 161–80; see (1058), and (701, 797, 1092).

467 McGovern, William M., Jr. 'Contract in medieval England: the necessity for *quid pro quo* and a sum certain', *AJLH*, XIII (1969), 173–201. These four articles, plus Milsom (476–8), are essential on contract law.

468 —— 'Contract in medieval England: wager of law and the effect of death', *Iowa Law Review*, LIV (1968), 19–62.

469 —— 'The enforcement of informal contracts in the later middle ages', *California Law Review*, LIX (1971), 1145–93.

470 —— 'The enforcement of oral covenants prior to assumpsit', *Northwestern University Law Review*, LXV (1970), 576–614.

471 McHardy, Alison K. 'The representation of the English lower clergy in parliament during the later fourteenth century', in Derek Baker (ed.), *Sanctity and secularity: the church and the world*. Oxford, 1973, pp. 97–108; see (1982).

472 McKisack, May. 'Borough representation in Richard II's reign', *EHR*, XXXIX (1924), 511—25.

473 —— 'The parliamentary representation of King's Lynn before 1500', *EHR*, XLII (1927), 583—9. And generally (137, 176, 196).

474 Meyer, Erwin F. 'Some aspects of *withernam* or the English medieval system of vicarious liability', *Speculum*, VIII (1933), 235—40.

475 Mills, H.J. 'John of Northampton's pardons [1386—91]', *EHR*, LII (1937), 474—9.

476 Milsom, Stroud F.C. 'Account stated in the action of debt', *LQR*, LXXXII (1966), 534—45. Excellent definition of fifteenth-century laws relating to debtor—creditor (549).

477 —— 'Reason in the development of the common law', *LQR*, LXXI (1965), 496—517. General but keen commentary on changes in legal actions, especially in the fifteenth century (286).

478 —— 'Sale of goods in the fifteenth century', *LQR*, LXXVII (1961), 257—84. See (364).

479 Moule, Henry J. 'Notes on a book called Domesday belonging to the mayor and corporation of Dorchester', *Proceedings of the Dorset Natural History and Antiquarian Field Club*, XI (1890), 34—45. Containing local laws, rentals, etc., for the fifteenth century; Moule also edited select materials for the boroughs of Weymouth and Melcombe Regis.

480 Myers, Alec R. 'The English parliament and the French estates-general in the middle ages', *Album Helen Maud Cam*, II (1961), 139—53. And generally (137, 176, 196).

481 —— 'A parliamentary debate of the mid-fifteenth century', *BJRL*, XXII (1938), 388—404. Found in BM, Harleian MS. 6849, f. 77; and (176, 196).

482 —— 'Parliamentary petitions in the fifteenth century', *EHR*, LII (1937), 385—404, 590—613.

483 —— 'Some observations on the procedure of the commons in dealing with bills in the Lancastrian period', *University of Toronto Law Journal*, III (1939—40), 51—73.

484 Neilson, Nellie. 'The early pattern of the common law', *AHR*, XLIX (1944), 199—212. General outline of the diversities of customs and jurisdictions outside royal law (286).

485 Newhall, Richard A. 'The war finances of Henry V and the duke of Bedford', *EHR*, XXVI (1921), 172—98. See (116, 689, 1539).

486 Otway-Ruthven, Annette J. 'The king's secretary in the fifteenth century', *TRHS*, 4th ser., XIX (1936), 81—100. Previews her book (337).

487 Owen, Leonard V.D. 'The borough of Nottingham 1284—1485', *ThorotonS*, L (1946), 25—35. See Stevenson (264); also (128).

488 —— 'The representation of Nottingham and Nottinghamshire in the early parliaments', *ThorotonS*, XLVII (1943), 20—8. And generally (137, 176, 196).

489 Palmer, J.J.N. 'The impeachment of Michael de la Pole in 1386', *BIHR*, XLII (1969), 96—101. See (454).

490 Pike, Luke O. 'Common law and conscience in the ancient court of chancery', *LQR*, I (1885), 443—54. Emphasizes lack of distinction in judicial functions between conciliar and common law exercises; see Avery (361—2) and Pronay (324), generally (127).

491 —— 'Feoffment and livery of incorporeal hereditaments', *LQR*, V (1889), 29—43. Based on Littleton (309).

492 —— and Leveson W.V. Harcourt. 'The trial of peers', *LQR*, XXIII (1907), 442—7; XXIV (1908), 43—8.

493 Plucknett, Theodore F.T. 'Impeachment and attainder', *TRHS*, 5th ser., III (1953), 145—58. See Bellamy (301), and esp. Lander (447), also (518, 527).

494 —— 'The Lancastrian constitution', in R.W. Seton-Watson (ed.), *Tudor studies presented . . . to Albert F. Pollard*. 1924, pp. 161—81. See (286).

495 —— 'The place of the council in the fifteenth-century', *TRHS*, 4th ser., I (1918), 157—89. For more concrete analyses, see Brown (380) and others named there.

496 ——— 'The rise of the English state trial', *Politica*, II (1937), 542—59.

497 ——— 'State trials under Richard II', *TRHS*, 5th ser., II (1952), 159—71.

498 Pollard, Albert F. 'Two notes on parliamentary history. (1) The chronology of Richard II's first parliament. (2) The clerk of Henry VI'S 'Re-adeption' parliament', *BIHR*, XVI (1939), 19—23; XV (1938), 137—61; XVI (1939), 65—87. See (176, 196); the second article surveys parliamentary clerks, and under-clerks are studied in the third.

499 Pollard, Graham. 'The medieval town clerks of Oxford', *Oxoniensia*, XXXI (1966), 43—76.

500 Post, John B. 'King's bench clerks in the reign of Richard II', *BIHR*, XLVII (1974), 150—63. And see (255).

501 Pronay, Nicholas. 'The hanaper under the Lancastrian kings', *LeedsS*, XII (1967), 73—86. See (127, 361—2, 324).

502 Putnam, Bertha H. 'The ancient indictments in the Public Record Office', *EHR*, XXIX (1914), 479—505. And generally (255).

503 ——— '*Suete de prisone*', *EHR*, XXV (1910), 307—8. Responding to Ronald Stewart-Brown's note one year earlier, pertinent to the payment to avoid pre-trial detention.

504 Reddaway, Thomas F. 'The king's mint and exchange in London 1343—1543', *EHR*, LXXXII (1967), 1—23. Important study of royal attempts to control bullion and currency flows (130, 312).

505 Reid, Rachel R. 'The office of warden of the marches; its origins and early history', *EHR*, XXXII (1917), 479—96. Previews (342).

506 Reynolds, Susan. 'The forged charters of Barnstaple', *EHR*, LXXXIV (1969), 699—720.

507 Rezneck, Samuel. 'Constructive treason by words in the fifteenth century', *AHR*, XXXIII (1928), 544—52. Attacks Thornley article (546); see Bellamy (301).

508 ——— 'The early history of the parliamentary declaration of treason', *EHR*, XLII (1927), 497—513; and, *LQR*, XLVI (1930), 80—102. See (137, 301).

509 Richardson, Henry G. 'The elections to the October parliament of 1399', *BIHR*, XVI (1939), 137—43. See (176, 196).

510 ——— 'John of Gaunt and the parliamentary representation of Lancashire', *BJRL*, XXII (1938), 175—222. See (556).

511 ——— 'Richard II's last parliament', *EHR*, LII (1937), 39—47. See (176, 692).

512 ——— and George O. Sayles. 'Parliamentary documents from formularies', *BIHR*, XI (1934), 147—62. And generally (137, 176, 196).

513 Riddell, William R. 'Erring judges of the fourteenth century', *Illinois Law Review*, XXI (1927), 543—58. The 1386 purge of the royal council.

514 Rogers, Alan. 'Clerical taxation under Henry IV, 1399—1413', *BIHR*, XLVI (1973), 123—44. See (116, 135, 221, 262).

515 ——— 'Henry IV, the commons and taxation', *Medieval Studies*, XXXI (1969), 44—70. See (176, 688).

516 ——— 'Late-medieval Stamford: a study of the town council 1465—1492', in Alan Everitt (ed.), *Perspectives in English urban history*. 1973, pp. 16—38.

517 ——— 'The Lincolnshire county court in the fifteenth century', *Lincolnshire History and Archaeology*, I (1966), 64—78. Uses sheriff's returns of writs for parliament to establish election procedures.

518 ——— 'Parliamentary appeals of treason in the reign of Richard II', *AJLH*, VIII (1964), 95—124. See (692, 527).

519 ——— 'Parliamentary elections in Grimsby in the fifteenth century', *BIHR*, XLII (1969), 212—20. See (176, 196).

520 ——— 'Parliamentary electors in Lincolnshire in the fifteenth century', *Lincolnshire History and Archaeology*, III (1968), 41—79; IV (1969), 33—53; V (1970), 47—58; VI (1971), 67—81. See (523).

521 ——— 'The political crisis of 1401', *Nottingham Mediaeval Studies*, XII (1968), 85—96. Examines conciliar advice to Henry IV and factional dissension.

522 Roskell, John S. 'The office and dignity of protector of England, with

special reference to its origins', *EHR*, LXVIII (1953), 193–233. Relative to Henry VI's minority.

523 —— 'The parliamentary representation of Lincolnshire during the reigns of Richard II, Henry IV, and Henry V', *Nottingham Mediaeval Studies*, III (1959), 53–77. See (520, 176, 196).

524 —— 'Perspectives in English parliamentary history', *BJRL*, XLVI (1963–4), 448–75. Challenges Geoffrey R. Elton's emphasis on the 1529–1536 parliament and the Tudor apologists generally, to which Elton responds in 'The body of the whole realm', Charlottesville, Va., 1969; and generally (137, 176, 196).

525 —— 'The problem of the attendance of the lords in medieval parliaments', *BIHR*, XXIX (1956), 153–204.

526 —— 'William Catesby, counsellor to Richard III', *BJRL*, XLII (1959–60), 145–74.

527 Ross, Charles D. 'Forfeiture for treason in the reign of Richard II', *EHR*, LXXI (1956), 560–75. Basically a critique of (392), and generally (301).

528 Sainty, J.C. 'The tenure of offices in the exchequer', *EHR*, LXXX (1965), 449–75. Excellent, wide-ranging administrative study particularly for fifteenth-century developments (158).

529 Savine, Alexander. 'Copyhold cases in the early [Henry VI] chancery proceedings', *EHR*, XVII (1902), 296–303. See the monograph on early Tudor copyhold by Charles M. Gray, Cambridge, Mass., 1963; and (127).

530 Scammell, Jean. 'The origin and limitations of the liberty of Durham', *EHR*, LXXXI (1966), 449–73. Careful, important history of evolving constitutional position of Durham relative to the crown.

531 Scott, Florence R. 'Chaucer and the parliament of 1386', *Speculum*, XVIII (1943), 80–6. See (176, 2191).

532 Serjeantson, Robert M. 'Court rolls of Higham Ferrers', *Reports and Papers Read at Meetings of the Architectural Societies*, XXXIII (1915–16), 95–141; XXXIV (1917–18), 47–102. A topical analysis of local, fifteenth-century law enforcement (120).

533 Sillem, Rosamond. 'Commissions of the peace, 1380–1485', *BIHR*, X (1933), 81–104. See (255, 415).

534 Simpson, Alan W.B. 'The circulation of year-books in the fifteenth century', *LQR*, LXXIII (1957), 492–505. See (280, 287).

535 —— 'The introduction of the action on the case for conversion', *LQR*, LXXV (1959), 364–80.

536 —— 'The penal bond with conditional defeasance', *LQR*, LXXXII (1966), 392–422.

537 —— 'The source and function of the later year-books', *LQR*, LXXXVII (1971), 94–118. But see Eric W. Ives' revision in *LQR*, LXXXIX, 1973, pp. 64–86.

538 Somerville, Robert. 'The Cowcher Books of the Duchy of Lancaster', *EHR*, LI (1936), 598–615. A register of title deeds for the Duchy, *c.* 1402; see his monograph (349).

539 Steel, Anthony B. 'The financial background of the wars of the roses', *History*, n.s., XL (1955), 18–30. His numerous articles on the Exchequer can be found in (350); and generally (116), but see (1379).

540 Stewart-Brown, Ronald. 'The jurybook of the county court of Chester', *EHR*, XLVIII (1933), 268–9. That is, the Book of the Gospels used in 1398.

541 Storey, Robin L. 'Ecclesiastical causes in chancery', in Donald A. Bullough and Robin L. Storey (eds.), *The study of medieval records: essays in honour of Kathleen Major*. Oxford, 1971, pp. 236–59. See (127, 357).

542 —— 'The wardens of the marches of England towards Scotland, 1377–1489', *EHR*, LXXII (1957), 593–615. For northern politics (735).

543 Tait, James. 'The common council of the borough', *EHR*, XLVI (1931), 1–29. See (128).

544 Tallent-Bateman, Charles T. 'The ancient Lancashire and Cheshire local courts of civil jurisdiction', *Lancs Antiq*, IV (1886), 61–79; V (1887), 231–41.

Fairly exhaustive list and description, the latter article pertinent to criminal matters (128).

545   Thorne, Samuel E. *'Statuti* in the post-glossators', *Speculum*, XI (1936), 452–61.

546   Thornley, Isobel D. 'Treason by words in the fifteenth century', *EHR*, XXXII (1917), 556–61. Emphasizes revival of such treasons, against the statute of 1352. See Rezneck (507), and (301).

547   Tout, Thomas F. 'The English parliament and public opinion, 1376–1388', in *Mélanges d'histoire offerts à Henri Pirenne . . . , II.* Brussels, 1926, pp. 545–62. Reprinted in *Collected papers of Thomas F. Tout*, vol. II; and (176, 843).

548   —— 'The household of the chancery and its disintegration', in Henry W.C. Davis (ed.), *Essays in history presented to Reginald L. Poole*. Oxford, 1927, pp. 46–85. See (127, 501).

549   Treiman, I. 'Escaping the creditor in the middle ages', *LQR*, XLIII (1927), 230–7. See (467–70, 476).

550   Virgoe, Roger. 'The Cambridgeshire election of 1439', *BIHR*, XLVI (1973), 95–101. And generally (176, 196).

551   —— 'The composition of the king's council, 1437–61', *BIHR*, XLIII (1970), 134–60. For related articles, see Brown (380).

552   —— 'A list of members of the parliament of February 1449', *BIHR*, XXXIV (1961), 200–10. See (176, 196).

553   —— (ed.). 'A new fragment of the Lord's journal of 1461', *BIHR*, XXXII (1959), 83–7. See (164, 176).

554   —— (ed.). 'Three Suffolk parliamentary elections of the mid-fifteenth century', *BIHR*, XXXIX (1966), 185–96.

555   Waugh, William T. 'The great statute of praemunire', *EHR*, XXXVII (1922), 173–205. See (357).

556   Wedgwood, Josiah C. 'John of Gaunt and the packing of parliament [1372–1382]', *EHR*, XLV (1930), 623–5. But see (510).

557   —— 'Staffordshire parliamentary history from the earliest times to . . . [1603]', *SaltS*, (1917), 122–271.

558   Williams, Charles H. 'A fifteenth-century lawsuit', *LQR*, XL (1924), 354–64. Babington vs. Venour, 1462, *re*: abduction.

559   —— 'A Norfolk parliamentary election, 1461', *EHR*, XL (1925), 79–86. See (176, 196).

560   Winfield, Percy H. 'Abridgments of the year-books', *Harvard Law Review*, XXXVII (1923–4), 214–44. Discusses those of Statham, Fitzherbert, Brooke, and the Book of Assizes; see (6).

561   Wolffe, Bertram P. 'Acts of resumption in the Lancastrian parliaments 1399–1456', *EHR*, LXXIII (1958), 583–613. Convincingly argues that the commons promoted such bills to correct exploitation of royal revenues by royal councillors (137).

562   —— 'The management of English royal estates under the Yorkist kings', *EHR*, LXXI (1956), 1–27. See his full studies (354–5).

563   Wood-Legh, Kathleen L. 'Chantries and corporation sole', *LQR*, LXXIV (1958), 272–84. See the debate in (440, 459, 461), and generally (357, 1955).

564   Wyon, Alfred B. 'On the great seals of Henry IV, Henry V, and Henry VI . . . ', *JBAA*, XXXIX (1883), 139–67; XL (1884), 275–89. Provides a list of extant seals, including those for Henry VI as king of France (335).

V. POLITICAL HISTORY

1 Printed sources

565   Armstrong, Charles A.J. (ed.). *The usurpation of Richard the Third. Dominicus Mancinus ad Angelum Catonem de occupatione regni Anglie per*

Ricardum Tercium libellus. 2nd ed., rev., 1969. A basic literary source, with (585—8, 596, 599, 616, 874).

566 —— (ed.). 'Verses by Jean Miélot on Edward IV and Richard, earl of Warwick', *Medium Aevum*, VIII (1939), 193—7. Miélot was servant to the dukes of Burgundy 1448—70.

567 Aston, Margaret E. (ed.). 'A Kent approver of 1440', *BIHR*, XXXVI (1963), 82—90. Alleged attempt to poison Henry VI.

568 Babington, Churchill (ed.). *Polychronicon Ranulphi Higden monachi Cestrensis; together with the English translations of John Trevisa and of an unknown writer of the fifteenth century* (Rolls Series, XLI). 1865—86, 9 vols. See Taylor (705), and Robinson (656); the Chronicles are thoroughly described in Gross (9), McKisack (104), Jacob (98), and Myers (106); also (1670).

569 Baildon, William P. (ed.). 'A wardrobe account of 16—17 Richard II, 1393—4', *Arch*, LXII (1911), 497—514.

570 Bateson, Mary (ed.). *George Ashby's poems* (EETS, e.s., LXXVI). 1899. Propaganda of the Yorkist era; see the 1971 ed. by V.J. Scattergood, *Politics and Poetry*; also Josef Kail ed. of poems *c*. 1400—1421 for *EETS*, CXXIV, 1904; and from the wars of the roses, see Frederic Madden, *Arch*, XXIX, 1842. Also (684).

571 Beauchamp, Frederick L. (ed.). *Liber regalis; seu, ordo consecrandi regem solum. Ordo consecrandi reginam cum rege. Ordo consecrandi reginam solam* (Roxburghe Club, 93). 1870. See Ullmann (676), and (332, 635, 665, 704, 728, 773, 818, 819, 830) on royal coronation, with (696).

572 Black, William H. (ed.). *Illustrations of ancient state and chivalry* (Roxburghe Club, 56). 1840. Contains narrative of the marriage of Richard, duke of York with Ann of Norfolk, the rules for wager of battle, and Johan Hill's treatise on gentlemen-in-arms; also (899, 993).

573 Bond, Edward A. (ed.). *Chronica monasterii de Melsa, a fundatione usque ad annum 1396, auctore Thoma de Burton, abbate [continuation to 1406]* (Rolls Series, XLIII). 1866—8, 3 vols.

574 Brie, Friedrich W.D. (ed.). *The brut, or the chronicles of England* (EETS, CXXXI, CXXXVI). 1906—8, 2 vols. See (580).

575 Bruce, John (ed.). *Historie of the arrivall of Edward IV. in England and the final recoverye of his kingdomes from Henry VI, A.D. M. CCCC. LXXI* (Camden Society, I). 1838. See (687, 774, 879); and John A.F. Thomson, *Speculum*, XLVI, 1971, pp. 84—93.

576 Buchon, Jean A.C. (ed.). 'Jean Le Beau's Chronique de Richard II, 1377—1399', *Collections des Chroniques Françaises*, XXV, Supp. 2 (1826), 1—79. See Wright (683, 692, 833, 861).

577 Carey, Edith F. (ed.). 'The accounts of Thomas Guille, Esq., captain and receiver to Richard Neville, earl of Warwick, 1450—2', *Report and Transactions of La Société Guernesiaise*, IX (1923), 224—48.

578 Clarke, Maude V. and Noel Denholm-Young (eds.). 'The Kirkstall chronicle, 1355—1400', *BJRL*, XV (1931), 100—37. Now see (671).

579 Cole, Charles A. (ed.). *Memorials of Henry the Fifth, king of England* (Rolls Series, XI). 1858. See Hearne (617, 618) and (621, 670, 680, 689, 784, 814, 824, 853) pertain to Henry V's contemporary biographies.

580 Davies, John S. (ed.). *An English chronicle of the reigns of Richard II, Henry IV, Henry V, and Henry VI* (Camden Society, LXIV). 1856. Continues the Brut chronicle to 1461 (574).

581 De Guerin, T.W.M. (ed.). 'Notes on some old documents, formerly in the possession of Sir Edgar MacCulloch', *Report and Transactions of La Société Guernesiaise*, VII (1914), 151—68. Relating to the earls of Warwick, 1338—1478 (713).

582 Dobson, Richard B. (ed.). *The Peasants' Revolt of 1381*. 1970. Excellent selection of sources with (702—3), and best used with Hilton (693); the recent German work by Horst Gerlach, 1969, overlooks much recent scholarship. For the royal itinerary during the revolt see W.H. Bird, *EHR*, XXXI, 1916, pp. 124—6.

583 Douce, Francis (ed.). *The customs of London, otherwise called Arnold's Chronicle*. 1811 (orig. ed., 1512). See (130).

584 Ellis, Henry (ed.). *Original letters illustrative of English history, including numerous royal letters [1074–1799]*. 1824–46, 11 vols. in 3 series. See Halliwell's selection (609).

585 —— (ed.). *Three books of Polydore Vergil's English history, comprising the reigns of Henry VI, Edward IV and Richard III* (Camden Society, XXIX). 1844. See the Denys Hay edition and translation for segment from 1485, in Camden Society, 3rd ser., LXXIV, 1950; and see Thysius (675), and Hay's critical evaluation in *Polydore Vergil: Renaissance historian and man of letters*. 1952.

586 —— (ed.). *John Hardyng's chronicle, from the earliest period of English history, together with the continuation by Richard Grafton to 34 Henry VIII*. 1812. But consult Charles L. Kingsford, *EHR*, XXVIII, 1912, pp. 462–82 and 740–53, because of Hardyng's two different versions.

587 —— (ed.). *Edward Hall's chronicle [1399–1547]*. 1809. Strongly influenced by the Tudor myths, like More (669) and Rous (616), with heavy dependence on Vergil (585, 675) for data.

588 —— (ed.). *The new chronicles of England and France, by Robert Fabyan, named by himself the concordance of histories [to 1485]*. 1811. See (626, 129).

589 —— (ed.). 'Copy of an historical document, printed by Machlinia, dated in 1475', *Arch*, XXXII (1847), 325–31. Relating to proposed marriage between Louis XI of France and Elizabeth, eldest daughter to Edward IV and later Henry VII's Queen.

590 Fahy, Conor (ed.). 'The marriage of Edward IV and Elizabeth Woodville: a new Italian source', *EHR*, LXXVI (1961), 660–72. From Modena, the *De mulieribus admirandis*.

591 Fellowes, Edmund H. (ed.). *The military knights of Windsor, 1352–1944*. Windsor, 1944. Also edits similar lists for Knights of the Garter, 1348–1939 (1626).

592 Flenley, Ralph (ed.). *Six town chronicles of England*. Oxford, 1911.

593 Fortescue, John. *The governance of England, otherwise called the difference between an absolute and a limited monarchy*, ed. by Charles Plummer. Oxford, 1885. See Wright (2450); for references to other work on Fortescue (738); also (665).

594 —— *De laudibus legum Angliae*, ed. and trans. by Stanley B. Chrimes. Cambridge, 1942. See Max Radin's review in *Michigan Law Review*, XLIII 1944, pp. 179–87; and there is another translation by Francis Grigor, publ. 1917.

595 Fortescue, Thomas (Lord Clermont) (ed.). *The works of Sir John Fortescue, chief justice of England and lord chancellor of king Henry VI*. 1869, 2 vols. The basic edition of all writings.

596 Fulman, William (ed.). 'Historiae Croylandensis continuatio', in *Rerum Anglicarum scriptores veterum*. Oxford, 1684, pp. 449–592. Covers 1149–1486; in the Bohn's Antiquarian Library, ed. and trans. by Henry T. Riley in 1854. See Edwards' article (753), and the new edition of the text by Nicholas Pronay; also, Ross (720), p. 430.

597 Furnivall, Frederick J. (ed.). *Arthur: a short sketch of his life and history in English verse . . . 1428 A.D.* (EETS, II). 1864.

598 Gairdner, James (ed.). *The historical collections of a London citizen* (Camden Society, n.s., XVII). 1876. William Gregory's chronicle to 1469, pp. 55–239; for which, see John A.F. Thomson, *British Museum Quarterly*, 1972; also (130, 626).

599 —— (ed.). *Letters and papers illustrative of the reigns of Richard III and Henry VII* (Rolls Series, XXIV). 1861–3, 2 vols. See (685).

600 —— (ed.). *Three fifteenth-century chronicles, with historical memoranda by John Stowe* (Camden Society, n.s., XXVIII). 1880. Includes the so-called 'Short English chronicle' and 'Brief Latin chronicle'.

601 Galbraith, Vivian H. (ed.). *The St Albans chronicle, 1406–1420*. Oxford,

1937. And see Riley (654), where the *Annales* for 1392—1406 immediately precede this; also, see Galbraith's article in *EHR*, XLVII, 1932, pp. 12—30.

602 —— (ed.). *The Anonimalle chronicle, 1333—81 from an MS at St. Mary's Abbey, York*. Manchester, 1970 (orig. ed. 1925). See reconsiderations in Du Boulay and Barron (315).

603 Giles, John A. (ed.). *The chronicles of the white rose of York . . . relating to the reign of King Edward the Fourth*. 1845. Includes the Warkworth chronicle (608) and various letters and papers; also (687).

604 —— (ed.). *Incerti scriptoris chronicon Angliae de regnis . . . Henrici IV., Henrici V. et Henrici VI*. 1848. Especially important for Henry VI's reign (722).

605 Griffiths, Ralph A. (ed.). 'Some partisans of Owain Glyndŵr at Oxford', *BBCS*, XX (1963), 282—92. See (97, 634, 655, 660, 691).

606 —— (ed.). 'Some secret supporters of Owain Glyn Dŵr', *BIHR*, XXXVII (1964), 77—100.

607 Grosjean, Paul (ed.). *Henrici VI Angliae Regis miracula postuma. Ex codice Musei Britannici Regio 13. c. VIII* (Société des Bollandistes, Subsidia Hagiographica 22). Brussels, 1935. Materials collected toward Henry VI's canonization; see also (625, 722). Extracts translated by Ronald Knox and J.R.S. Leslie (eds.), *The miracles of king Henry VI*, Cambridge, 1923; see Leonard Smith, *Dublin Review*, CLXVIII, 1921, pp. 41—53; and esp., John W. McKenna's excellent article in Beryl Rowland (ed.), *Chaucer and middle English studies*, 1974.

608 Halliwell, James O. (ed.). *A chronicle of the first thirteen years of the reign of Edward IV, by John Warkworth* (Camden Society, X). 1839. See (603, 687).

609 —— (ed.). *Letters of the kings of England [1189—1649]*. 1846—8, 2 vols.

610 —— (ed.). 'Observations upon the history of certain events in England during the reign of King Edward the Fourth [1461]', *Arch*, XXIX (1842), 127—38. See (687).

611 Harriss, Gerald L. and M.A. (eds.). 'John Benet's chronicle for the years 1400 to 1462', *Camden Miscellany XXIV* (Camden Society, 4th ser., IX). 1972, pp. 151—233. Previewed by him in *BIHR*, XXXVIII, 1965, pp. 212—18.

612 Haselden, Reginald B. and H.C. Schulz (eds.). 'Summary report on the Hastings manuscripts', *Huntingdon Library Bulletin*, V (1934), 1—67.

613 Haydon, Frank S. (ed.). *Eulogium historiarum sive temporis . . . [continuations to 1490]* (Rolls Series, IX). 1858—63, 3 vols.

614 Hearne, Thomas (ed.). *Duo rerum Anglicarum scriptores veteres, viz. Thomas Otterbourne [chronicle, to 1420] et Johannes Whethamstede, ab origine gentis Britannicae usque ad Eduardum IV*. Oxford, 1732, 2 vols. For Wheathampstead's *Registrum*, see Riley (654); more about Hearne is in Herbert E. Salter (ed.), *Oxford Historical Society*, LXVII, 1915.

615 —— (ed.). *Historia vitae et regni Ricardi II. Angliae regis, a monacho quodam de Evesham consignata. Accesserunt, praeter alia, Joannis Rossi Historiola de comitibus warwicensibus . . . .* Oxford, 1729. See (692).

616 —— (ed.). *J. Rossi antiquarii Warwicensis historia regum Angliae [to 1485]*. Oxford, 1716.

617 —— (ed.). *Thomae de Elmham Vita et gesta Henrici Quinti, Anglorum regis*. Oxford, 1727. This pseudo-Elmham biography, probably written about 1445, remains an essential source with (618, 621, 680), and (689).

618 —— (ed.). *Titi Livii Foro-Juliensis vita Henrici Quinti*. Oxford, 1716. Although written after 1437, Livius de Frulovisiis gives a vital portrait, but see Charles L. Kingsford's ed. of the 1513 English version, Oxford, 1911; and (579, 617, 670, 680, 689, 824).

619 —— (ed.). 'Chronicon (anonymi) Godstovianum [to 1431]', in *William Roper's Vita Thomae Mori*. Oxford, 1716, pp. 180—246.

620 Hingeston, Francis C. (ed.). *The chronicle of England [to 1417] by John Capgrave* (Rolls Series, I). 1858. For Capgrave (1726).

621 —— (ed.). *Liber de illustribus Henricis [per] Johannem Capgrave* (Rolls Series, VII), 1858. See (579, 689).

622　—— (ed.). *Royal and historical letters during the reign of Henry the Fourth, king od England and of France and lord of Ireland . . . 1399—[1413]* (Rolls Series, XVIII). 1860, 2 vols.

623　Hope, William H. St John and [Harold A.L.] Viscount Dillon (eds.). 'Inventory of goods belonging to Thomas, duke of Gloucester, seized in his castle at Pleshy, Essex, 1397, with their values, as shown in the escheators' accounts', *AJ*, LIV (1897), 275—308. Also (742).

624　Ives, Eric W. (ed.). 'Andrew Dymmock and the papers of Antony, earl Rivers, 1482—3', *BIHR*, XLI (1968), 216—29.

625　James, Montague R. (ed.). *Henry the Sixth: a reprint of John Blacman's memoir*. Cambridge, 1919. Encomium on his spiritual virtues and saintliness; see Grosjean (607) and Hearne (614); also (722).

626　Kingsford, Charles L. (ed.). *Chronicles of London*. Oxford, 1905. See (130, 583, 598, 647, 674, 734, 1481).

627　—— (ed.). 'Two forfeitures in the year of Agincourt', *Arch*, LXX (1920), 71—100. By Henry Le Scrope and Richard Gurmyn.

628　Kirby, John L. (ed.). 'An account of Robert Southwell, receiver-general of John Mowbray, earl marshall, 1422—3', *BIHR*, XXVII (1954), 192—8.

629　Laing, David (ed.). *The orygYnale cronykil of Scotland by Andrew of Wyntoun*. Edinburgh, 1872—9, 3 vols. Also, Skene (1520); the Fordun-Bower chronicle, ed. by W. Goodall, 1759; T. Thomson (ed.), *The Auchinleck chronicle*, 1819, 1877; and John de Fordun's chronicle, ed. by W.F. Skene, 1871—2.

630　Leighton, William A. (ed.). 'Early chronicles of Shrewsbury 1372—1603', *ShropsT*, III (1880), 239—352. Found in Library of Royal Free Grammar School, known as Dr Taylor's ms. (162).

631　Lumby, Joseph R. (ed.). *Henry Knighton's Chronicon vel cnitthon [959—1395] monachi Leycestrensis* (Rolls Series, XCII). 1889—95, 2 vols.

632　Macray, William D. (ed.). *Chronicon abbatiae de Evesham ad annum 1418* (Rolls Series, XXIX). 1863.

633　Madden, Frederic (ed.). 'Letter containing intelligence of the proceedings of the court and nobility at the commencement of the year 1454' *Arch*, XXIX (1842), 305—17.

634　Mathews, T. (ed.). *Welsh records in Paris*. Carmarthen, 1910. Includes letters of Owain Glyn Dŵr (605, 97).

635　McKenna, John W. (ed.). 'The coronation oil of the Yorkist kings', *EHR*, LXXXII (1967), 102—4. Important note on the sanctity and symbolism of kingship, with (571, 830).

636　McKisack, May (ed.). 'Historia sive narracio de modo et forma mirabilis parliamenti apud Westmonasterium . . . [1386] per Thomam Favent clericum indictata', *Camden Miscellany XIV* (Camden Society, 3rd ser., XXXVII). 1926.

637　Monro, Cecil (ed.). *Letters of Queen Margaret of Anjou and Bishop Beckington and others, written in the reigns of Henry V. and Henry VI.* (Camden Society, LXXXVI). 1863. See (642—3, 707, 875).

638　Moore, Stuart A. (ed.). *Letters and papers of John Shillingford, mayor of Exeter, 1447—50* (Camden Society, n.s., II). 1871.

639　Myers, Alec R. (ed.). *The household of Edward IV: the black book and the ordinance of 1478*. Manchester, 1959. The authoritative edition, but see also (646, 687). And now see D.A.L. Morgan's important article in *TRHS*, 5th ser., XXIII, 1973, pp. 1—22.

640　—— (ed.). 'An official progress through Lancashire and Cheshire in 1476', *Lancs Historic*, CXV (1963), 1—29. Recorded in the duchy of Lancaster council register.

641　—— (ed.). 'The household of Queen Elizabeth Woodville, 1466—7', *BJRL*, L (1967—8), 207—35, 443—81. See Nicolas (650), and (659).

642　—— (ed.). 'The household of Queen Margaret of Anjou, 1452—3', *BJRL*, XL (1957—8), 79—113, 391—431.

643　—— (ed.). 'The jewels of Queen Margaret of Anjou', *BJRL*, XLII (1959—60), 113—31.

644 —— (ed.). 'Some household ordinances of Henry VI [1445 ?] ', *BJRL*,
XXXVI (1953–4), 449–67.

645 Nelson, Lynn H. and Carolyn (eds.). 'A lost fragment of the *Defensio juris
domus Lancastriae*', *Speculum*, XL (1965), 290–3.

646 Nichols, John (ed.). *A collection of ordinances and regulations for the government of the royal household . . . Edward III to King William and
Queen Mary*. 1790. Also edited the wills of English kings and queens,
1780.

647 Nichols, John G. (ed.). *Chronicle of the grey friars of London* (Camden
Society, LIII). 1852. Covering 1189–1556; but see later edition in Rolls
Series by Richard Howlett, *Monumenta Franciscana*, II, 1882, pp. 143–
260; also (130, 626).

648 —— (ed.). *The boke of noblesse. Addressed to King Edward the Fourth on
his invasion of France, 1475*. 1857. Another edition in Roxburghe Club,
No. 77, 1860; (1500), and read Ferguson (1060).

649 —— (ed.). 'Chronicle of the rebellion in Lincolnshire, 1470', *Camden
Miscellany I* (Camden Society, XXXIX). 1847.

650 Nicolas, Nicholas H. (ed.). *Privy purse expenses of Elizabeth of York: wardrobe accounts of Edward the Fourth*. 1830. And with Edward Tyrrell,
edited *A chronicle of London, 1189–1483*, publ. 1827. not to be confused with (583, 598, 626, 674); see (641, 687).

651 Ord, Craven (ed.). 'An account of the entertainment of king Henry the Sixth
at the abbey of Bury St Edmund's', *Arch*, XV (1806), 65–71.

652 Pollard, Alfred W. and Charles Sayles (eds.). *John Wyclif's De officio regis*.
1887. See references in (571); more on Wycliffe in (1750).

653 Rickert, Edith (ed.). 'Some English personal letters of 1402', *Review of
English Studies*, VIII (1932), 257–63. Written by Elizabeth, lady Zouche.

654 Riley, Henry T. (ed.). *Chronica monasterii S. Albani* (Rolls Series, XXVIII).
1863–76, 11 vols. Segment of 1272–1422 by Thomas Walsingham;
1259–96, 1307–24, 1392–1406 by John de Trokelowe and Henry de
Blaneford; 1421–40 by John Amundesham; note that the third vol. contains the *Annales* of Richard II and Henry IV, a vital source for the era;
and (673).

655 Roberts, Glyn (ed.). 'The Anglesey submissions of 1406', *BBCS*, XV (1954),
39–61. Lists supporters of Owen Glyn Dŵr (605, 97).

656 Robinson, Joseph A. (ed.). 'An unrecognized Westminster chronicler, 1381–
94', *PBA*, III (1907–8), 61–92. Argues John Malvern continued Higden
for 1346–81, completed by a Westminster monk; for Higden see (568),
and for Westminster Abbey (1802).

657 Scofield, Cora L. (ed.). 'Five indentures between Edward IV and Warwick the
kingmaker', *EHR*, XXXVI (1921), 67–70. See (713).

658 Scott, James R. (ed.). 'Fauconberge's Kentish rising in 1471', *ArchCant*, XI
(1877), 359–64. His letter and the city of London's response (575).

659 Smith, George (ed.). *The coronation of Elizabeth Wydevile, Queen Consort
of Edward IV, on May 26th, 1465. A contemporary account* . . . . 1935.
See (687, 717).

660 Smith, J. Beverley (ed.). 'The last phase of the Glyndŵr rebellion', *BBCS*,
XXII (1967), 250–60. See (605, 97).

661 Smith, John G. (ed.). 'Transcript of a manuscript relating to Henry the Fifth
of England, preserved in the King's Library at Paris', *Transactions of the
Royal Society of Literature*, I, pt 2 (1829), 57–73. See (579, 689).

662 Smith, John J. (ed.). 'Abbreviata cronica ab anno 1377 usque ad annum
1469', *Cambridge Antiquarian Society, Quarto Publications*, I, no. II
(1840), 1–22.

663 Smith, Lucy T. (ed.). *Expeditions to Prussia and the Holy Land made by
Henry, earl of Derby (afterwards king Henry IV.) in the years 1390–1 and
1392–3: being the accounts kept by his treasurer* (Camden Society, n.s.,
LII). 1894. See (688).

664 —— (ed.). *The maire of Bristowe is kalendar. By Robert Ricart, town clerk
of Bristol 18 Edward IV* (Camden Society, n.s., V). 1872. See (134).

665 Steele, Robert (ed.). *Lydgate and Burgh's Secrees of old philosoffres; a*

version of the 'Secreta secretorum' (EETS, e.s., LXVI, LXXIV), 1894–8, 2 vols. The "Governance of kings and princes"; also (571, 593).

666 Stevenson, Joseph (ed.). *Letters and papers illustrative of the wars of the English in France during the reign of Henry VI* (Rolls Series, XXII). 1861–4, 2 vols. in 3 pts. Includes the *Annales rerum Anglicarum*, for which see McFarlane (798), also (722).

667 —— (ed.). *Narratives of the expulsion of the English from Normandy, 1449–50*. (Rolls Series, XXXII). 1863. See (922), and (1523, 1527).

668 Stewart-Brown, Ronald (ed.). 'Two Liverpool medieval affrays [1345 and 1425]', *Lancs Historic*, LXXXV (1933), 71–87.

669 Sylvester, Richard S. (ed.). *St Thomas More, The history of king Richard III*. New Haven, Conn., 1963. This is volume II of Yale University's excellent edition of the *Complete works of Sir Thomas More*, which fully replaces Joseph R. Lumby's 1883 ed.; also (685).

670 Taylor, Frank (ed.). 'The chronicle of John Strecche for the reign of Henry V (1414–1422)', *BJRL*, XVI (1932), 137–87. Adds interesting, anecdotal material (579, 689).

671 Taylor, John (ed.). 'The Kirkstall Abbey chronicles', *Thoresby Society*, XLII (1952), 1–133. The so-called *Short chronicle*, covers Richard II's reign (578, 692).

672 Thompson, Edward M. (ed.). *Chronicon Adae de Usk, 1377–1421*. 2nd ed., 1904. See (851, 97).

673 —— (ed.). *Chronicon Angliae, 1328–88, auctore monacho quodam Sancti Albani* (Rolls Series, LXIV). 1874. Most important for events of Richard II's reign, and (654, 692).

674 Thornley, Isobel D. and Arthur H. Thomas (eds.). *The great chronicle of London*. 1938. Magnificent parchment edition of a most basic source (130, 626), different from *A chronicle . . .* (650).

675 Thysius, J. (ed.). *Polydore Vergil's Anglicae historiae libri XXVII [to 1538]*. Leyden, 1651. This early edition is followed by Ellis (585); Denys Hay's edition and translation for events after 1485, explains the ms., its provenance and published versions.

676 Ullmann, Walter (ed.). *Liber regie cappelle* (Henry Bradshaw Society, XCII). 1961. Written in the early fifteenth century for the English Royal household, and (571).

677 Vale, Malcolm G.A. (ed.). 'A fifteenth-century interrogation of a political prisoner', *BIHR*, XLIII (1970), 78–85.

678 Ware, James (ed.). 'Henry of Marlborough's chronicle of Ireland [1285–1421]', in *Historie of Ireland*, pt. 3. Dublin, 1633, pp. 207–23. Generally (1, 133).

679 Williams, Benjamin (ed.). *Chronicque de la traïson et mort de Richart Deux, roy d'engleterre, mise en lumière d'après un manuscrit de la Bibliothèque royale de Paris, autrefois conservé dans l'abbaye de S. Victor* (English Historical Society). 1846. See (692).

680 —— (ed.). *Henrici Quinti Angliae regis gesta [1413–16]* (English Historical Society). 1850. This is the so-called chaplain's biography and has been newly edited by Frank Taylor and John S. Roskell, 1973; also (579, 617, 618, 689).

681 Wood, Mary A.E. [Mary A.E. Green] (ed.). *Letters of royal and illustrious ladies of Great Britain [1103–1558]*. 1846, 3 vols. And see (875).

682 Woodruff, Charles E. (ed.). 'The chronicle of William Glastynbury, monk of the priory of Christ Church, Canterbury, 1418–48', *ArchCant*, XXXVII (1925), 121–51.

683 Wright, Thomas (ed.). *Alliterative poem on the deposition of King Richard II; Ricardi Maydiston, De concordia inter Ric. II et civitatem London* (Camden Society, III). 1838. See Jones (779), Buchon (576), and the monograph by C. Ziepel, Berlin, 1874; also (692).

684 —— (ed.). *A collection of political poems and songs relating to English history, from the accession of Edward III to the reign of Henry VIII* (Rolls Series, XIV). 1859–61, 2 vols. See Bateson (570) and the more recent selection edited by Rossell H. Robbins, 1959.

2 Surveys

685 Gairdner, James. *History of the life and reign of Richard the Third*. Cambridge, 1898, rev. ed. Remains an authoritative study for a most controversial era, but see Charles D. Ross's new biography. The specific items are (565, 599, 669, 708, 712, 718, 725, 744, 770, 791, 803).

686 Ramsay, James H. *Lancaster and York: a century of English history, A.D. 1399—1485*. Oxford, 1892, 2 vols.

687 Scofield, Cora L. *The life and reign of Edward the Fourth*. 1923, 2 vols. Still a thorough and reliable history for the era, as are her numerous *EHR* articles publ. between 1906 and 1922; and read Thomas G. Paget's biography of Edward's mistress, Jane Shore, *The Rose of London*. See Ross (691, 720) for the definitive biography of Edward IV; other relevant items are (575, 590, 603, 608, 610, 639, 648, 650, 659, 711, 774, 787, 845, 874, 1492, 2288, 2429).

688 Wylie, James H. *History of England under Henry the Fourth*. 1884—98. 4 vols. Standard studies for detailed political history of both reigns; see A.L. Brown's recent essay (691); other specific items are (663, 715, 764, 859, 939, 956, 2450).

689 —— *The reign of Henry the Fifth*. Cambridge, 1914—1929. 3 vols. Important items are (579, 617, 618, 621, 661, 670, 680, 709, 714, 784, 796, 804, 863, 865, 866, 924, 954, 957, 962, 968, 978, 980, 1533, 2325, 2385).

3 Monographs

690 Carlyle, Robert W. and Alexander J. *A history of medieval political theory in the west*, VI, *Political theory from 1300 to 1600*. 1936.

691 Chrimes, Stanley B., Charles D. Ross, and Ralph A. Griffiths (eds.). *Fifteenth-century England: studies in politics and society*. Manchester, 1972. Excellent collection of synthetic essays: on Henry IV by Alfred L. Brown, Henry VI by Bertram P. Wolffe, Ross on Edward IV, Robin L. Storey on northern politics, Griffiths surveying Welsh politics, and a copiously documented survey of the aristocracy by Thomas B. Pugh that commands the topic with (701).

692 Goodman, Anthony. *The loyal conspiracy: the lords appellant under Richard II*. 1971. Other basic work on Richard II is in (576, 615, 671, 673, 679, 683, 695, 699, 706, 723, 727, 733, 792, 813, 833, 861, 862, 889, 901, 925, 937, 2136, 2341, 2435).

693 Hilton, Rodney H. *Bond men made free. Medieval peasant movements and the English rising of 1381*. 1973. The best synthesis of social and political themes, also Dobson (582), and (702—3).

694 —— and Hyman Fagan. *The English rising of 1381*. 1950. Somewhat tendentious economic determinism argued from solid evidence; read the more general accounts by George G. Coulton, 1934, or Charles W. Oman, 1906; in Russian, See Dimitri M. Petrushevskii's 1897—1901 volumes, revised 1914 and 1927 (1358).

695 Jones, Richard H. *Royal policy of Richard II: absolutism in the later middle ages* (Oxford Studies in Mediaeval History, X). Oxford, 1968.

696 Kantorowicz, Ernst H. *The king's two bodies: a study in medieval political theology*. Princeton, 1957. Classic analysis for general political theory of kingship; also (571, 704, 799).

697 Keen, Maurice H. *The outlaws of medieval legend*. 1961. Argues that aristocracy used common law against the peasantry; for the debate (752).

698 Kriehn, George. *The English rising in 1450*. Strassburg, 1892. Careful and authoritative study; see also the book by B.B. Orridge, 1869.

699 Mathew, Gervase. *The court of Richard II*. 1968. Emphasizes the literary patronage, painting and illuminations, with only slight attention to political institutions (2313).

700 McFarlane, Kenneth B. *Lancastrian kings and Lollard knights*. Oxford, 1972.

Important reassessment of character for Henry IV and Henry V, plus a continuation to his Wycliffe book (1925).

701 —— *The nobility of later medieval England*. Oxford, 1973. Fundamental to our knowledge and understanding of the aristocracy, these are a posthumous col'ection of lectures and papers; and see Pugh (691).

702 Powell, Edgar. *The rising in East Anglia in 1381; with an appendix containing the Suffolk poll-tax lists for that year*. Cambridge, 1896. Expansion of article in *TRHS*, n.s., VIII, 1894, pp. 203–49; also publ. a collection of documents on the topic with George M. Trevelyan, 1899. Other important articles are (751, 757, 786, 806, 812, 832, 842, 850, 1015, 1161).

703 Réville, André. *Le soulèvement des travailleurs d'Angleterre en 1381; études et documents, publiés avec une introduction historique par Charles Petit-Dutaillis*. Paris, 1898. Now use Dobson (582).

704 Schramm, Percy E. *A history of the English coronation*, trans. by Leopold G.W. Legg. Oxford, 1937. But see (571, 635, 830), plus Bertie Wilkinson's Historical Association pamphlet, G.23.

705 Taylor, John. *The 'universal chronicle' of Ranulf Higden*. Oxford, 1966. Essential analysis for chronicles generally, with his (18), and for Higden (568).

706 Tuck, [J.] Anthony. *Richard II and the English nobility*. 1973. A most important and clear evaluation, and see Caroline Barron's analysis (733).

4 Biographies

707 Bagley, John J. *Margaret of Anjou, queen of England*. 1948. Rather shallow, fanciful but interesting; see other biographies by Philippe Erlanger, Mary A. Hookham, or Karl Schmidt; and (637, 643, 875).

708 Buck, George. *The life and reign of Richard III*. 1646. Reprinted in White Kennet, *Complete History of England*, I, 1706, pp. 514–77; also, Caroline A. Halsted's two vols., 1844, contain much data. Now see Ross (720) and (685).

709 Earle, Peter. *Life and times of Henry V*. 1972. Most recent biography, with good illustrations from mss., emphasizing life at court; another biography that is readable and reliable is by Harold F. Hutchison, 1967. The Historical Association's pamphlet by Christopher T. Allmand is succinct and current; and (579, 689).

710 Fowler, Kenneth. *The age of Plantagenet and Valois*. 1967.

711 Habington, William. *The historie of Edward IV*. 1640. Like Buck, of historiographical interest, reprinted in White Kennet, *Complete History of England*, I, 1706, pp. 429–81 (687).

712 Kendall, Paul M. *Richard the Third*. 1955. To be used with care despite its intelligent, sympathetic, well-written character, so see Levine (791) and the biography noted in Ross (720); also, there is the excellent museum catalogue, *Richard III*, by Pamela Tudor-Craig, National Portrait Gallery, 1973.

713 —— *Warwick the kingmaker*. 1957. Replaces books by Walther Bensemann and Charles W. Oman. See Philip B. Chatwin, *Transactions of the Birmingham Archaeological Society*, LIX, 1938, 2–8; and (581, 657, 732, 739, 783, 827).

714 Kingsford, Charles L. *Henry V: the typical mediaeval hero*. New York, 1901. Similarly, see H.S. Kennedy-Skipton in *Bristol-Gloucs*, XX, 1896, 108–13; and (100, 579, 689).

715 Kirby, John L. *Henry IV of England*. 1970. Interesting, learned but conventional political biography; and see Arthur Goodman's monograph on the 1403 marriage with Joan of Navarre, Winchester, 1934; and (688).

716 Lloyd, John E. *Owen Glendower: Owen Glyn Dŵr*. Oxford, 1931. This is the classic study, summarized in his Historical Association Leaflet 87, 1932; add references in (605, 749, 97); and see Glanmor Williams, Oxford, 1966.

717 MacGibbon, David. *Elizabeth Woodville, 1437–1492; her life and times*. 1938. See Katharine Davies' 1937 biography and especially the sound monograph on her coronation by Smith (659).

718   Markham, Clements R. *Richard III: his life and character reviewed in the light of recent research*. 1906. Classic revivifying of Richard's reputation that evoked various restatements and researches in the 'black' tradition, Gairdner (685). See summary (791) and Josephine Tey's amusing fictions in *Daughter of Time*. Debate began in *EHR*, VI, 1891, pp. 250–83.

719   Mitchell, Rosamund J. *John Tiptoft (1427–70); The declamacion of noblesse. Translated by J. Tiptoft from the Controversia de nobilitate of Buonaccorso da Montemagno*. 1938. On Tiptoft's library see (2498) and her article, *Library*, 4th ser., XVIII, 1937, pp. 67–83; also (648, 1500).

720   Ross, Charles D. *Edward IV*. 1974. Previewed in (691), now the authoritative study, as is his *Richard III*, 1976; see (687).

721   Routh, Enid M.G. *Lady Margaret: a memoir of Lady Margaret Beaufort, countess of Richmond & Derby, mother of Henry VII*. 1924. Also, William B. Hannon's 1916 biography, and the 1839 effort of Caroline A. Halsted.

722   Saltmarsh, John. *King Henry VI and the royal foundations*. Cambridge, 1972. A biography by Bertram P. Wolffe is in progress; other basic materials for Henry VI are (604, 607, 625, 644, 666, 691, 758, 772, 788, 799, 828, 864, 881, 882, 896, 906, 922, 941, 944, 972–3).

723   Steel, Anthony. *Richard II*. 1941. See extensive review by Vivian H. Galbraith, *History*, n.s., XXVI, 1942, pp. 223–39, and Harold F. Hutchison, *The hollow crown*, in 1961 and esp. see Henri Wallon's 1864 biography in 2 vols; on Richard's marriage to Anna, see Churchill G. Chamberlayne, Halle, 1906, and (805); see generally (692).

724   Vickers, Kenneth H. *Humphrey, duke of Gloucester: a biography*. 1907. See (741, 768, 782, 837, 1474, 2395, 2400, 2444, 2473).

725   Walpole, Horace. *Historic doubts on the life and reign of Richard III*. 1768. Original 'revisionist' interpretation followed by Markham (718), and Kendall (712), but see Gairdner's (685) counter view.

726   Williams, Ethel C. *My lord of Bedford, 1389–1435*. 1963. Excellent and readable study of John of Lancaster, who was Regent of France; also (810, 1558, 1589).

5 Articles

727   Amyot, Thomas. 'An inquiry concerning the death of Richard the Second', *Arch*, XX (1824), 424–42; XXIII (1831), 277–98; XXV (1834), 394–7; XXVIII (1840), 75–95. More gruesome details by P.W. Dillon in the last article; for other royal exhumations (755, 764, 772, 834); and for Richard II's deposition (679, 683, 743, 779, 841, 849).

728   Armstrong, Charles A.J. 'The inauguration ceremonies of the Yorkist kings and their title to the throne', *TRHS*, 4th ser., XXX (1948), 51–73. See (571).

729   —— 'The piety of Cicely, duchess of York: a study in late-mediaeval culture', in Douglas Woodruff (ed.), *For Hilaire Belloc: essays in honour of his 72nd birthday*. 1942, pp. 73–94. See (687).

730   —— 'Politics and the battle of St Albans, 1455', *BIHR*, XXXIII (1960), 1–72. Careful study of the origins of Yorkist political power.

731   Barber, Madeline J. 'John Norbury (*c*. 1350–1414): an esquire of Henry IV', *EHR*, LXVIII (1953), 66–76. Successful royal retainer, mercenary, and keeper of the privy wardrobe.

732   Barnard, Ettwell A.B. 'Salwarpe and the Talbots', *Transactions of the Worcestershire Archaeological Society*, n.s., XV (1938), 27–44. Especially concerned with Richard Beauchamp, earl of Warwick (713).

733   Barron, Caroline M. 'The tyranny of Richard II', *BIHR*, XLI (1968), 1–18. Intelligent, sure study with special emphasis on royal policy in London; also, Leonard C. Hector's note on Richard II's temperament, *EHR*, LXVIII, 1953, pp. 62–5; generally (692).

734   Baskerville, Geoffrey. 'A London chronicle of 1460', *EHR*, XXVIII (1913), 124–7. See (130, 626).

735 Bean, John M.W. 'Henry IV and the Percies', *History*, XLIV (1959), 212–27.
Other recent work on northern politics (151, 165, 542, 691, 736, 767,
777, 789, 844) and for Scotland (1, 107, 629, 856).

736 Bellamy, John G. 'The northern rebellions in the later years of Richard II',
BJRL, XLVII (1964–5), 254–74.

737 Bittmann, Karl. 'La campagne lancastrienne de 1463: Un document italien',
Revue Belge de philologie et d'histoire, XXVI (1948), 1059–83.

738 Blayney, Margaret S. 'Sir John Fortescue and Alain Chartier's *Traité de
l'Ésperance*', *Modern Language Review*, XLVIII (1953), 385–90. For
Fortescue see important materials in (593–5, 740, 761, 763, 771, 776,
848); Blayney has edited the text for the EETS, 1974.

739 Brown, Alfred L. and Bruce Webster. 'The movements of the earl of Warwick
in the summer of 1464 – a correction', *EHR*, LXXXI (1966), 80–2.
Generally (687, 713).

740 Chrimes, Stanley B. 'Sir John Fortescue and his theory of dominion', *TRHS*,
4th ser., XVII (1934), 117–47. And see Charles F. Arrowood, *Speculum*,
X, 1935, pp. 404–10; and (738), plus Max A. Shepard's general arguments in *Essays in history and political theory in honor of Charles H.
McIlwain*. Cambridge, Mass., 1936.

741 —— 'The pretensions of the duke of Gloucester in 1422', *EHR*, XLV
(1930), 101–3. See (724).

742 Christy, Miller. 'Where in Essex are Froissart's "Bondelay" and "Behode"?'
Essex Review, XXXI (1922), 138–46. Pertaining to the murder of
Thomas of Woodstock, duke of Gloucester (623).

743 Clarke, Maude V. and Vivian H. Galbraith. 'The deposition of Richard II',
BJRL, XIV (1930), 125–81. See (683, 692, 727).

744 Conway, Agnes E. 'The Maidstone sector of Buckingham's Rebellion, Oct.
18, 1483', *ArchCant*, XXXVII (1925), 97–119. See (685).

745 Cooper, William D. 'John Cade's followers in Kent', *ArchCant*, VII (1868),
233–71; *SussexS*, XVIII (1866), 17–36.

746 Coulborn, A.P.R. 'The economic and political preliminaries of the crusade of
1383', *BIHR*, X (1933), 40–4.

747 Crotch, Walter J.B. 'An Englishman of the fifteenth century [William
Caxton]', *Economica*, X (1930), 56–73. Also editor of Caxton's *Pro-
logues and Epilogues*, 1928 (2463).

748 Davies, John. 'Sir John Oldcastle (Lord Cobham)', *ArchCamb*, 4th ser., VIII
(1877), 124–34.

749 Davies, R.R. 'Owain Glyn Dŵr and the Welsh squirearchy', *Transactions of
the Honourable Society of Cymmrodorion* (1968), 150–69. Recon-
structs and analyses the bases for his support; also (605, 766, 775, 809,
97).

750 Davies, Richard G. 'Some notes from the register of Henry de Wakefield,
bishop of Worcester, on the political crisis of 1386–1388', *EHR*,
LXXXVI (1971), 547–58. See (1761).

751 Dilks, Thomas B. 'Bridgwater and the insurrection of 1381', *SomersetP*,
LXXIII (1927), 57–69. See (582, 693, 702).

752 Dobson, Richard B. and John Taylor. 'The medieval origins of the Robin
Hood legend: a reassessment', *Northern History*, VII (1972), 1–30. Sum-
marizes the controversy amongst Maurice H. Keen (697), Rodney H.
Hilton and James C. Holt in *Past and Present*, XIV, 1958, pp. 30–44;
XVIII, 1960, pp. 89–110; and XIX, 1961, pp. 16–18; and (2194).

753 Edwards, [J.] Goronwy. 'The "second" continuation of the Crowland
chronicle: Was it written "in ten days"?' *BIHR*, XXXIX (1966), 117–29.
See (596).

754 Evans, Howell T. 'William Herbert, earl of Pembroke [executed 1469]',
Transactions of the Honorable Society of Cymmrodorion (1909–10),
137–79. See (97, 687).

755 Evans, Joan. 'Edmund of Langley and his tomb', *Arch*, XLVI (1881), 297–
328. Reports on modern exhumation of the first Yorkist, died 1402;
other exhumations in (727).

756 Ferguson, Arthur B. 'The problem of counsel in *Mum and the sothsegger*', *Studies in the Renaissance*, II (1955), 67–83. See (696, 1060).

757 Flaherty, William E. 'The great rebellion in Kent, 1381, illustrated from the public records', *ArchCant*, III (1860), 65–96; IV (1861), 67–86. See (702).

758 Flood, William H.G. 'King Henry VI as musician', *Dublin Review*, CLXXIV (1924), 66–72. Generally (722).

759 Flower, Cyril T. 'The Beverley town riots (1381–2)', *TRHS*, n.s., XIX (1905), 79–99.

760 Gairdner, James. 'Jack Cade's rebellion', *Fortnightly Review*, XIV (1870), 442–55. The action that Hubert Hall perceived as nihilistic in *Antiquary*, XII, 1885, pp. 57–61, 118–21.

761 Gilbert, Felix. 'Sir John Fortescue's *dominium regale et politicum*', *Medievalia et Humanistica*, II (1944), 88–97. Expands Stanley B. Chrimes' suggestion that the origin of Fortescue's concept is in Aquinas' *De regimine principium*, while in the same journal, VII, 1952, pp. 89–94, George L. Mosse emphasizes Fortescue's exaltation of the papacy; also (738).

762 Gill, Harry. 'A local patron of architecture in the reign of Henry VI', *ThorotonS*, XIX (1915), 105–40. Ralph Cromwell died 1456 (2372).

763 Gill, Paul E. 'Politics and propaganda in fifteenth-century England: the polemical writings of Sir John Fortescue', *Speculum*, XLVI (1971), 333–47. See (738, 1569).

764 Godfrey-Faussett, Thomas G. 'Tomb of King Henry IV in Canterbury Cathedral', *ArchCant*, VIII (1872), 294–9. Reports exhumation records for 1832 in detail (727, 688).

765 Griffiths, Ralph A. 'Gruffydd ap Nicholas and the fall of the house of Lancaster', *WHR*, II (1965), 213–31. See (97, 691).

766 —— 'The Glyndŵr rebellion in north Wales through the eyes of an Englishman', *BBCS*, XXII (1967), 151–68. See Smith (660), and for Wales in the second half of the fifteenth century see Griffiths (691), also (97, 749).

767 —— 'Local rivalries and national politics: the Percies, the Nevilles, and the Duke of Exeter, 1452–1455', *Speculum*, XLIII (1968), 589–632. And see (735).

768 —— 'The trial of Eleanor Cobham: an episode in the fall of Duke Humphrey of Gloucester', *BJRL*, LI (1968–9), 381–99. See (724, 837).

769 —— 'William Botiller: a fifteenth-century civil servant', *Bristol-Gloucs*, LXXXIII (1964), 70–7.

770 Hanham, Alison. 'Richard III, Lord Hastings and the historians', *EHR*, LXXXVII (1972), 233–48. Revises date of Hastings' arrest, thus of Richard's usurpation; but see the new biography of *Richard III* by Charles D. Ross; and Bertram P. Wolffe's refutation of Hanham's dating, in *EHR*, LXXXIX, 1974, pp. 835–44; Hanham's reply, *EHR*, XC, 1975, pp. 821–7.

771 Hinton, Raymond W.K. 'English constitutional theories from Sir John Fortescue to Sir John Eliot', *EHR*, LXXV (1960), 410–25. Exposition on Fortescue's implications for early seventeenth century conflicts; similarly, see Caroline A.J. Skeel, *TRHS*, 3rd ser., X, 1916, 77–114, and (738).

772 Hope, William H. St John. 'The discovery of the remains of Henry VI in St. George's Chapel, Windsor Castle', *Arch*, LXII (1911), 533–42. See (722, 727).

773 —— 'The king's coronation ornaments [to 1485]', *Ancestor*, I (1902), 127–59. See references in (571).

774 Huizinga, Johan. 'Koning Eduard IV van Engeland in ballingschap', in *Mélanges d'histoire offerts à Henri Pirenne . . .* , I. Brussels, 1926, pp. 245–56. That is, his exile 1470–1 (575, 687).

775 Jack, R. Ian. 'Owain Glyn Dŵr and the lordship of Ruthin', *WHR*, II (1965), 303–22; *BBCS*, XXI (1965), 163–6. See (97, 605, 766).

776 Jacob, Ernest F. 'Sir John Fortescue and the law of nature', *BJRL*, XVIII (1934), 359–76. See (738).

777 Jeffs, Robin M. 'The Poynings–Percy dispute: an example of the interplay of open strife and legal action in the fifteenth century', *BIHR*, XXXIV (1961), 148–64. Similarly see Joel T. Rosenthal in *Nottingham Mediaeval*

Studies, XIV, 1970, pp. 84—90, regarding the Hastings family feuds in land, 1458.

778 Johnston, C.E. 'Sir William Oldhall', *EHR*, XXV (1910), 715—22. Yorkist supporter, died 1460.

779 Jones, Evan J. 'An examination of the authorship of *The deposition and death of Richard II*, attributed to Créton', *Speculum*, XV (1940), 460—77. See Buchon (576, 743, 861).

780 Jones, Morris C. 'The feudal barons of Powys', *Collections Historical & Archaeological Relating to Montgomeryshire*, I (1868), 257—423. See (97, 793).

781 Jones, Thomas A. 'Owen Tudor's marriage', *BBCS*, XI (1943), 102—9. And Stanley B. Chrimes, *Henry VII*, 1972, p. 5, for some corrections.

782 Kendrick, Thomas D. 'Humphrey, duke of Gloucester, and the Gardens of Adonis', *AntiqJ*, XXVI (1946), 118—22. See (724).

783 Kingsford, Charles L. 'The earl of Warwick at Calais in 1460', *EHR*, XXXVII (1922), 544—6. See (713).

784 —— 'The early biographies of Henry V', *EHR*, XXV (1910), 58—92. See (579, 689).

785 —— 'An historical collection of the fifteenth century', *EHR*, XXIX (1914), 505—15; XXXI (1916), 126—8. The second note concerns Robert Bale, a chronicler of London (130, 626).

786 Kriehn, George. 'Studies in the sources of the social revolt in 1381', *AHR*, VII (1902), 254—85, 458—84. See (582, 693, 702).

787 Lander, Jack R. 'Edward IV: the modern legend: and a revision', *History*, n.s., XLI (1956), 38—52. See (687, 720).

788 —— 'Henry VI and the duke of York's second protectorate, 1455 to 1456', *BJRL*, XLIII (1960—1), 46—69. See (722).

789 —— 'Marriage and politics in the fifteenth century: the Nevilles and the Wydevilles', *BIHR*, XXXVI (1963), 119—52. See (735, 767).

790 Leadman, Alexander D.H. 'The insurrection and death of archbishop Scroope, and the battle of Bramham Moor', *YorksJ*, XI (1891), 189—99. See (800).

791 Levine, Mortimer. 'Richard III — usurper or lawful king?' *Speculum*, XXXIV (1959), 391—401. Challenges Kendall's exculpatory biography of Richard III (712), and adds sound synthetic comments in *Tudor dynastic problems 1460—1571*, 1973; and generally (685, 2091).

792 Lewis, M.B. 'Simon Burley and Baldwin of Raddington', *EHR*, LII (1937), 662—9. Underchamberlain and controller of the wardrobe, respectively, to Richard II (692).

793 Lloyd, William V. 'A Powysian at Agincourt: Sir Griffith Vaughan', *Collections Historical & Archaeological Relating to Montgomeryshire*, II (1869), 139—72. See (97, 793).

794 Longford, William W. 'Some notes on the family history of Nicholas Longford, sheriff of Lancashire in 1413', *Lancs Historic*, LXXXVI (1934), 47—71.

795 McFarlane, Kenneth B. 'The English nobility in the later middle ages', in *XIIe Congrès international des sciences historiques, Rapports*, I (1965), 337—45. And (691, 701).

796 —— 'Henry V, bishop Beaufort, and the red hat, 1417—1421', *EHR*, LX (1945), 316—48. See (464, 689).

797 —— 'The wars of the roses', *PBA*, L (1965), 87—119. An important synthesis, defining the role of nobility in the dynastic struggles.

798 —— 'William of Worcester, a preliminary survey', in James C. Davies (ed.), *Studies presented to Sir [Charles] Hilary Jenkinson*. 1957, pp. 196—221. Proving that he did not write the *Annales* (666), and (1013).

799 McKenna, John W. 'Henry VI of England and the dual monarchy: aspects of royal political propaganda, 1422—1432', *Journal of the Warburg and Courtauld Institutes*, XXVIII (1965), 145—62. Analysis toward a definition of kingship, with (571, 696, 722, 828, 944).

800 McNiven, Peter. 'The betrayal of archbishop Scrope', *BJRL*, LIV (1971—2), 173—213.

801 —— 'The Cheshire rising of 1400', *BJRL*, LII (1969—70), 375—96.

802 Myers, Alec R. 'The captivity of a royal witch: the household accounts of Queen Joan of Navarre, 1419–21', *BJRL*, XXIV (1940), 263–84; XXVI (1941), 82–100.

803 —— 'Richard III and historical tradition', *History*, LIII (1968), 181–202. Poorly written but interesting historiographical essay (685); better still, read his essay on Richard III's character reprinted in Christopher M.D. Crowder's collection of articles from 'History Today', 1967.

804 Old, William W. 'Historical notices of the cradle of Henry V', *TRHS*, IV (1876), 231–59. See (689).

805 Palmer, J.J.N. 'The background to Richard II's marriage to Isabel of France [1396]', *BIHR*, XLIV (1971), 1–17.

806 Palmer, William M. and Herbert W. Saunders (eds.). 'The peasants' revolt of 1381 as it affected the villages of Cambridgeshire', in *Documents Relating to Cambridgeshire Villages*, II. Cambridge, 1926, pp. 17–36. Generally (582, 693, 702).

807 Perceval, Charles S. 'Inaccuracies in the ordinary accounts of the early years of the reign of Edward IV', *Arch*, XLVII (1883), 265–94. Summarizes events 1461–5 to correct the early Tudor chroniclers.

808 Perry, George G. 'Bishop Beckington and king Henry VI', *EHR*, IX (1894), 261–74. See (227, 896).

809 Phillips, J.R.S. 'When did Owain Glyndŵr die?', *BBCS*, XXIV (1970), 59–77. Generally (605, 97).

810 Pocquet du Haut-Jussé, Barthélemy. 'Anne de Bourgogne et le testament de Bedford [1429]', *Bibliothèque de l'École des Chartes*, XCV (1934), 284–326.

811 Pollard, Albert F. 'The making of Sir Thomas More's "Richard III" ', in John G. Edwards, Vivian H. Galbraith and Ernest F. Jacob (eds.), *Historical essays in honour of James Tait*. Manchester, 1933, pp. 223–38. And his review of the William E. Campbell edition, *History*, n.s., XVII, 1932, pp. 317–23; also (669, 685).

812 —— 'The authorship and value of the "Anonimalle" chronicle', *EHR*, LIII (1938), 577–603. Especially for its account of the peasants' revolt, 1381; see Galbraith (315, 602).

813 Poole, Mrs Reginald L. 'Notes on the history in the seventeenth century of the portraits of Richard II', *AntiqJ*, XI (1931), 145–59. Regarding the Wilton Dyptych (2313), and see (2341).

814 Previté-Orton, Charles W. 'The earlier career of Titus Livius de Frulovisiis', *EHR*, XXX (1915), 74–8. Henry V's contemporary biographer (579, 618).

815 Radford, Cecily. 'Fight at Clyst in 1455', *DevonA*, XLIV (1912), 252–65. Between retinues of Thomas Courtenay, earl of Devon, and William Bonville; and now John A.F. Thomson, *BIHR*, XLV, 1972, pp. 234–8.

816 —— 'Nicholas Radford, 1385?–1455', *DevonA*, XXXV (1903), 251–78. Royal servant and recorder of Exeter, murdered by Thomas Courtenay.

817 —— 'An unrecorded royal visit to Exeter', *DevonA*, LXIII (1931), 255–63. By Henry IV and his second wife, Joan of Navarre in 1403.

818 Richardson, Henry G. 'The coronation in medieval England', *Traditio*, XVI (1960), 111–202. Much earlier, but relevant background (571).

819 —— 'The English Coronation Oath', *Speculum*, XXIV (1949), 44–75.

820 —— 'Illustrations of English history in the mediaeval registers of the parlement of Paris', *TRHS*, 4th ser., X (1927), 55–85. Particularly during the latter stages of the 100 years' war.

821 Richmond, Colin F. 'Fauconberg's Kentish rising of May 1471', *EHR*, LXXXV (1970), 673–92. See (575).

822 Robbins, Edgar C. 'The cursed Norfolk justice. A defence of Sir William Yelverton (c. 1400–1477)', *NA*, XXVI (1936), 1–51.

823 Roskell, John S. 'John, lord Wenlock of Someries', *Bedfordshire Historical Record Society*, XXXVIII (1958), 12–48. Lancastrian supporter, killed at Tewkesbury, 1471.

824 —— and Frank Taylor. 'The authorship and purpose of the *Gesta Henrici*

Quinti', *BJRL*, LIII (1970–1), 428–64; LIV (1971–2), 223–40. Important and detailed interpretation previewing their edition of the work (680).

825 Roth, Cecil. 'Sir Edward Brampton: an Anglo-Jewish adventurer during the wars of the roses', *Transactions of the Jewish Historical Society of England*, XVI (1952), 121–7; IX (1918–20), 143–62. The second article makes a connection between Brampton and Perkin Warbeck.

826 —— 'Sir Edward Brampton, alias Duarte Brandão: governor of Guernsey, 1482–1485', *Reports and Transactions of La Société Guernesiaise*, XVI (1956), 160–70. Portuguese Jew, possibly bastard of the Brandon family.

827 Round, John H. 'The arms of the King-Maker', *Ancestor*, IV (1903), 143–7; V (1903), 195–202; VIII (1904), 202–4. Richard Neville, earl of Warwick, died 1471 (713).

828 Rowe, Benedicta J.H. 'King Henry VI's claim to France in picture and poem', *Library*, 4th ser., XIII (1932), 77–88. And see (799).

829 Rowse, Alfred L. 'The turbulent career of Sir Henry de Bodrugan', *History*, n.s., XXIX (1944), 17–26. Yorkist Cornishman, attainted by Henry VII.

830 Sandquist, T.A. 'The holy oil of St Thomas of Canterbury', in T.A. Sandquist and Michael R. Powicke, *Essays in medieval history presented to Bertie Wilkinson*. Toronto, 1969, pp. 330–44. See references in (571).

831 Solly-Flood, Frederick. 'The story of prince Henry of Monmouth [1402–5] and chief justice Gascoigne', *TRHS*, n.s., III (1886), 47–152; IV (1889), 125–41.

832 Sparvel-Bayly, John A. 'Essex in insurrection, 1381', *EssexT*, n.s., I (1878), 205–19. Reprinted in *Antiquary*, XIX, 1889, pp. 11–14, 69–73; also (702).

833 Stamp, Alfred E. 'Richard II and the death of the duke of Gloucester', *EHR*, XXXVIII (1923), 249–51; XLVII (1932), 453, 726. See (742, 838, 852).

834 Stanley, Arthur P. 'On an examination of the tombs of Richard II and Henry III in Westminster Abbey', *Arch*, XLV (1880), 309–27; XLVI (1881), 281–96. Somewhat gruesome, detailed report on the exhumed remains, with noteworthy comments on English royal burial customs; the second article concerns Katherine de Valois's corpse; also (727, 755, 764, 772).

835 Starkey, H.W. 'Two Saffron Walden men of the 14th century', *Essex Review*, XXIX (1920), 46–50. Roger Walden, Richard II's secretary and lord treasurer, and Thomas Waldensis, Henry V's confessor and councillor.

836 Stewart-Brown, Ronald. 'The Scrope and Grosvenor controversy, 1385–1391', *Lancs Historic*, LXXXIX (1938), 1–22. See (1516).

837 —— 'The imprisonment of Eleanor Cobham, duchess of Gloucester', *Lancs Historic*, LXXXV (1933), 89–97. See (724, 768).

838 Tait, James. 'Did Richard II murder the duke of Gloucester?' in Thomas F. Tout and James Tait (eds.), *Historical essays*. Manchester, 1902 (re-issued 1907), pp. 193–216. And see Richard L. Atkinson, *EHR*, XXXVIII, 1923, pp. 563–4; also (742, 833, 852).

839 Tanner, Lawrence E. 'The princes in the Tower', in his *Recollections of a Westminster antiquary*. 1969, pp. 153–65. And see Dennis E. Rhodes, *EHR*, LXXVII, 1962; part of the larger debate (685, 718).

840 —— and William Wright. 'Recent investigations regarding the fate of the princes in the Tower', *Arch*, LXXXIV (1935), 1–26. An additional example of scientific analysis currently available is in Martin A. Rushton's study of Anne Mowbray's teeth, from this time, in *British Dental Journal*, CXIX, 1965, pp. 355–9.

841 Thompson, Edward M. 'A contemporary account of the fall of Richard the Second', *The Burlington Magazine*, V (1904), 160–72, 267–70. Jean Creton's chronicle, being B.M. Harleian ms. 1319 (861, 727).

842 Tillotson, J.H. 'Peasant unrest in the England of Richard II: some evidence from royal records', *Historical Studies*, XVI (1974), 1–16. See (693, 702).

843 Tuck, J. Anthony. 'The Cambridge parliament, 1388', *EHR*, LXXXIV (1969), 225–43. See (176, 196, 392).

844 ——— 'Richard II and the border magnates', *Northern History*, III (1968),
27—52. Emphasizing his support of the Nevilles, and not the Percies,
against the Scots (735).

845 Van Tromp, Harold. ' "Scogin's jests." As gathered by Andrew Board', *Sussex
County Magazine*, VIII (1934), 422—6. Jokebook of Edward IV's court
jester; also, William E. Farnham, *Modern Language Review*, XVI, 1921;
and on Edward IV's style of literary patronage, see Margaret Kekewich,
Modern Language Review, LXVI, 1971, pp. 481—7.

846 Virgoe, Roger. 'The death of William de la Pole, duke of Suffolk [2 May
1450]', *BJRL*, XLVII (1964—5), 489—502.

847 ——— 'William Tailboys and Lord Cromwell: crime and politics in Lancastrian
England', *BJRL*, LV (1973), 459—82. Excellent reconstruction of the
realities of retainers and the law, with an edition of interrogatories and
confessions of William Stanes.

848 Welch, Anne M. 'Sir John Fortescue, buried at Ebrington, Glouc. [died
1476]', *Bristol-Gloucs*, XXIV (1901), 193—250. See (738).

849 Wilkinson, Bertie. 'The deposition of Richard II and the accession of Henry
IV', *EHR*, LIV (1939), 215—39. Argues that Henry IV did not base his
claim on parliamentary title, against the conclusions of Stubbs and
Lapsley; also (688, 692, 727).

850 ——— 'The peasants' revolt of 1381', *Speculum*, XV (1940), 12—35. See
(582, 693, 702).

851 Williams, William L. 'Adam of Usk', *Y Cymmrodor*, XXXI (1921), 135—60.
Born about 1352, died about 1430, and provided additions to Higden's
Polychronicon for period after Edward III (568, 672, 705, 97).

852 Wright, Herbert G. 'Richard II and the death of the duke of Gloucester', *EHR*,
XLVII (1932), 276—80, 726; *BJRL*, XXIII (1939), 151—65. The second
article analyses Richard II's Tower protestation in 1399; see (833, 692).

853 Wylie, James H. 'Decembri's version of the *Vita Henrici quinti* by Tito Livio',
EHR, XXIV (1909), 84—9. See (618, 579, 689).

VI. FOREIGN RELATIONS

1 Printed sources

854 Allmand. Christopher T. (ed.). 'Documents relating to the Anglo-French
negotiations of 1439', *Camden Miscellany XXIV* (Camden Society, 4th
ser., IX). 1972, pp. 79—149. See (942).

855 Anon. (ed.). *Ancient petitions of the chancery and the exchequer' ayant
trait aux Îles de la Manche, conservées au Public Record Office à Londres*.
1902. That is, for the Channel Islands, 1292—1454 (938).

856 Bain, Joseph (ed.). *Calendar of documents relating to Scotland preserved in
the Public Record Office, London [1108—1509]*. Edinburgh, 1881—8, 4
vols. See Hancock (1) and (629, 863); for printed sources in Scottish
government see their editors: J.H. Burton (privy council), M. Livingstone
(secret seal), J. Stuart (exchequer), J.M. Thomson (great seal), T.
Thomson (lords in council), T. Thomson and C. Innes (parliament).

857 Beaune, Henri and Jean J. d'Arbaumont (ed.). *Mémoires d'Olivier de la
Marche, maître d'hotel et capitaine des gardes de Charles le téméraire*,
(Société de l'Histoire de France). Paris, 1883—8, 4 vols.

858 Benham, William G. (ed.). ' "Colchester merchants" sea adventure in 1388',
Essex Review, XLIII (1934), 78—81. Diplomacy with Zeeland (970,
1264, 1285, 1296).

859 Bond, Edward A. (ed.). 'Original letter addressed to Henry IV., king of
England, by Elisabetta, duchess of Bavaria, dated Nov. 24, 1400', *AJ*, XII
(1855), 377—9. Suggesting marriage alliance through her niece (688).

860 Buchon, Jean A.C. (ed.). *Jean Juvénal des Ursins' Histoire de Charles VI,
1380—1422*. Paris, 1838.

861 ——— (ed.). *Jean Créton's Histoire du roy d'Angleterre Richard II* (Collection

des chroniques Françaises, XXIV). Paris, 1826. See Jones (779), and an English translation by John Webb is in *Arch*, XX, 1824, pp. 1–423; generally (692).

862 Bueno de Mesquita, Daniel M. (ed.). 'The foreign policy of Richard II in 1397: some Italian letters', *EHR*, LVI (1941), 628–37.

863 *Calendars of French rolls, 1–10 Henry V* (Forty-Fourth Annual Report of the Deputy Keeper of the Public Records, App. III, pp. 543–638). 1883. And for Scottish papers, see Illingworth (878), and for relevant Scottish chronicles (1, 629); other materials in (689, 897, 903, 910, 961, 1520).

864 *Calendar of French rolls, Henry VI* (Forty-Eighth Annual Report of the Deputy Keeper of the Public Records, App. II, pp. 217–450). 1887. Important for protections granted individuals in diverse military retinues, but also includes trade and diplomatic licenses, safe-conducts, as do the Norman Rolls (722, 881).

865 *Calendar of Norman rolls, Henry V. (First Part)* (Forty-First Annual Report of the Deputy Keeper of the Public Records, App. II, pp. 671–810). 1880. See Hardy (876), and generally (579, 689).

866 *Calendar of Norman rolls, Henry V (Second Part and Glossary)* (Forty-Second Annual Report of the Deputy Keeper of the Public Records, App. II, pp. 313–472). 1881. See Hardy (876).

867 *Calendar of state papers, Milan*, ed. by Allen B. Hinds [HMSO]. 1912. Materials from 1359 to 1618, with (880, 891).

868 *Calendar of state papers, Venetian*, ed. by Rawdon Brown, G. Cavendish Bentinck, and Horatio F. Brown, I [HMSO]. 1964. Materials from 1202 to 1509.

869 Champollion-Figeac, Jacques J. (ed.). *Lettres de rois, reines, et autras personnages des cours de France et d'Angleterre, depuis Louis VII, jusqu'a Henri IV*. Paris, 1839–47, 2 vols.

870 Douet-D'arcq, Louis C. (ed.). *Choix de pièces inédites relatives au règne de Charles VI* (Société de l'Histoire de France). Paris, 1863–4, 2 vols.

871 —— (ed.). *La chronique d'Enguerran de Monstrelet . . . 1400–1444* (Société de l'Histoire de France). Paris, 1858–62, 6 vols. Also an English ed. by Thomas Johnes, 1809, 5 vols.

872 Dupont, Mlle. [L.M.E.] (ed.). *Anchiennes cronicques d'Engleterre par Jehan de Waurin* (Société d l'Histoire de France). Paris, 1858–63, 3 vols. Or, English ed. by William J. and Edward L.C.P. Hardy for the Rolls Series, XXXIX–XL, 1864–91, 7 vols.

873 —— (ed.). *Mémoires de Pierre de Fenin, comprenant le récit des evénements qui se sont passés en France et en Bourgogne . . . (1407–1427)* (Société de l'Histoire de France). Paris, 1837.

874 —— (ed.). *Mémoires de Philippe de Commynes* (Société de l'Histoire de France). Paris, 1840–7, 3 vols. There is a good paperback translation by Michael Jones, 1972; for the actual text, use the Dupont or the Bernard de Mandrot ed., Paris, 1901–3, 2 vols.; also, Mandrot's important study of Commynes' reliability, *Revue historique*, LXXIII, 1900, pp. 241–57, and LXXIV, 1901, pp. 1–38; and (687).

875 Green, Mrs Everett [Mary A.] (ed.). 'Letters of Margaret d'Anjou and Prince Edward, in the archives at Paris', *AJ*, VII (1850), 166–71. About 1461, found in the *Documens relatif à l'Angleterre* collections in the Bibliothèque Nationale; also (637).

876 Hardy, Thomas D. (ed.). *Rotuli Normanniae in turri Londinensi asservati [1200–1205, 1417]* (Record Commission). 1835.

877 Hennessy, William M. (ed.). *Annals of Loch Cé: a chronicle of Irish affairs [1014–1590]* (Rolls Series, LIV). 1871, 2 vols. Also edited *Annals of Ulster . . . 431–1541*, Dublin, 1887–1901, 4 vols.; and see John O'Donovan, Dublin, 1851, 7 vols.; for Ireland (1, 133, 2046, 2068, 2397).

878 Illingworth, William, John Caley, and David Macpherson (eds.). *Rotuli Scotiae in turri Londinensi et in domo capitulari Westmonasteriensi asservati, II* (Record Commission). 1819. Transcripts of Scottish relations, Richard II – Henry VIII (1, 863).

879 Jerningham, Edward (ed.). 'Account of king Edward the Fourth's second

invasion of England, in 1471, drawn up by one of his followers, with the king's letter to the inhabitants of Bruges upon his success', *Arch*, XXI (1827), 11—23. From ms. in the public library in Ghent, with (575).

880 Kendall, Paul M. and Vincent Ilardi (eds. and trans.). *Dispatches, with related documents, of Milanese ambassadors in France and Burgundy, 1450—1483*. 1970—, 6 vols. To date 1971, two volumes published in this most valuable collection, see (867, 891).

881 Le Cacheux, Paul (ed.). *Actes de la chancellerie d'Henri VI concernant la Normandie sous la domination anglaise (1422—1435). Extraits des registres du trésor des chartes aux Archives Nationales*. Rouen and Paris, 1907—8, 2 vols. See (722, 864).

882 —— (ed.). *Rouen au temps de Jeanne d'Arc et pendant l'occupation anglaise (1419—1449)*. Rouen, 1931. See review in *Journal des Savants*, 1933, pp. 158—165; also (911, 932, 1527); the two monographs by Raymond Quenedey, 1923 and 1932 are especially useful.

883 Lefèvre-Pontalis, Germain (ed.). *Chronique d'Antonio Morosini: extraits relatifs a l'histoire de France [1396—1433]* (Société de l'Histoire de France). Paris, 1898—1902, 4 vols.

884 Le Vavasseur, Achille (ed.). *Chronique d'Arthur de Richemont, connétable de France, duc de Bretagne (1393—1458)* (Société de l'Histoire de France). Paris, 1890.

885 Lewis, Peter S. (ed.). *The recovery of France in the fifteenth century*. 1971.

886 Lopez de Ayala, Pedro. *Cronicas de los reyes de Castilla, Don Pedro, Don Enrique II, . . .* Madrid, 1779, 2 vols. See (937).

887 Luce, Siméon (ed.). *Chronique des quatre premiers Valois (1327—1393)* (Société d l'Histoire de France). Paris, 1862.

888 —— (ed.). *Chronique du Mont-Saint-Michel (1343—1468)* (Société des Anciens Textes Français). 1879—83, 2 vols.

889 ——, *et al.* (eds.). *Chroniques de J. Froissart* (Société de l'Histoire de France). Paris, 1869—1966, 14 vols. Complete English version, translated by John Bourchier, lord Berners, and originally publ. in 1523—5, 2 vols.; republished by Thomas Johnes in 1803—5, 4 vols., and by W.P. Ker in 1901—3, 6 vols.; consult the authoritative *Oeuvres*, ed. by Baron Joseph M.B.C. Kervyn de Lettenhove, 1867—77; and (2205).

890 Madden, Frederic (ed.). 'Narratives of the arrival of Louis de Bruges, seigneur de la Gruthuyse, in England, and of his creation as earl of Winchester, in 1472', *Arch*, XXVI (1836), 265—86. Found in B.M., Add. ms. 6113, f. 103.

891 Mandrot, Bernard De (ed.). *Dépèches des ambassadeurs Milanais en France sous Louis XI et Francois Sforza [1461—1466]* (Société de l'Histoire de France). Paris, 1916—23, 4 vols. And see Curt Bühler in *Speculum*, XXX, 1955, pp. 239—40, for a letter from Edward IV to Sforza (867, 880). Mandrot also edited Commynes' *Mémoires* (874).

892 —— (ed.). *Journal de Jean de Roye, connu sous le nom de Chronique scandaleuse 1460—1483* (Société de l'Histoire de France). Paris, 1894—6, 2 vols.

893 Morand, Francois (ed.). *Chronique de Jean Le Fèvre, seigneur de Saint-Rémy [1408—1435]* (Société de l'Histoire de France). Paris, 1876—81, 2 vols. With the English at Agincourt, providing an important source.

894 Moranvillé, Henri (ed.). *Chronographia regum Francorum* (Société de l'His-toire de France). Paris, 1891—7, 3 vols. Particularly vol III covering 1380—1405.

895 Newhall, Richard A. (ed.). *The Chronicle of Jean de Venette* (Records of Civilization, no. 50). New York, 1953.

896 Nicolas, Nicholas H. (ed.). *A journal by one of the suite of Thomas Becking-ton, during an embassy to negotiate a marriage between Henry VI. and a daughter of the count of Armagnac, A.D. 1442*. 1828. A translation of the Latin text is published by Benjamin Williams; also (277).

897 Palgrave, Francis [Francis Cohen] (ed.). *Scotland. Documents and records illustrating the history of Scotland . . . and England [to 36 Henry VI]* (Record Commission). 1837. See (1, 863, 878).

898   Palmer, J.J.N. (ed.). 'Articles for a final peace between England and France, 16 June 1393', *BIHR*, XXXIX (1966), 180—5.

899   Pannier, Leopold and Paul Meyer (eds.). *Le débat des hérauts d'armes et d'Angleterre* (Société des Anciens Textes Francais). 1877. English edition in 1870 by Henry Pyne; also (572, 993, 1045, 1500, 1535).

900   Parry, Clive and Charity Hopkins (eds.). *Index to British treaties 1101—1968.* 1970, 3 vols. See Rymer (905).

901   Perroy, Edouard (ed.). *The diplomatic correspondence of Richard II.* (Camden Society, 3rd ser., XLVIII). 1933. Generally (692).

902   Phillipps, Thomas (ed.). 'Account of the ceremonial of the marriage of the princess Margaret, sister of king Edward the Fourth, to Charles duke of Burgundy, in 1468', *Arch*, XXXI (1846), 326—38. From a private ms. owned by the Wriothesley family; and (949).

903   Public Record Office. *List of diplomatic and Scottish documents and papal bulls.* 1923, no. 49. For Scotland (1, 863, 629).

904   Quicherat, Jules E.J. (ed.). *Histoire des règnes de Charles VII, et de Louis XI, par Thomas Basin (Évêque de Lisieux)* (Société de l'Histoire de France). Paris, 1855—9, 4 vols.

905   Rymer, Thomas (ed.). *Foedera, conventiones, letterae et cujuscunque generis acta publica inter reges Angliae et alios quosuis imperatores, reges, pontifices, principes, vel communitates.* 1727—35, 20 vols. Revised ed. by Adam Clark *et al.* covers 1066—1383, publ. 1816—19, 4 vols; for guidance begin with Thomas D. Hardy (ed.), *Rymer's Foedera: syllabus in English with index 1066—1654*, 1869—85, 3 vols.

906   Thoms, William J. *et al.* (eds.). 'Instructions given by King Henry VI to Edward Grimston and others, his ambassadors to the duchess of Burgundy, 1449; and notice of a portrait of Edward Grimston, painted by Peter Christus in 1446', *Arch*, XL (1866), 451—82; XLV (1877), 124—6. See (722).

907   Tuetey, Alexandre (ed.). *Journal d'un bourgeois de Paris, 1405—1449.* Paris, 1881.

908   Vaësen, Joseph and Étienne Charavay (eds.). *Lettres de Louis XI, roi de France* (Société d l'Histoire de France). Paris, 1883—1909, 11 vols.

909   Waters, William G. and Emily (eds.). *The Vespasiano memoirs*, 1926. That is, a translation of Vespasiano da Bistices, *Vite di uomini illustri del secolo xv.*

910   Weiss, Roberto (ed.). 'The earliest account of the murder of James I of Scotland', *EHR*, LII (1937), 479—84. Given eight days after the event, 1437; for James' English captivity, see Evan W.M. Balfour-Melville's Historical Association Leaflet no. 77, 1929.

2 Monographs

911   Amiet, Marie L. *La condamnation de Jeanne d'Arc vue à la lumière des grands événements du moyen age.* Paris, 1934. See (1518); of the dozens of books available, the best biographies are by Henri Wallon, Paris, 1876, by Victoria Sackville-West, 1936, and by W.S. Scott, 1974; for the best and most recent work on Joan see Pernoud (932), and (882, 979, 1498, 1527, 2285).

912   Beaucourt, Gaston du Fresne de. *Histoire de Charles VII.* Paris, 1881—91, 6 vols. Covers Anglo-French relations in the reigns of Henry V and Henry VI; now see Malcolm G.A. Vale's biography, 1974.

913   Behault de Dornon, Armand de. *Bruges séjour d'exil des rois d'Angleterre, Edouard IV (1471) et Charles II (1656—1658).* Bruges, 1931.

914   Bémont, Charles. *La Guienne pendant la domination anglaise, 1152—1453.* Paris, 1920. Also, Désiré Brissaud, *Les Anglais en Guyenne*, Paris, 1875; and Henri Ribadieu, 1866; also (959).

915   Bonenfant, Paul. *Du meutre de Montereau au traité de Troyes.* Brussels, 1958. Burgundian diplomacy, particularly with Henry V, September 1419 to June 1420.

916   Bossuat, André. *Perrinet Gressart et François de Surienne, agents de l'Angleterre. Contribution à l'étude des relations de l'Angleterre et de la*

Bourgogne avec la France sous le règne de Charles VII. Paris, 1936. See (919), and the revisions proposed by Maurice H. Keen and M.J. Daniel, *History*, LIX, 1974, pp. 375—91.

917 Boutruche, Robert. *La Crise d'une société: seigneurs et paysans du Bordelais pendant la guerre de cent ans.* Paris, 1947. See (1048, 1526).

918 Calmette, Joseph L.A. and Georges Perinelle. *Louis XI et l'Angleterre (1461—1483).* Paris, 1930. See review by Henri Prentout, *Journal des Savants*, 1932, pp. 261—73.

919 Champion, Pierre F. and Paul de Thoisy. *Bourgogne—France—Angleterre au [1420] traité de Troyes. Jean de Thoisy . . . 1350—1453.* Paris, 1943. See (930, 940, 944, 967, 1369, 1370, 1529).

920 Denquin, Marcel. *Calais sous la domination anglaise, 1347—1558.* Calais, 1939. Also, Georges Daumet's monograph, Arras, 1902; and (956, 957, 424).

921 Dickinson, Joycelyne G. *The Congress of Arras, 1435: a study in medieval diplomacy.* Oxford, 1955. Careful study of personnel and especially of procedures, as in *History*, n.s., XL, 1955, pp. 31—41; more recently, see Reginald Brill, *Studies in Medieval and Renaissance History*, VII, 1970, pp. 211—47; also Malcolm G.A. Vale, *Nottingham Mediaeval Studies*, XVII, 1973, pp. 78—84.

922 Ferguson, John. *English diplomacy, 1422—1461.* Oxford, 1972. Excellent reconstruction of final phases of the Hundred Years' War (722).

923 Frondeville, Henri de. I: *Le vicomté d'Orbec pendant l'occupation anglaise, 1417—1419*; II: *Compte de Jean le Muet, vicomte d'Orbec pour la Saint-Michel, 1444.* Caen, 1936.

924 Gierth, Wilhelm. *Die vermittlungsversuche K. Sigmunds zwischen Frankreich und England, 1416.* Halle, 1895. German scholarship on Emperor Sigismund's mediation and visit to Canterbury also includes monographs by Paul Hagemann, 1905, Jacob Caro, 1880, and Max Lenz, 1874; and see Charles L. Kingsford's note, *EHR*, XXVI, 1911, pp. 750—1; also (981).

925 Heeren, John J. *Das Bündis zwischen König Richard II. von England und König Wenzel vom Jahre 1381.* Halle, 1910. See (692).

926 Jones, Michael. *Ducal Brittany, 1364—1399: relations with England and France during the reign of Duke John IV.* Oxford, 1971. Narrative political history on English occupation of Brest and Richmond.

927 Knowlson, George A. *Jean V, duc de Bretagne et l'Angleterre 1399—1442.* Cambridge, 1964. Thorough for the Breton side of diplomacy with (933); and see Eugène Cosneau, *Le connétable de Richemont (Artur de Bretagne), 1393—1458,* Paris, 1886.

928 Lewis, Peter S. *Later medieval France.* New York, 1968.

929 Lodge, Eleanor C. *Gascony under English rule.* 1926. See Vale (941).

930 Owen, Leonard V.D. *The connection between England and Burgundy during the first half of the fifteenth century.* Oxford, 1909. See (919).

931 Palmer, J.J.N. *England, France and Christendom 1377—99.* 1972. Diplomacy and domestic politics during an intensive phase of the Hundred Years' War, partially described in *TRHS*, 5th ser., XVI, 1966, pp. 81—94.

932 Pernoud, Regine. *Jeanne devant les Cauchons.* Paris, 1970. The most vigorous recent scholarship by the author of numerous, reliable monographs; essential to any biography of Joan of Arc is Paul Doncoeur, *Documents et recherches rélatifs à Jeanne la Pucelle*, Melun and Paris, 1952—61, 5 vols.

933 Pocquet du Haut-Jussé, Barthélemy A.M.J. *François II, duc de Bretagne, et l'Angleterre (1458—1488),* (Mémoires de la Société d'histoire et d'archeologie de Bretagne, IX). Paris, 1928 [1929].

934 Poullain, H. *Orleans. L'invasion anglaise en 1428: notice rétrospective.* Orleans, 1913. See (1527, 1531).

935 Renouard, Yves. *Bordeaux sous les rois d'Angleterre.* Bordeaux, 1965.

936 —— *Études d'histoire médiévale,* II, *Septième partie: Sud-ouest et relations Franco-Anglaises.* Paris, 1968.

937 Russell, Peter E. *The English intervention in Spain and Portugal in the time of Edward III and Richard II.* Oxford, 1955. See (692, 886).

938 Saunders, Arthur C. *Jersey in the 15th and 16th centuries.* Jersey, 1933.

939 Stranders, Vivian. *Die Frankreichpolitik Heinrichs IV von England, 1399–1413*. Berlin, 1941. See (688).

940 Thielemans, Marie-Rose. *Bourgogne et Angleterre. Relations politiques et économiques entre les Pays-Bas Bourguignons et l'Angleterre, 1435–1467* (Travaux de la Faculté de Philosophie et Lettres de l'Université libre de Bruxelles, XXX). Brussels, 1966. Excellent scholarship that includes comments on trade regulations and their enforcement, but criticized in (1369); and see (919).

941 Vale, Malcolm G.A. *English Gascony 1399–1453*. Oxford, 1970. Partly described in *TRHS*, 5th ser., XIX, 1969, pp. 119–38 (1262).

3 Articles

942 Allmand, Christopher T. 'The Anglo-French negotiations, 1439', *BIHR*, XL (1967), 1–33. See (854, 922).

943 Anquetil, Eugène. 'Girot Davy de Bayeux. Épisode de l'occupation anglaise du XVe siècle', *Bulletin de la Société des Antiquaires de Normandie*, XII (1902), 136–44.

944 Armstrong, Charles A.J. 'La double monarchie France-Angleterre et la maison de Bourgogne (1420–1435). Le déclin d'une alliance', *Annales de Bourgogne*, XXXVII (1965), 81–112. See (404, 799).

945 Behrens, Betty. 'Origins of the office of English resident ambassador in Rome', *EHR*, XLIX (1934), 640–56. Read Garrett Mattingly, *Renaissance diplomacy*, 1955; also (964).

946 —— 'Treatises on the ambassador written in the fifteenth and early sixteenth centuries', *EHR*, LI (1936), 616–27.

947 Bonenfant, Paul. 'Actes concernant les rapports entre les Pays-Bas et la Grande-Bretagne de 1293 à 1468, conservés au château de Mariemont', *Académie Royale de Belgique, Commission Royale d'histoire, Bulletin*, CIX (1944), 53–125.

948 Braddy, Haldeen. 'New documentary evidence concerning Chaucer's mission to Lombardy [1378]', *Modern Language Notes*, XLVIII (1933), 507–11; LII (1937), 33–4. And John Manly's addendum in *ibid.*, XLIX, 1934, pp. 209–16; Braddy also notes the Clifford mission to France in 1391.

949 Calmette, Joseph L.A. 'Le mariage de Charles le téméraire et de Marguerite d'York', *Annals de Bourgogne*, I (1929), 193–214. See (902).

950 Clough, Cecil H. 'The relations between the English and Urbino courts, 1474–1508', *Studies in the Renaissance*, XIV (1967), 202–18.

951 Dickinson, Joycelyne E. ' "Blanks" and "blank charters" in the fourteenth and fifteenth centuries', *EHR*, LXVI (1951), 375–87. Particularly for diplomatic efficiency, saving extra time and posting (29, 337).

952 Doucet, Roger. 'Les finances anglaises en France à la fin de la guerre de cent ans, 1413–35', *Le Moyen Âge*, XXXVI (1926), 265–332. See (116, 485).

953 Halecki, Oscar. 'Gilbert de Lannoy and his discovery of east central Europe [embassy of 1421]', *Polish Institute of Arts and Sciences in America Bulletin*, II (1944), 314–31.

954 Jacob, Ernest F. 'The collapse of France in 1419–20', *BJRL*, XXVI (1942), 307–26. See (689, 968, 972, 978).

955 Jones, Michael. 'The ransom of Jean de Bretagne, count of Penthièvre; an aspect of English foreign policy 1386–8', *BIHR*, XLV (1972), 7–26.

956 Kirby, John L. 'Calais sous les Anglais, 1399–1413', *Revue du Nord*, XXXVII (1955), 19–30. Particularly the fiscal importance (920); and generally (116, 688).

957 —— 'The financing of Calais under Henry V', *BIHR*, XXIII (1950), 165–77.

958 Lacour, René. 'Une incursion anglaise en Poitou en Novembre 1412. Compte d'une aide de 10,000 écus accordée du duc de Berry pour résister à cette incursion', *Archives Historiques du Poitou*, XLVIII (1934), 1–87.

959 La Martinière, Jules de. 'Instructions secrètes données par Charles VI au sire d'Albret, pour soulever la Guyenne contre Henri IV (fin d'octobre 1399–janvier 1400)', *Bibliothèque de l'École des Chartes*, LXXIV (1913), 329–40. See (914).

960 Le Patourel, John. 'Le rôle de la ville de Caen dans l'histoire de l'Angleterre', *Annales de Normandie*, XI (1961), 171–7.

961 Macrae, C. 'The English council and Scotland in 1430', *EHR*, LIV (1939), 415–26. See (629, 856).

962 McFarlane, Kenneth B. 'Anglo-Flemish relations in 1415/16', *Bodleian Quarterly Record*, VII (1935), 41–5.

963 Mirot, Léon. 'Isabelle de France, reine d'Angleterre, comtesse d'Angoulême, duchesse d'Orléans (1389–1409). Épisode des relations entre la France et l'Angleterre pendant la guerre de cent ans', *Revue d'Histoire Diplomatique*, XVIII (1904), 545–73; XIX (1905), 60–95, 161–91, 481–522.

964 —— and Eugène Déprez. 'Les ambassades anglaises pendant la guerre de cent ans: catalogue chronologique, 1327–1450', *Bibliothèque de l'École des Chartes*, LIX (1898), 550–77; LX (1899), 177–214; LXI (1900), 20–58. Using PRO Exchequer accounts; but see important revisions by Alfred Larson, *EHR*, LV, 1940, pp. 423–31.

965 Moranvillé, Henri. 'Aide imposée par le roi d'Angleterre à Paris en 1432', *Bulletin de la Société de l'histoire de Paris*, XXX (1903), 112–26.

966 —— 'Conférences entre la France et l'Angleterre, 1388–93', *Bibliothèque de l'École des Chartes*, L (1889), 355–80.

967 Myers, Alec R. 'The outbreak of war between England and Burgundy in February 1471', *BIHR*, XXXIII (1960), 114–15. See (919).

968 Newhall, Richard A. 'Henry V's policy of conciliation in Normandy, 1417–1422', in C.H. Taylor (ed.). *Anniversary essays in medieval history by students of Charles H. Haskins*. Boston, 1929, pp. 205–29. Generally (579, 689).

969 —— 'Payment to Pierre Cauchon for presiding at the trial of Jeanne d'Arc', *Speculum*, IX (1934), 88–90.

970 Owen, Leonard V.D. 'England and the Low Countries, 1405–1413', *EHR*, XXVIII (1913), 13–33. See (858).

971 Perroy, Edouard. 'Franco-English relations, 1350–1400', *History*, n.s., XXI (1936), 148–54. General survey of diplomacy (1542).

972 Rowe, Benedicta J.H. 'The *Grand Counseil* under the duke of Bedford, 1422–1435', in Frederick M. Powicke (ed.), *Oxford essays in medieval history presented to Herbert E. Salter*. Oxford, 1934, pp. 207–34. See (722, 954).

973 —— 'The states of Normandy under the duke of Bedford, 1422–1435', *EHR*, XLVI (1931), 551–78; XLVII (1932), 583–600.

974 Sayers, Jane E. 'Proctors representing British interests at the papal court, 1198–1415', in Stephan Kuttner (ed.), *Proceedings of the Third International Congress of Medieval Canon Law*. Vatican City, 1971, pp. 143–64.

975 Tournouer, Henri. 'Les anglais à Longny à la fin de la guerre de cent ans', *Bulletin des Société historique et archéologique de l'Orne*, XXIV (1905), 169–88.

976 Troplong, Edouard. 'De la fidelité des Gascons aux Anglais pendant le moyen âge (1152–1453)', *Revue d'Histoire Diplomatique*, XVI (1902), 51–68, 238–66, 410–37, 481–521.

977 Tuck, [J.] Anthony. 'Some Evidence for Anglo-Scandinavian relations at the end of the fourteenth century', *Mediaeval Scandinavia*, V (1972), 75–88. See (1189, 1352).

978 Waugh, William T. 'The administration of Normandy, 1420–22', in Andrew G. Little and Frederick M. Powicke (eds.), *Essays in medieval history presented to Thomas F. Tout*. Manchester, 1925, pp. 349–59. See (689, 954).

979 —— 'Joan of Arc in English sources of the fifteenth century', in John G. Edwards, Vivian H. Galbraith, and Ernest F. Jacob (eds.), *Historical essays in honour of James Tait*. Manchester, 1933, pp. 387–98. See (911).

980 Wylie, James J. 'Memorandum concerning a proposed marriage between Henry V and Catherine of France in 1414', *EHR*, XXIX (1914), 322–33. See (689).

VII. SOCIAL HISTORY

1 Printed sources

981   Altmann, Wilhelm (ed.). *Eberhart Windecke's Denkwürdigkeiten zur Geschichte des Zeitalters Kaiser Sigmunds*. Berlin, 1893. Record of visit to England in 1416 (924); other visitors to England who kept records are (1019, 1021, 1036, 1041); more visitors are (1010, 1055, 1099, 1128, 1974) and see Thrupp on alien residents (1143).

982   Amyot, Thomas (ed.). 'Transcript of two rolls containing an inventory of effects formerly belonging to sir John Fastolfe', *Arch*, XXI (1927), 232–80.

983   Anon. *Index of wills, etc., from the dean and chapter's court at York, 1321–1636*, (YorksRS, XXXVIII). Worksop, 1907. Numerous collections of wills have been indexed, and a few calendared, usually according to ecclesiastical jurisdictions. The following editors, with dates of publ., have produced separate volumes of indices: Francis Collins (York registry), 1889; Frederick A. Crisp (Ipswich), 1895; Leland L. Duncan (Kent), 1890; Frederick A. Emmison (Essex), 1958; Margaret A. Farrow (Norwich), 1943–5; Marc Fitch (London), 1969; Charles W. Foster (Lincoln), 1902–14; Edward A. Fry (Worcester), 1904; Frederick J. Furnivall (London), 1882; Alfred Gibbons (Lincoln), 1888; Walter H. Godfrey (Sussex), 1935–41; T.W. Oswald-Hicks (Suffolk), 1913; Henry R. Plomer (Canterbury registry), 1920; James Raine and John W. Clay (York registry), 1835–1902; Reginald R. Sharpe (London hustings), 1889–90; J.C.C. Smith (Canterbury court), 1893–5; Frederic W. Weaver (Somerset), 1901; and, John R.H. Weaver and Alice Beardwood (Oxfordshire), 1958. For other wills indexed in periodicals see (995, 1004, 1117).

984   —— *Index of Wiltshire fines, 1 Edward III to Richard III*. N.p., Middle Hill Press, n.d. The fine records agreements involving freehold property and is therefore important for family and economic history. The following editors, with dates of publ., have indexed fine records extant for their counties in separate volumes: Lucy Drucker (Warwickshire), 1943; William Farrer (Lancaster), 1899–1910; Robert C. Fowler (Essex), 1949; Edward A. and George S. Fry (Dorset), 1896–1910; Emanuel Green (Somerset), 1902–6; William J. Hardy and William Page (London–Middlesex), 1892–3; Frank B. Lewis (Surrey), 1894; Thomas Phillipps (Worcestershire), 1865; Percy H. Reaney and Marc Fitch (Essex), 1947–64; Walter Rye (Norfolk), 1885–6; Walter Rye (Suffolk), 1900; Harry Tapley-Soper (Cornwall), 1950; and, George J. Turner (Huntingdon), 1913. For other fines indexed in periodicals see (1034, 1035, 1047).

985   Atchley, Edward G.C.F. (ed.). 'Some more Bristol inventories', *StPaulS*, n.s., IX (1922–8), 1–50. That is, addenda to the basic ed. published in 1900.

986   Austin, Thomas (ed.). *Two fifteenth-century cookery books* (EETS, LIV). 1888. See (1009, 1046, 1070, 1131).

987   Baildon, William P. (ed.). 'Three inventories: the earl of Huntingdon, 1377; brother John Randolf, 1419; sir John de Boys, 1426', *Arch*, LXI (1908), 163–76.

988   —— and John W. Clay (eds.). *Inquisitions post mortem relating to Yorkshire of the reigns of Henry IV and Henry V* (YorksRS, LIX). 1918. See (996, 997, 1006, 1018, 1030, 1042, 1043); for plague (1466).

989   Baillie-Grohman, William A. and Florence (eds.). *The master of game. By Edward, second duke of York. The oldest English book on hunting*. 1904. Also, Alice Dryden (ed.), Northampton, 1908; and (1060, 1104, 2425), esp. *The boke of Saint Albans*, attributed to Dame Juliana Berners.

990   Bandinel, Bulkeley (ed.). *The itineraries of William Wey, fellow of Eton College. To Jerusalem, A.D. 1458 and A.D. 1462; and to Saint James of Compostella, A.D. 1456 [and] map of the Holy Land* (Roxburghe Club,

76, 88). 1857—67, 2 vols. See (1013, 1020); for travel generally (981, 1002, 1079, 1086, 1088, 1096, 1136, 1137, 1555).

991   Bateson, Edward (ed.). 'Notes on a journey from Oxford to Embleton and back, in 1464', *ArchAel*, n.s., XVI (1894), 113—20. Found in Merton College, Oxford, deed no. 2853.

992   Beamont, William (ed.). *Annals of the lords of Warrington for the first five centuries after the conquest* (Chetham Society, LXXXVI, LXXXVII). Manchester, 1872.

993   Bentley, Samuel (ed.). *Excerpta historica, or, illustrations of English history.* 1831. For the narrative of the 'Tournament between Anthony Neville, lord Scales, and the Bastard of Burgundy, 1467', pp. 171—212; also (572, 899, 1010, 1045, 1071, 1147, 1500, 1501).

994   Botfield, Beriah (ed.). *Manners and household expenses of England in the thirteenth and fifteenth centuries.* 1841. Accounts and memoranda of John, 1st duke of Norfolk, 1462—1471; another ed. by Thomas H. Turner for Roxburghe Club, 1841; see John P. Collier's ed., covering 1484—90, for Roxburghe Club, 1844; also (1024, 1029, 1038, 1044).

995   Brigg, William (ed.). 'Testamenta Leodiensia', *Thoresby Society, Miscellanea I* (1891), 98—110, 205—14. From York probate registry, 1391—1494 (983).

996   *Calendar of inquisitions post mortem and other analogous documents preserved in the Public Record Office.* Vols XV—XVI: 1—14 *Richard II.* 1970—3, 2 vols. See (988).

997   Caley, John and John Bayley (eds.). *Calendarium inquisitionum post mortem sive excaetarium.* 1806—28, 4 vols. Also, 3 vols. in 1823—34 for the Record Commission, calendaring same for the Duchy of Lancaster, ed. by Caley, R.J. Harper and W. Minchin; (988).

998   Chambers, Raymond W. (ed.). *A fifteenth century courtesy book* (EETS, CXLVIII). 1914. See (1007, 1008, 1028, 1031, 1060, 2408).

999   Collier, John P. (ed.). *Trevelyan papers prior to A.D. 1558* (Camden Society, LXVII). 1857.

1000   Cooper, William D. (ed.). 'Proofs of age of Sussex families, temp. Edw. II to Edw. IV', *SussexS*, XII (1860), 23—44; XV (1863), 211—14. Similarly (411, 1016).

1001   Coulton, George G. (ed.). *Social life in Britain from the conquest to the reformation.* Cambridge, 1918 (repr. 1968).

1002   Cronne, Henry A. and Rodney H. Hilton (eds.). 'The Beauchamp household book: an account of a journey from London to Warwick in 1432', *UBHJ*, II (1949—50), 208—18. See (990).

1003   Davis, Norman (ed.). *Paston letters and papers of the fifteenth century.* Oxford, 1971. First of projected four volumes, to replace Gairdner (1011). See Davis in *PBA*, XL, 1954, pp. 119—44 and in *Review of English Studies*, n.s., III, 1952, pp. 209—21; also Curt Bühler in *Review of English Studies*, XIV, 1938, pp. 129—42. The other collections of family letters are (1017, 1026, 1039).

1004   Foster, Charles W. (ed.). 'Lincolnshire wills proved in the prerogative court of Canterbury', *Reports and Papers of the Architectural and Archaeological Societies*, XLI (1932—3), 61—114, 179—218. See (983).

1005   France, Reginald S. (ed.). 'A Stanley account roll, 1460', *Lancs Historic*, CXIII (1961), 203—9.

1006   Fry, Edward A. (ed.). *A calendar of inquisitions post mortem for Cornwall and Devon, 1216—1649* (Devon and Cornwall Record Society). 1906. See (988).

1007   Furnivall, Frederick J. (ed.). *The boke of curtasye.* (EETS, XXXII, and e.s., III). 1868, 2 vols. From B.M., Sloane ms. 1986, dated 1430—40, and includes verse descriptions of royal household officers and their duties; also (998, 1031).

1008   —— (ed.). *The boke of nurture, by John Russell, about 1460—1470 A.D.* (Roxburghe Club, 87). 1867.

1009   —— (ed.). *A booke of precedence* (EETS, e.s., VIII). 1869. Subtitled

Queen Elizabethes achademy, providing the order for royal feasts and the courses served (986).

1010 —— and Richard E.G. Kirk (eds.). *Analogues of Chaucer's Canterbury pilgrims (April 1386) and his putting-up joust-scaffolds, etc., in West Smithfield (May 1390)* (Chaucer Society, 2nd ser., XXXVI). 1903. Daily expenses of Aragonese embassy for 58 days in England (21 July—16 September 1415) and costs for scaffolding on 30 January 1442; also (981, 993, 1500).

1011 Gairdner, James (ed.). *The Paston letters, 1422—1509*. 1872—5; repr. with corrections in 1896, 3 vols.; supp. ed., 1901, 4 vols.; rev. ed., 1904, 6 vols. The last edition is best, but see Davis (1003); the original edition, 1787—1823 in 5 vols., is by John Fenn. A good biography of William Paston, 1378—1444, publ. in 1932, was written by Edgar C. Robbins. And see *Arch*, XLI, 1867, pp. 33—74, for initial reports on authenticity of Paston letters, and Gairdner on that subject in *Fortnightly Review*, II, 1865, pp. 579—94; and see (375, 1050, 1051, 1102, 2097).

1012 *Harleian Society*. 1869—. Editions in many volumes of diverse sixteenth and seventeenth century heraldic visitations in most counties, establishing authenticity of coats-of-arms; also edits marriage license registers, genealogies, obituaries, pedigrees, and parish registers, especially for London; see Wagner (1045, 1083).

1013 Harvey, John H. (ed.). *Itineraries [of] William of Worcester*. Oxford, 1969. Records antiquarian treks in southern England, 1478—80; and (990); the previous ed. was J. Nasmith, 1778; see (2449).

1014 Haward, Winifred I. and Helen M. Duncan (eds.). *Village life in the fifteenth century* (Texts for Students, XLI). 1928. Collection of documents for students.

1015 Hoare, Christobel M. (ed.). *The history of an east Anglian soke: studies in original documents. Including hitherto unpublished material dealing with the peasants' rising of 1381, and bondage and bond tenure*. Bedford, 1918. See (693, 702).

1016 Hodgson, John C. (ed.). 'Proofs of age of heirs to estates in Northumbria', *ArchAel*, XXII (1900), 116—30; XXIV (1903), 126—7; 3rd ser., III (1907), 297—305. Dating from 1328—40 and 1401—72 (411, 1000).

1017 Kingsford, Charles L. (ed.). *The Stonor letters and papers, 1290—1483* (Camden Society, 3rd ser., XXIX, XXX). 1919, 2 vols; [and,] *Camden Miscellany XIII* (Camden Society, 3rd ser., XXXIV). 1924. See (1003, 1026, 1039).

1018 Langton, William (ed.). *Abstracts of inquisitions post mortem* (Chetham Society, XCV, XCIX). 1875—6, 2 vols. Mainly fifteenth century but dating between 1297 and 1637 (988).

1019 Letts, Malcolm H.I. (ed.). *The diary of Jörg von Ehingen*. 1929. Translates part of Franz Pfeiffer's ed. of 1842, esp. recording the visit to England in 1458 with portraits of Henry VI and James II of Scotland (981).

1020 —— (ed.). *Mandeville's travels: texts and translations* (Hakluyt Society, 2nd ser., CI, CII). 1953, 2 vols. Includes essay by Eva G.R. Taylor on cosmography; an earlier ed. for EETS in CLIII, CLIV, CCLLIII, 1919—63, 3 vols.; also (990).

1021 —— (ed.). *Travels of Leo von Rozmital* (Hakluyt Society, 2nd ser., CVIII). 1957. To Edward IV's court in 1465; but see (1036), also (981).

1022 Lodge, Eleanor C. and Robert Somerville (eds.). *John of Gaunt's register, 1379—1383* (Camden Society, 3rd ser., LVI, LVII). 1937, 2 vols.

1023 Lyte, Henry C. Maxwell (ed.). 'An account relating to sir John Cobham, 1408', *AntiqJ*, II (1922), 339—43. Made by estate administrators.

1024 Macray, William D. (ed.). *Beaumont papers. Letters relating to the family of Beaumont, of Whitley, Yorkshire from the fifteenth to the seventeenth centuries* (Roxburghe Club, 113). 1884. See (994).

1025 Malden, Arthur R. (ed.). 'A Salisbury fifteenth-century death register', *Ancestor*, IX (1904), 28—35. Unique register, here only extracted, covering 1467—75.

1026 Malden, Henry E. (ed.). *The Cely papers: Selections from the correspondence of the Cely family, merchants of the staple, 1475—88* (Camden Society, 3rd ser., I). 1900. Also, *TRHS*, 3rd ser., X (1916), 159—65. See Hanham (1101), (2195), and (1003, 1017, 1039).

1027 Nichols, John (ed.). *Illustrations of the manners and expences of antient times in England, deduced from the accompts of churchwardens.* 1797.

1028 Offord, Marguerite Y. (ed.). *The book of the knight of the tower* (EETS, Supp. Ser. II). 1971. Earlier ed. by Thomas Wright in EETS, IV, 1868, of this superb source about courtly virtue; see (998, 1500).

1029 Redstone, Vincent B. (ed.). *The household book of dame Alice de Bryene of Acton Hall, Suffolk, Sept. 1412—Sept. 1413.* Ipswich, 1931. See (994).

1030 Renshaw, Mary A. (ed.). *'Inquisitiones post mortem* relating to Nottinghamshire 1437—1485', *Thoroton Society Record Series*, XVII (1956), 1—99. See (988, 1043).

1031 Rickert, Edith (ed.). *The babees' book; medieval manners for the young.* 1908 (reissued 1923). And (998, 1007, 2462); this is a major compilation of sources for education and home life, originally published in 1868 and followed by (1009). See Frederick J.H. Darton's broad survey of children's books, Cambridge, 1958; and (2408, 2451, 2461).

1032 Riley, Henry T. (ed.). *Memorials of London and London life, in the XIIIth, XIVth and XVth centuries . . . 1270—1419.* 1868. See (130, 249).

1033 Rye, Walter (ed.). *Calendar of the freemen of Norwich, 1317—1603.* 1888. See (117, 132).

1034 —— (ed.). *'Pedes finium*: or fines, relating to the county of Cambridge, levied in the king's court (1196—1485)', *Cambridge Antiquarian Society*, XX (1891), 1—157. See (984).

1035 Salzmann, Louis F. (ed.). 'An abstract of feet of fines relating to the county of Sussex from 1 Edward II to 24 Henry VII', *Sussex Record Society*, XXIII (1916), 1—304. See (984).

1036 Schmeller, Johann A. (ed.). *Des böhmischen Herrn Leo's von Rozmital Ritter-, Hof- und Pilger-Reise durch die Abendlande 1465, 1466 und 1467. Beschrieben von zweien seiner Begleiter.* Stuttgart, 1844. Includes both Schaschek's and Gabriel Tetzel's accounts of the same visit to England by Rozmital's suite (981, 1021, 1041).

1037 Scott, James R. (ed.). 'Receipts and expenditure of sir John Scott, in the reign of Edward IV [in 1463 and 1466]', *ArchCant*, X (1876), 250—8.

1038 Smith, Lucy T. (ed.). *A common-place book of the fifteenth century, containing a religious play and poetry, legal forms, and local accounts.* 1886. See (994).

1039 Stapleton, Thomas (ed.). *Plumpton correspondence: a series of letters, chiefly domestic, written in the reigns of Edward IV, Richard III, Henry VII, and Henry VIII* (Camden Society, IV). 1839. See (1003, 1017, 1026).

1040 Steer, Francis W. (ed.). 'The statutes of Saffron Walden almshouses', *EssexT*, n.s., XXV (1958), 161—221.

1041 Stenzel, Gustav A. (ed.). *Scriptores rerum silesiacarum III.* Breslau, 1847. Nikolaus von Popplau's diary of his visit to England in 1484, with detailed descriptions of English manners; based on Samuel B. Klose's copy made in the eighteenth century in his *Darstellung der inneren Verhältnisse der Stadt Breslau vom Jahre 1458 bis zum Jahre 1526*; see (981).

1042 Stokes, Ethel (ed.). *Abstracts of inquisitions post mortem for Gloucestershire returned into the court of chancery . . . 1359—1413* (British Record Society, Index Library, XLVII). 1914. See (988).

1043 Train, Keith S.S. (ed.). 'Abstracts of the inquisitions post mortem relating to Nottinghamshire 1350—1436', *Thoroton Society, Record Series*, XII (1948—51), 1—204. See (1030, 988).

1044 Turnbull, William B.D.D. (ed.). *Compota domestica familiarum de Buckingham et d'Angoulême.* Edinburgh, 1836. Household books for 1443—4 and 1463—4; also (994).

1045 Wagner, Anthony R. *A catalogue of English medieval rolls of arms.* (Harleian Society, C). Oxford, 1950. And (89, 899, 993, 1012, 1069, 1083, 1098, 1104, 1118, 1147, 1494, 1500, 1535).

1046 Webb, Margaret J. (ed.). *Early English recipes. Selected from the Harleian MS.
279 of about 1430 A.D.* Cambridge, 1937. See Mary S. Serjeantson's notes
on this ms.'s vocabulary, *Essays and Studies*, XXIII, 1938, pp. 25—37;
and J.J. Dickenmann's report on fourteenth-century sources, in *Anglia*,
XXVII, 1904, pp. 453—515; see (986, 1070).

1047 Wrottesley, George (ed.). 'Final concords, or *pedes finium*, Staffordshire,
1327—1547', *SaltS*, 1st ser., XI (1891), 127—292. See (984).

2 Monographs

1048 Allmand, Christopher T. *Society at war: the experience of England and
France during the Hundred Years' War*. New York, 1973. Includes select
bibliography and documents; see similar study by John Barnie for 1337—
99, published 1974. For France, read Boutruche (917) and esp.,
Contamine (1526).

1049 Bardsley, Charles W. *English surnames: their sources and signification*. 1873.
For place-names (77, 80, 81); and Bardsley's *A dictionary of English and
Welsh surnames*, 1901.

1050 Bennett, Henry S. *The Pastons and their England: studies in an age of transition*. Cambridge, 1922; rev., 1932. See (1003, 1011).

1051 —— *Six medieval men and women*. Cambridge, 1955. Humphrey, duke of
Gloucester, Thomas Hoccleve, Margery Kempe, Sir John Fastolf, Margaret
Paston, and Richard Bradwater (724, 2450, 1763, 1011).

1052 Beresford, Maurice W. *The lost villages of England*. 1971, 5th ed., rev. (orig.
ed. 1954). Brilliant pioneering study in literary and archaeological evidence for depopulation and demographic movement; also (74—5, 78, 83,
1076, 1085, 1141).

1053 —— and John G. Hurst (eds.). *Deserted medieval villages: studies*. 1971.

1054 Chambers, Jonathan D. *Population, economy, and society in pre-industrial
England* (ed. by W.A. Armstrong). 1972. Single best analytical survey
available, a detailed and rigorous synthesis (1059, 1076).

1055 Colvin, Ian D. *The Germans in England, 1066—1598*. 1915. See (981, 1143).

1056 DeWindt, Edwin B. *Land and people in Holywell-cum-Needingworth: structures of tenure and patterns of social organization in an East Midlands
village, 1252—1457*. Toronto, 1972. Excellent study, inspired by Raftis
(1122—4, 1281), details local government, family, and economic
relationships.

1057 Dugdale, William. *The baronage of England*. 1675. See (163).

1058 Dunham, William H., Jr. *Lord Hastings' indentured retainers 1461—1483*
(Transactions of Connecticut Academy of Arts and Science, XXXIX).
New Haven, 1955. Direct challenge to MacFarlane (466) and Roskell
views on bastard feudalism.

1059 Ekwall, B.O. Eilert. *Studies on the population of medieval London*. Stock-
holm, 1956. See (1052—4, 1076, 1141).

1060 Ferguson, Arthur B. *The indian summer of English chivalry*. Durham, North
Carolina, 1960. Careful and stimulating essays on knighthood in literature
and society, like his *The articulate citizen and the English Renaissance*,
Durham, N.C., 1965; also (756, 989, 998, 1028, 1045, 1066, 1070, 1071,
1081, 1083, 1115, 1142, 2444).

1061 Green, Mary A.E. *Town life in the fifteenth century*. New York, 1894, 2 vols.
Remains the most thorough and synthetic study of urban society (117, 353).

1062 Hartley, Dorothy and Margaret M. Elliot. *Life and work of the people of
England: the fifteenth century*. New York, 1926. See (109).

1063 Hilton, Rodney H. *The decline of serfdom in medieval England*. 1969.
Succinct survey; and for earlier study see Edward P. Cheyney, *EHR*, XV,
1900, pp. 20—37; on villeinage, see Thomas W. Page's monograph, 1900.

1064 —— *The English peasantry in the later middle ages: the Ford Lectures for
1973, and five related studies*. 1975.

1065 Hollaender, Albert E.J. and William Kellaway (eds.). *Studies in London history presented to Philip Edmund Jones*. 1969. Especially the articles by
Betty R. Masters on pre-1600 mayors' households, Jean M. Imray on

Mercer Company membership, Olive Coleman on London customers serving Richard II (324), and Sylvia L. Thrupp on aliens in London (1143).

1066 Kendall, Paul M. *The Yorkist age: daily life during the wars of the roses.* New York, 1962.

1067 Kingsford, Charles L. *Prejudice and promise in XVth-century England.* Oxford, 1925. A classic collection of essays designed to correct distortions created by Tudor authors, including Shakespeare, with an optimistic emphasis on mercantile and London activities.

1068 Lobel, Mary D. (General ed.). *Historic towns . . . from earliest times to c. 1800.* 1969. Projected multi-volume series (2 available, 1972) with maps and plans.

1069 London, Hugh S. *The life of William Bruges, the first Garter King of Arms* (Harleian Society, CXI, CXII). 1970. Died in 1450; here Anthony R. Wagner supplies excellent bibliographical notes (1045, 1083, 1570).

1070 Mitchell, Rosamund J. *The medieval feast: the story of the coronation banquet of king Henry IV in Westminster Hall, 13th October 1399.* 1958. Also, William E. Mead, *The English medieval feast*, 1931; and (986).

1071 —— *The medieval tournament: the story of the tournament at Smithfield on 11th June, 1467.* 1958. See the important study by F.H. Cripps-Day, 1918, and also Robert C. Clephan, 1919, for general history of tournaments; and Sidney Painter in *Modern Language Notes*, XLVIII, 1933, pp. 82–3; and (993, 1500).

1072 Myers, Alec R. *London in the age of Chaucer.* Norman, Oklahoma, 1972. Preferable to Robertson (1074).

1073 Nathan, Mathew. *The annals of West Coker [Somerset].* Cambridge, 1957. Excellent local, family history, with bibliography ed. by Michael M. Postan.

1074 Robertson, Durant W. *Chaucer's London.* New York, 1968. Sometimes misinformed and impressionistic but generally useful; also see (2191), Edith Rickert's 1948 collection of documents, and (1072). Now see Derek Brewer's valuable collection of essays, 1974; also, the earlier monographs of Charles Pendrill, 1925 and 1928.

1075 Rodgers, Edith C. *Discussion of holidays in the later middle ages* (Columbia University Studies in History, Economics, and Public Law, XLVII). New York, 1940. See (24, 1934).

1076 Russell, Josiah C. *British medieval population.* Albuquerque, New Mexico, 1948. The beginning for all British demographic studies, but see Thrupp (1141); and Russell's article in *Speculum*, XX, 1945, pp. 157–71; also (1052–4, 1059, 1108, 2143).

1077 Salter, Herbert E. *Medieval Oxford.* Oxford, 1936. Also edits numerous muniments of Oxford institutions (254).

1078 Salusbury, Goronwy T. [Jones, G.T.S.]. *Street life in medieval England.* Oxford, 1939; 1948, 2nd ed. Popular study in social history and municipal records.

1079 Salzmann, Louis F. *English life in the middle ages.* 1926. Excellent mss. illustrations and solid, general, topical text (1089, 1109, 1147); also, Jean J. Jusserand, *English wayfaring life in the middle ages*, 4th ed., 1950, remains useful (990).

1080 Thrupp, Sylvia L. *The merchant class of medieval London.* Ann Arbor, Michigan, 1948. Single most important study of late-medieval urban society, immensely learned and a model for scholarship. For alien merchants pre-1377, see Alice Beardwood's monograph, 1931; and (1143).

1081 Ticehurst, Norman F. *The mute swan in England.* 1957 [1958]. Studies customs of swan-keeping and its social significance (1060).

1082 Tierney, Brian. *Medieval poor law: a sketch of canonical theory and its application in England.* 1959. Studies proscriptions and their justifications, not enforcement, but still of essential importance for social and institutional history (357, 1922).

1083 Wagner, Anthony R. *Heralds and heraldry in the middle ages.* 2nd ed., 1956. See his (89, 1045, 1060, 1069); also (1494, 1500, 1535).

3 Articles

1084 Alexander, John J. 'Tavistock in the fifteenth century', *DevonA*, LXIX (1937), 247—85; LXXII (1940), 283—303. The second article describes the local aristocracy in Devon *circa* 1434.

1085 Allison, K.J., Maurice W. Beresford, and John G. Hurst. 'The deserted villages of Oxfordshire' (Leicester, Dept. of English Local History. Occasional Papers no. 17). 1965. Similarly for Northamptonshire, 1966, and (1052).

1086 Armstrong, Charles A.J. 'Some examples of the distribution and speed of news in England at the time of the wars of the roses', in Richard W. Hunt, William A. Pantin, and Richard W. Southern (eds.), *Studies in medieval history presented to Frederick M. Powicke*. 1948, pp. 429—54. See (990, 1105).

1087 Baldwin, James F. 'The household administration of Henry Lacy and Thomas of Lancaster', *EHR*, XLII (1927), 180—200.

1088 Barber, Madeline J. 'The Englishman abroad in the fifteenth century', *Medievalia et Humanistica*, XI (1957), 69—77. Records the use and abuse of licenses to travel; also (990).

1089 Barron, Oswald. 'Fifteenth-century costume', *Ancestor*, IX (1904), 113—36; X (1904), 120—32; XII (1905), 125—42. Superb illustrations and sources, as (1079, 1147, 2207, 2297).

1090 Bennett, M.J. 'A county community: social cohesion amongst the Cheshire gentry, 1400—1425', *Northern History*, VIII (1973), 24—44. Somewhat inflated generalizing from important evidence, especially from 1412 at Macclesfield, about intermarriage and control of offices.

1091 Butcher, A.F. 'The origins of Romney freemen, 1433—1523', *EcHR*, 2nd ser., XXVII (1974), 16—27. Important survey of urban—rural migrations, using local taxation and governmental records; similar materials in (132).

1092 Cam, Helen M. 'The decline and fall of English feudalism'. *History*, n.s., XXV (1940), 216—33. Provides conventional view, emphasizing early Tudor fiscal and legal centralization (466, 701, 1235), in contrast with preceding chaos.

1093 Carr, Anthony D. 'Sir Lewis John — a medieval London Welshman', *BBCS*, XXII (1967), 260—70. Generally (97).

1094 Charlesworth, Dorothy. 'Northumberland in the early years of Edward IV', *ArchAel*, 4th ser., XXXI (1953), 69—81.

1095 Cooper, J.P. 'The social distribution of land and men in England, 1436—1700', *EcHR*, 2nd ser., XX (1967), 419—40. And see George G. Chisholm's study of the distribution of towns and villages, *Geographical Journal*, IX, 1896, and X, 1897; and (1076, 1403).

1096 Cooper, Thomas P. 'The mediaeval highways, streets, open ditches, and sanitary conditions of the city of York', *YorksJ*, XXII (1913), 270—86. For London, see Sabine (1131—2); for travel (990), and for York (153).

1097 Fry, Timothy. 'A medieval defense of women', *American Benedictine Review*, III (1952), 122—34. Written between 1405 and 1410 in *Dives et Pauper*, printed in 1496; on women see (1011, 1102, 1135, 1317, 1331, 1476, 1489) and nunneries (1619).

1098 Giffin, Mary E. 'Cadwalader, Arthur and Brutus in the Wigmore manuscript', *Speculum*, XVI (1941), 109—20. See (1045, 1060, 97); Giffin describes the Mortimer family's use thereof.

1099 Gray, Howard L. 'Greek visitors to England in 1455—1456', in C.H. Taylor (ed.), *Anniversary essays in medieval history by students of Charles H. Haskins*. Boston, 1929, pp. 81—116.

1100 Hall, George D.G. 'The abbot of Abingdon and the tenants of Winkfield', *Medium Aevum*, XXVIII (1959), 91—5. Claim of serfdom made by the Abbot, 1393—4 (1063).

1101 Hanham, Alison. ' "Make a careful examination": some fraudulent accounts in the Cely papers', *Speculum*, XLVIII (1973), 313—24; *BIHR*, XLVI (1973), 123—44. And see (1026).

1102 Haskell, Anne S. 'The Paston women on marriage in fifteenth-century England', *Viator*, IV (1973), 459—72. And see (1011, 1097, 1135).

1103   Hulbert, N.F. 'A survey of the Somerset fairs', *SomersetP*, LXXXII (1936),
        83–159; LXXXIV (1938), 171–2. Detailed historical catalogue, with
        addenda and corrections by Ivan F.H. Jones in *ibid.*, XCI, 1945, pp. 71–
        81; also (1112, 1145–6).

1104   Jacob, Ernest F. 'The book of St Albans', *BJRL*, XXVIII (1944), 99–118.
        That is, Dame Juliana Berners, *Book of hawking, hunting and the blasing
        of arms*, printed first in 1486, and in facsimile, 1905; also (1045, 1500,
        2425). See Rachel Hands' facsimile ed., Oxford, 1975.

1105   —— 'To and from the court of Rome in the early fifteenth century', in
        *Studies in French language and literature presented to Professor Mildred
        K. Pope*. Manchester, 1939, pp. 161–81. See (981, 1086).

1106   Kenyon, Nora. 'Labour conditions in Essex in the reign of Richard II', *EcHR*,
        IV (1932–4), 429–51.

1107   Kerling, Nelly J.M. 'Aliens in the county of Norfolk, 1436–1485', *NA*,
        XXXIII (1965), 200–15. See Thrupp (1065, 1080, 1143).

1108   Krause, John. 'The medieval household: large or small?', *EcHR*, 2nd ser., IX
        (1956), 420–32. Wide-ranging critique of Russell (1076).

1109   Lewer, Henry W. 'The king's book of sports: Sunday games', *Essex Review*,
        XXII (1913), 173–88. Based on ms. illuminations from fourteenth and
        fifteenth centuries, and on sixteenth and seventeenth centuries' arch-
        diaconal visitations; also (1111, 1126, 1147).

1110   Linnoll, Charles L.S. 'The commonplace book of Robert Reynys of Acle',
        NA, XXXII (1961), 111–27. Calendar of Bodleian, Tanner ms. 407, con-
        taining 64 folios dated between 1474 and 1500.

1111   Magoun, Francis P., Jr. 'Football in medieval England and in middle-English
        literature', *AHR*, XXXV (1930), 33–45. See (1109).

1112   McCutcheon, Kenneth L. 'Yorkshire fairs and markets to the end of the
        eighteenth century', *Thoresby Society*, XXXIX (1939), 1–177. For
        Sussex, see Frederick E. Sawyer's lists, *SussexS*, XXXVI, 1888, pp.
        180–92; the entire topic of markets is best covered by Alan Everitt in
        chapter VIII, Joan Thirsk (ed.), *The agrarian history . . . 1500–1640*,
        Cambridge, 1967, pp. 466–592; and see (1103, 1145–6). For fairs and
        markets in York, see H. Richardson, St. Anthony's Hall Publication, no.
        20, 1961.

1113   McFarlane, Kenneth B. 'England and the Hundred Years' War', *Past and
        Present*, XXII (1962), 3–18. Compare with Postan's assessment
        (1120).

1114   Mills, A.D. 'Notes on some middle English occupational terms', *Studia Neo-
        philologica*, XL (1968), 35–48. Also (50, 55).

1115   Mitchell, Rosamund J. 'Italian *nobilità* and the English idea of the gentleman
        in the fifteenth century', *English Miscellany*, IX (1958), 23–37. See (701,
        1060).

1116   Myatt-Price, E.M. 'The Cromwell household accounts, 1417–1476', in
        Ananias C. Littleton and Basil S. Yamey (eds.), *Studies in the history of
        accounting*. 1956, pp. 99–113. In the same, see Dorothea Oschinsky's
        description of 'medieval treatises on estate accounting', pp. 91–8, and see
        (1205).

1117   Owst, Gerald R. 'Everyday life in medieval St Albans: some notes on a 15th
        century register of wills', *Transactions of the St Albans and Hertfordshire
        Architectural and Archaeological Society*, (1926), 190–206.

1118   Planché, James R. 'On the badges of the house of Lancaster', *JBAA*, VI
        (1851), 374–93; XX (1864), 18–33. The latter illustrates Yorkist badges
        (1045, 1495).

1119   Pollard, Graham. 'Mediaeval loan chests at Cambridge', *BIHR*, XVII (1940),
        113–29.

1120   Postan, Michael M. 'Some social consequences of the Hundred Years' War',
        EcHR, XII (1942), 1–12. See (1113, 1379).

1121   Power, Eileen E. 'The effects of the black death on rural organization in
        England', *History*, n.s., III (1918), 109–16. See (1466).

1122   Raftis, J. Ambrose. 'Changes in an English village after the black death',
        Mediaeval Studies, XXIX (1967), 158–77.

1123 —— 'The concentration of responsibility in five villages', *Mediaeval Studies*, XXVIII (1966), 92–118.

1124 —— 'Social structures in five east midland villages: a study of possibilities in the use of court roll data', *EcHR*, 2nd ser., XVIII (1965), 83–100.

1125 Redstone, Vincent B. 'Social conditions of England during the wars of the roses', *TRHS*, XVI (1902), 159–200. Marks continuity in cultural life in Norfolk, as does Alice E. Radice in *Antiquary*, XL, 1904, pp. 229–35, 269–74, 330–7, 356–62.

1126 Ross, Alan S.C. 'Pize-ball', *LeedsS*, XIII (1968), 55–77. Popular game similar to stool-ball and tut-ball, or to modern rounders and baseball; also, George R. Stephens in *Speculum*, XII, 1937, pp. 264–7; and (1109).

1127 Ross, Charles D. 'The household accounts of Elizabeth Berkeley, countess of Warwick, 1420–1', *Bristol-Gloucs*, LXX (1951), 81–105.

1128 Ruddock, Alwyn A. 'Alien hosting in Southampton in the fifteenth century', *EcHR*, XVI (1946), 30–7; *EHR*, LXI (1946), 1–17. See (1143).

1129 —— 'John Payne's persecution of foreigners in the town court of Southampton in the fifteenth century. A study in municipal misrule', *Proceedings of the Hants. Field Club and Archaeological Society*, XVI (1944), 23–37.

1130 Rushforth, Gordon M. 'Burials of Lancastrian notables in Tewkesbury Abbey after the battle, 1471', *Bristol-Gloucs*, XLVII (1925), 131–49.

1131 Sabine, Ernest I. 'Butchering in mediaeval London', *Speculum*, VIII (1933), 335–53. For diet and recipes (986).

1132 —— 'Latrines and cesspools of mediaeval London', *Speculum*, IX (1934), 303–21; XII (1937), 19–43.

1133 Salzmann, Louis F. 'The property of the earl of Arundel, 1397', *SussexS*, XCI (1953), 32–52.

1134 Shaw, Ronald C. 'Two fifteenth-century kinsmen: John Shaw of Dukinfield, mercer, and William Shaw of Heath Chornock, surgeon', *Lancs Historic*, CX (1958), 15–30; CXII (1960), 155–8.

1135 Sheehan, Michael M. 'The formation and stability of marriage in the four-teenth century: evidence of an Ely register', *Mediaeval Studies*, XXXIII (1971), 228–64. Fundamental research and careful analysis make this a most perceptive and persuasive model for social studies; also (1097, 1102), and Sheehan's earlier study of canon law and married women's property rights, *Mediaeval Studies*, XXV, 1963, pp. 109–24.

1136 Stretton, Grace. 'Some aspects of mediaeval travel, notably transport and accommodation, with special reference to the wardrobe accounts of Henry, earl of Derby, 1390–93', *TRHS*, 4th ser., VII (1924), 77–97. Again, in *Mariner's Mirror*, XI, 1925, pp. 307–15; and (981, 990).

1137 —— 'The travelling household in the middle ages', *JBAA*, n.s., XL (1935), 75–103.

1138 Thomas, Arthur H. 'Life in medieval London', *JBAA*, n.s., XXXV (1929), 122–47; 3rd ser., II (1937), 99–120.

1139 Thrupp, Sylvia L. 'The gilds', in *The Cambridge economic history of Europe from the decline of the Roman Empire, III*. Cambridge, 1963, pp. 230–80, 624–34. See (1240) and her earlier article in *Journal of Economic History*, II, 1942, pp. 164–73, remains important, as is the more general article in *International encyclopedia of the social studies*, VI, 1968, pp. 184–7. For parochial, religious gilds (1621).

1140 —— 'Plague effects in medieval Europe', *Comparative Studies in Society and History*, VIII (1966), 474–83. See (1302, 1466).

1141 —— 'The problem of replacement rates in late medieval English population', *EcHR*, 2nd ser., XVIII (1965), 101–19. A basic analytical and methodo-logical guide for demographic studies (1054, 1076).

1142 —— 'The problem of conservatism in fifteenth-century England', *Speculum*, XVIII (1943), 363–8.

1143 —— 'A survey of the alien population of England in 1440', *Speculum*, XXXII (1957), 262–73. With her article (1065), the definitive analysis of foreigners in London and environs; also (1080, 1107, 1128, 1129) and references in (981).

1144   Tingey, John C. 'The journals of John Dernell and John Boys, carters at the Lathes in Norwich', *NA*, XV (1904), 114–63. From 10 May 1417 to 20 November 1417, and 1428–9: a unique source.

1145   Tupling, George H. 'The origin of markets and fairs in mediaeval Lancashire . . . and their tolls', *Lancs Antiq*, XLIX (1933), 75–94; L (1934–5), 107–37; LI (1936), 86–110. Includes list of all markets and fairs in third segment; see (1112, 1146).

1146   Watkins, (Mrs) Owen S. 'The mediaeval market and fair in England and Wales', *Y Cymmrodor*, XXV (1915), 21–74. Describes laws governing same, rates of toll, and basic organization (1112, 1145).

1147   Way, Albert. 'Illustrations of mediaeval manners and costume from original documents. Jousts of peace, tournaments, and judicial combats', *AJ*, IV (1847), 226–39; V (1848), 258–72. For Lancastrian era, citing numerous mss., as (1079, 1089, 1109); for tournaments and heraldry (993, 1045).

VIII. ECONOMIC HISTORY

1 Printed sources

1148   Anderton, H.I. (ed.). 'A Blackburnshire puture roll', *Lancs Historic*, LXIV (1912), 273–86. That is, manorial lords owing meat for men, horses, and dogs, 1440–62 (120).

1149   Barker, Eric E. (ed.). *Talbot deeds 1200–1682* (Record Society for Lancashire and Cheshire, CIII). 1948. Similar collection of the Moore family, ed. by John Brownbill in this series, LXVII, 1913; more cartulary and family muniments in (26, 152, 274, 1152, 1171, 1187, 1201, 1209, 1709).

1150   Beamont, William (ed.). *Warrington in M.CCCC.LXV.* (Chetham Society, XVII). 1849. Based on the rent roll for the Legh family from 1465.

1151   Beardwood, Alice (ed.). *The statute merchant roll of Coventry, 1392–1416* (Dugdale Society, XVII). 1939. And see (190).

1152   Brooke, Christopher N.L. and Michael M. Postan (eds.). *Carte nativorum. A Peterborough cartulary of the fourteenth-century* (Northamptonshire Record Society, XX). 1960. Excellent introduction, with evidence of peasant land transactions (1149).

1153   Bunyard, Barbara D.M. (ed.). *The brokage book of Southampton, from 1439–40* (Southampton Record Society, XL). 1941. Unique record of tolls paid on goods entering and departing the town, in great detail; additional Southampton records in (118).

1154   Carus-Wilson, Eleanora M. (ed.). *The overseas trade of Bristol in the later middle ages* (Bristol Record Society, VII). 1937. See (134, 1290).

1155   —— and Olive Coleman (eds.). *England's export trade 1275–1547*. Oxford, 1963. Especially useful compilations from customers' accounts; and more material on customers accounts, royal and local (1157, 1169, 1195, 1211, 1227, 1234, 1252, 1294, 1339) and esp. (1316).

1156   Cobb, Henry S. (ed.). *The local port book of Southampton for 1439–40* (Southampton Record Series, V). 1961. See (118, 1153).

1157   Coleman, Olive (ed.). *The brokage book of Southampton from 1443–1444* (Southampton Record Series, IV, VI). 1960–1, 2 vols. See her general survey of Southampton's trade, *EcHR*, 2nd ser., XVI, 1963–4, pp. 9–22.

1158   Coote, Henry C. (ed.). 'The ordinances of some secular guilds of London, 1354–1496', *London-Midd*, IV (1871), 1–59. For the glovers, blacksmiths, and dutchmen (130, 1139).

1159   Corbett, John S. (ed.). 'Caerphilly: minister's accounts, 1428–9', *ArchCamb*, 6th ser., XIX (1919), 19–34. And (97, 1213).

1160   Courthope, Elinor J. and Beryl E.R. Fermoy (eds.). 'Lathe court rolls and views of frankpledge in the rape of Hastings, A.D. 1387–1474', *Sussex Record Society*, XXXVII (1934), 1–210. See (120).

1161   Cox, John C. (ed.). 'A poll-tax roll of the East Riding, with some account of the peasant revolt of 1381', *Transactions of the East Riding Antiquarian Society*, XV (1909), 1–70. See (116, 702).

1162 Cunningham, William (ed.). 'Compotus roll of the manor of Anstie, 2–3 Henry IV', in his *Growth of English Industry and Commerce*, I. Cambridge, 1910, pp. 591–610. See (120).

1163 Denney, Anthony H. (ed.). *The Sibton Abbey estates; select documents 1325–1509* (Suffolk Record Society, II). 1960. More on monastic economy in (1247, 1250, 1259, 1273, 1281, 1289, 1297, 1406, 1901, 1917, 1946, 1981, 2016, 2090, 2186).

1164 Drinkwater, Charles H. (ed.). 'Shrewsbury gild merchant rolls of the fourteenth and fifteenth centuries', *ShropsT*, 3rd ser., V (1905), 35–54, 81–100. See (162).

1165 Ellis, Henry (ed.). *Registrum vulgariter nuncupatum 'The record of Caernarvon'*. 1838. Includes *valor* of Bangor diocese 22 Richard II (205, 1351, 1437, 97).

1166 Elvey, Elizabeth M. (ed.). 'Aylesbury in the fifteenth century: a bailiff's notebook', *Records of Buckinghamshire*, XVII (1965), 321–35. Similarly *Transactions of the Old Stafford Society*, 1941, pp. 15–25.

1167 Espinas, Georges and Henri Pirenne (eds.). *Recueil de documents relatifs à l'histoire de l'industrie drapière en Flandre*. Brussels, 1906–23, 4 vols.

1168 Fenton, Frank H. (ed.). *Court rolls of the manors of Bruces, Dawbeneys, Pembrokes (Tottenham): 1 Richard II to 1 Henry IV (1377–1399)*. Tottenham, 1961. Virtually complete series for all three manors (120).

1169 Foster, Brian (ed.). *The local port book of Southampton for 1435–6* (Southampton Record Series, VII). 1963. See (118, 1156).

1170 Gidden, Harry W. (ed.). *The stewards' books of Southampton, from 1428 [to 1439]* (Southampton Record Society, XXXV, XXXIX). 1935–9, 2 vols.

1171 Giuseppi, Montague S. *et al.* (eds.). *Chertsey Abbey cartularies* (Surrey Record Society, XII). 1933–63, 2 vols. in 5 pts. See (1149).

1172 Green, Emanuel (ed.). 'Bath lay subsidies, Henry IV–Henry VIII', *Proceedings of the Bath Natural History and Antiquarian Field Club*, VI (1889), 379–411. See (116, 259).

1173 Hall, Hubert and Frieda J. Nicholas (eds.). 'Select tracts and tablebooks relating to English weights and measures (1100–1742)', *Camden Miscellany XV* (Camden Society, 3rd ser., XLI). 1929, pp. 1–68 of Part 5. With a bibliography of mss. and secondary sources; see (60, 1385).

1174 Hall, James (ed.). 'The book of the abbot of Combermere, 1289 to 1529', *Miscellanies II* (Record Society for Lancashire and Cheshire, XXXI). 1896, pp. 1–74. Containing indentures and rentals.

1175 Hall, Thomas W. (ed.). *Sheffield, Hallamshire. A descriptive catalogue (3rd volume) of Sheffield manorial records from the court roll, 1427 to 1497*. Sheffield, 1934. See (120).

1176 Harland, John (ed.). 'Three Lancashire documents . . . III. Custom roll and rental of the manor of Ashton-Under-Lyne, November 11, 1422', *Chetham Society*, LXXIV (1868), pp. 93–134.

1177 Hilton, Rodney H. (ed.). *Ministers' accounts of the Warwickshire estates of the duke of Clarence, 1479–80* (Dugdale Society, XXI). 1952.

1178 HMSO. *Inquisitions and assessments relating to feudal aids, with other analogous documents, 1284–1431*. 1899–1921, 6 vols.

1179 —— *Public Record Office: list of rentals and surveys and other analogous documents*. 1908–68, 2 vols.; No. 25, and No. 14 in Supp. Series. See (120, 229, 7).

1180 Hobson, Thomas F. (ed.). *Adderbury 'Rectoria'. The manor at Adderbury belonging to New College, Oxford: the building of the chancel 1408–1418: account rolls, deeds, and court rolls* (Oxfordshire Record Society, VIII). 1926. See (120).

1181 Hodgson, John C. (ed.). *Percy bailiff's rolls of the fifteenth century [1471–2]* (Surtees Society, CXXXIV). 1921.

1182 Hone, Nathaniel J. (ed.). *The manor and manorial records*. 1912, 2nd ed., rev. Includes extensive lists of manorial court roll mss. (7, 120).

1183 Hunt, Timothy J. (ed.). *Mediaeval customs of the manors of Taunton and Bradford on Tone*. 1962. See (120).

1184 Jack, R. Ian (ed.). 'The Grey of Ruthin valor . . . 1467—8', *Bedfordshire Historical Record Society*, XLVI (1965), 1—158.

1185 Jeayes, Isaac H. (ed.). 'On the compotus rolls [1365—1473] of the manor of Oundle', *JBAA*, XXXIV (1878), 384—90. See (120).

1186 Jones, Gwilym P. (ed.). *The extent of Chirkland (1391—1393)*. 1933. See (97).

1187 Kerry, Charles (ed.). 'Discovery of the register and chartulary of the mercers' company, York [1429—1523]', *Antiquary*, XXII (1890), 266—70; XXIII (1891), 27—30, 70—3. See (1198, 153, 1149).

1188 Kingdon, John A. (ed.). *Facsimile of the first volume of ms. archives of the . . . company of grocers, 1345—1463*. 1886. See Thrupp (1279); for London (130).

1189 Kunze, Carl (ed.). *Hanseakten aus England, 1275 bis 1412* (Verein für hansische Geschichte, Band 6). Halle, 1891. More on the Hansa in (1216, 1245, 1248, 1265, 1279, 1288, 1291, 1292, 1327, 1372, 1399, 1407, 1410).

1190 —— and Walter Stein (eds.). *Hansisches Urkundenbuch 1361—1485, Vols. IV—X* (Verein für hansische Geschichte). Halle, 1876.

1191 Lancaster, William T. (ed.). 'A fifteenth-century rental of Leeds', *Miscellanea VII* (Thoresby Society, XXIV), 1915—18, pp. 6—22, 281—303. Dated 1425 as parcel of the Duchy of Lancaster, the latter for Rothwell.

1192 —— (ed.). 'A fifteenth-century rental of Nostell Priory', *Miscellanea I* (YorksRS, LXI). 1920, pp. 108—35.

1193 Lapsley, Gaillard T. (ed.). 'Account roll of a fifteenth-century iron master [1408—1409]', *EHR*, XIV (1899), 509—29.

1194 Leighton, William A. (ed.). 'The guilds of Shrewsbury: mercers, ironmongers, and goldsmiths' company', *ShropsT*, VII (1885), 269—412. Company book begins 1424—5 (162).

1195 Lewis, Edward A. (ed.). 'A contribution to the commercial history of mediaeval Wales, with tabulated accounts, 1301—1547', *Y Cymmrodor*, XXIV (1913), 86—188. Complete list of extant customs accounts for Welsh ports (1155, 97).

1196 —— (ed.). 'The court rolls of the manor of Broniarth (Co. Mont.), 1429—1464', *BBCS*, XI (1941), 54—73. See (120, 97).

1197 Lister, John (ed.). *The early Yorkshire woollen trade. Extracts from the Hull customs' rolls, and complete transcripts of the ulnagers' rolls* (*YorksRS* LXIV). Leeds, 1924. More on wool and cloth trade in (1207, 1208, 1257, 1272, 1278, 1362, 1368, 1373, 1374).

1198 Lyell, Laetitia (ed.). *Acts of court of the mercers' company, [London] 1453—1527*. Cambridge, 1936. See (130, 1065).

1199 *Manorial society's publications and monographs*. 1907—23, 12 vols. Extensive lists of privately owned court rolls, steward's accounts, rentals, surveys; there are two out-of-date lists and bibliographies, by Frances G. Davenport and by Margaret F. Moore, 1912; generally (120).

1200 Markland, James H. (ed.). 'Some remarks on the rent-roll of Humphrey, duke of Buckingham. 26 and 27 Henry VI, 1447, 1448', *AJ*, VIII (1851), 259—81.

1201 Moore, Stuart A. (ed.). *Cartularium monasterii sancti Johannis Baptiste de Colecestria* (Roxburghe Club, 131). 1897. See (1149).

1202 Mollat, Michel (ed.). *Les sources de l'histoire maritime en Europe de moyen âge au XVIIIe siècle*. Paris, 1962. Absolutely essential papers on extant evidence, with useful bibliographical notes; more on English foreign trade in (1154—5, 1189, 1197, 1207—8, 1221, 1262, 1284, 1294, 1298, 1309, 1330, 1332, 1334, 1341, 1346, 1361, 1366, 1368, 1390, 1396, 1411); for Italian sources (1284).

1203 Muhlfeld, Helen E. (ed.). *A survey of the manor of Wye [Kent]*. New York, 1933.

1204 Nevill, Edmund R. (ed.). 'Salisbury in 1455 (*Liber Niger*)', *WiltsMag*, XXXVII (1912), 66—91.

1205 Oschinsky, Dorothea (ed.). *Walter of Henley and other treatises on estate management and accounting.* Oxford, 1971. Or Elizabeth Lamond's ed., 1890. Oschinsky's articles in *EcHR*, XVII, 1947, pp. 52—61, and 2nd ser., VIII, 1956, pp. 296—309, survey ms. treatises (1116).

1206 Owen, Leonard V.D. (ed.). 'An annual account roll of the manors of Scarrington, Car-Colstron, Screveton and Orston, 1413—1414', *Thoroton Society, Record Series*, XI (1945), 167—75.

1207 Posthumus, Nicholas W. (ed.). *Bronnen tot de geschiedenis van de Leidsche textielnijverheid, 1335—1795.* The Hague, 1910—22, 6 vols. And see (1197, 1221).

1208 —— (ed.). *De geschiedenis van de Leidsche lakensindustrie.* The Hague, 1908. Both are essential for British trade, esp. Leiden—Calais wool and cloth data.

1209 Powell, Edward (ed.). 'Ancient charters presented at Scarisbrick Hall, in the county of Lancaster', *Lancs Historic*, XLVIII (1896), 259—94; XLIX (1897), 185—230. See (1149).

1210 Quaife, Jill (ed.). 'Reeve's account of the manor of Burnham 14—15 Richard II, A.D. 1390—1391', *EssexT*, 3rd ser., II (1968), 147—58. Includes a good glossary of terms.

1211 Quinn, David B. (ed.). *The port books or local customs accounts of Southampton for the reign of Edward IV [1469—1481]* (Southampton Record Society, XXXVII—XXXVIII). 1937—8, 2 vols. See (118, 1155).

1212 Reddaway, Thomas F. and Alwyn A. Ruddock (eds.). 'The accounts of John Balsall, purser of the *Trinity of Bristol*, 1480—1', *Camden Miscellany XXIV* (Camden Society, 4th ser., VII). 1969, pp. 1—28. More on shipping (1226, 1347, 1359, 1390, 1396, 1402, 1411).

1213 Rees, William (ed.). 'Records relating to the lordship of Senghenydd with Caerphilly', *South Wales and Monmouthshire Record Society*, IV (1957), 33—50. Contains diverse accounts, Edward I to Henry VIII (97, 1159).

1214 —— (ed.). 'Receiver's accounts for a coalmine in the lordship of Kilvey, near Swansea, 1399—1400', *South Wales and Monmouthshire Record Society*, I (1949), 180—92.

1215 Rope, Irenen M. (ed.). 'The earliest book of the drapers' company [from 1461], Shrewsbury', *ShropsT*, 4th ser., III (1913), 135—262; IV (1914), 195—247; IX (1924), 258—77; X (1925), 193—208; XI (1927), 141—84. See (162).

1216 Ropp, Goswin von der (ed.). *Hanserecesse von 1431—1476* (Verein für Hansische Geschichte). Leipzig, 1876—92, 7 vols. See (1189).

1217 Rye, Walter (ed.). 'Some Norfolk guild certificates [1389]', *NA*, XI (1892), 105—136.

1218 Saltmarsh, John (ed.). 'Hand-list of the estates of King's College, Cambridge', *BIHR*, XII (1935), 32—8. Almost all are fifteenth century manorial records (120).

1219 Searle, Eleanor and Barbara Ross (eds.). 'The cellarers' rolls of Battle Abbey 1275—1513', *Sussex Record Society*, LXV (1967), 1—172. Includes an excellent glossary, and much data relating to prices and wages; also publ. separately in Sydney, 1967; now see (1289, 2158). For prices, generally (1236).

1220 Sellers, Maud (ed.). *The York mercers and merchant adventurers, 1356—1917* (Surtees Society, CXXIX). 1918. See (153, 1187)

1221 Smit, Homme J. (ed.). *Bronnen tot de geschiedenis van den handel met Engeland, Schotland en Ireland, 1150—1485* (Rijks geschiedkundige publicatiën, LXV). The Hague, 1928, 2 vols. Documents on Anglo-Dutch trade taken from English archives; see Posthumus (1202, 1207—8).

1222 Stansfeld, John (ed.). 'Rent roll of Kirkstall Abbey [1459]', *Thoresby Society, Miscellanea I* (1891), 1—21.

1223 Steer, Francis W. (ed.). *Scriveners' company common paper 1357—1628* (London Record Society, IV). 1968. Contains membership lists and regulations (130).

1224 Stevenson, William H. (ed.). *Rental of all the houses in Gloucester, A.D. 1455; from a roll in the possession of the corporation of Gloucester.* Gloucester, 1890.

1225   Stewart-Brown, Ronald (ed.). 'The disafforestation of Wirral [1376—84]',
        Lancs Historic, LIX (1907), 165—80; LXXXIX (1937), 23—7.

1226   Studer, Paul (ed.). *The oak book of Southampton of c. 1300* (Southampton
        Record Society, VI). 1910—11, 3 vols. Miscellany of town and maritime
        regulations, including the so-called 'Rolls of Oleron' (118, 1212, 1521).

1227   —— (ed.). *The port books of Southampton, or (Anglo-French) accounts of
        Robert Florys, water-bailiff and receiver of petty customs, A.D. 1427—
        1430* (Southampton Record Society, XV). 1913. Essential for view of
        town's import and export trade (118, 1155).

1228   Taylor, Frank (ed.). 'Court rolls, rentals, surveys and analogous documents in
        the John Rylands Library', *BJRL*, XXXI (1948), 345—78. Listed and
        calendared (120).

1229   Templeman, Geoffrey (ed.). *The register (records) of the guild of the Holy
        Trinity, St Mary, St John the Baptist and St Katherine of Coventry,
        Volume II* (Dugdale Society, XIX). 1944. City corporation materials, to
        1533, following Mary D. Harris's ed. of the 1340—1450 register from the
        same, Dugdale Society, XIII, 1935; and (190).

1230   Torr, Cecil (ed.). *Wreyland documents*. Cambridge, 1910. Extensive fifteenth
        century manorial documents pertaining to Devonshire (120).

1231   Walker, Violet W. (ed.). 'An extent of Upton, 1431', *Thoroton Society,
        Record Series*, XIV (1950), 26—38. Belonging to the archbishop of York.

1232   Walton, William (ed.). 'Accompts of the manor of the Savoy, temp. Richard
        II', *Arch*, XXIV (1832), 299—316.

1233   Williams, John F. (ed.). 'A bailiff's roll of Thetford, 1403—1404', *NA*, XXIV
        (1932), 7—12.

1234   Wilson, Keven P. (ed.). *Chester customs accounts 1301—1566* (Record
        Society for Lancashire and Cheshire, CXI). 1969. And see (132, 1155,
        1413).

2 Monographs

1235   Bean, John M.W. *The estates of the Percy family 1416—1537*. 1958. Careful
        reconstruction of large, unified landholdings that challenges the Postan
        pessimism (1275, 1382—3). Similarly, for other lordships and large
        estates (1249, 1256, 1258, 1260, 1283, 1318, 1323, 1336, 1378, 1386,
        1387, 1393, 1394, 1431, 1434, 1437, 1438); for monastic estates (1163).

1236   Beveridge, William. *Prices and wages in England from the twelfth to the nine-
        teenth century*. 1939. First serious attempt, now useful only with (1219,
        1254, 1269, 1282, 1306, 1307, 1311, 1357, 1375—7, 1404).

1237   Bridbury, Anthony R. *Economic growth: England in the later middle ages*.
        1962; repr. with new introduction, 1974. Controversial for optimism con-
        cerning expansion of economic and urban stability, persuasively argued
        but not thoroughly documented (93, 1275).

1238   —— *England and the salt trade in the later middle ages*. Oxford, 1955. And
        Berry (1305).

1239   *Cambridge economic history of Europe*, II, *Trade and industry in the middle
        ages* (ed. by Michael M. Postan and Hrothgar J. Habakkuk). Cambridge,
        1952.

1240   —— III, *Economic organization and policies in the middle ages* (ed. by
        Michael M. Postan, Edwin E. Rich, and Edward Miller). Cambridge, 1963.

1241   Carus-Wilson, Eleanora M. *The expansion of Exeter at the close of the middle
        ages*. Exeter, 1963. Brief but vivid description of one town possessing
        superb evidence (314).

1242   —— *Medieval merchant venturers: collected studies*. 2nd ed., 1967. Import-
        ant essays defining English roles in European trade, mainly pre-fifteenth
        century, all publ. earlier as articles in *EcHR* and *BIHR*.

1243   —— *Merchant adventurers of Bristol in the fifteenth-century* (Historical
        Association, no. 4, Bristol Branch). Bristol, 1962. From *TRHS*, 4th ser.,
        XI, 1928, pp. 61—82; but see (1290), and generally (134).

1244   Cooke, Alfred H. *The early history of Mapledurham* (Oxfordshire Record

Society, VII). Oxford, 1925. Although only extracts of court rolls and accounts 1416—93, the book does provide full muniments list (7, 120).

1245 Daenell, Ernst. *Die Blütezeit der deutschen Hanse: hansische Geschichte von der zweiten Hälfte des XIV. bis zum letzten Viertel des XV. Jahrhunderts*. Berlin, 1905—6, 2 vols. (reprinted 1973). See (1189).

1246 Davenport, Frances G. *The economic development of a Norfolk manor [of Forncett], 1086—1565*. Cambridge, 1906. More local studies in (120, 1244, 1253, 1261, 1312, 1324, 1326, 1333, 1342, 1350, 1367, 1442).

1247 Dobson, Richard B. *Durham priory 1400—1450*. Cambridge, 1973. Superb study for economic and monastic analysis; also (1163, 1671), and although his study is for an earlier period, Ian Kershaw's *Bolton Priory: the economy of a northern monastery*, 1973, provides another excellent model in economic history.

1248 Dollinger, Philippe. *La Hanse (XIIe–XVIIe siècle)*. Paris, 1964. Translation by D.S. Ault and S.H. Steinberg, Stanford, Calif., 1970, is most recent survey available in English; in German, see Karl Pagel's survey, 3rd ed., 1963; and (1189).

1249 Du Boulay, Francis R.H. *The lordship of Canterbury: an essay on mediaeval society*. 1966. Important, unconvincing analysis of economic and social management in a large landed system (1235, 1323).

1250 Finberg, Herbert P.R. *Tavistock Abbey: a study in the social and economic history of Devon* (Cambridge Studies in Medieval Life and Thought, n.s., II). Cambridge, 1951 (corrected ed. 1969). Excellent regional, monastic economic history (1163).

1251 Girling, Frank A. *English merchants' marks: a field survey of marks used by merchants and tradesmen in England between 1400 and 1700*. Oxford, 1964. See John P. Rylands, *Lancs Historic*, LXII, 1910, pp. 1—34; and William C. Ewing, *NA*, III, 1852.

1252 Gras, Norman S.B. *The early English customs system* (Harvard Economic Studies, no. 18). Cambridge, Mass., 1918. See (1155, 1316).

1253 —— *The economic and social history of an English village: Crawley, Hampshire A.D. 909—1928* (Harvard Economic Studies, no. 34). Cambridge, Mass., 1930. See (1246).

1254 —— *The evolution of the English corn market*. Cambridge, Mass., 1915. See Ernst Kneisel's critique in *Journal of Economic History*, XIV, 1954, pp. 46—52; on prices (1236).

1255 Hatcher, John. *English tin production and trade before 1550*. Oxford, 1973. Significantly adds to the classic monograph by George R. Lewis, *The stannaries: a study of the medieval tin miners of Cornwall and Devon* (Harvard Economic Studies, no. 3), Cambridge, Mass., 1903.

1256 —— *Rural economy and society in the duchy of Cornwall, 1300—1500*. Oxford, 1970. Basic reconstruction of lay estate management, with analytical complexities clearly defined and tentative conclusions revising Postan's thesis; previewed in *EcHR*, 2nd ser., XXII, 1969, pp. 208—27; also (1235).

1257 Heaton, Herbert. *Yorkshire woollen and worsted industries, from earliest times up to the Industrial Revolution*. 1966, 2nd ed. See (1197).

1258 Hilton, Rodney H. *The economic development of the Leicestershire estates in the 14th and 15th centuries* (Oxford Historical Series). 1947. See (1235).

1259 Hockey, Stanley F. *Quarr Abbey and its lands, 1132—1631*. Leicester, 1970. Located on Isle of Wight, exemplifies careful research and analysis into Cistercian economy and administration (1163, 1297).

1260 Holmes, George A. *The estates of the higher nobility in fourteenth century England*. Cambridge, 1957. See (1235).

1261 Hoskins, William G. *The midland peasant. The economic and social history of a Leicestershire village*. 1957. Village of Wigston Magna, from sixth to nineteenth centuries; also (1246).

1262 James, Margery K. *Studies in the mediaeval wine trade* (ed. by Elspeth M. Veale). Oxford, 1971. Particularly the Anglo-Gascon commerce (1202, 941).

1263   Kahl, William F. *The development of London livery companies* (Kress Library of Business and Economics, XV). Boston, 1960. Complete with an inventory of primary sources (130, 1139).

1264   Kerling, Nelly J.M. *Commercial relations of Holland and Zealand with England from the late 13th century to the close of the middle ages*. Leiden, 1954. Similarly for Scotland and the Netherlands, see Matthiis Rooseboom, The Hague, 1910; and (1285, 858).

1265   Keutgen, Friedrich. *Die Beziehungen der Hanse zu England im letzten Drittel des 14. Jahrhunderts*. Giessen, 1890. Also, books by Johann M. Lappenberg, Hamburg, 1851, and Pagel (1248); generally (1189).

1266   Knoop, Douglas and Gwilym P. Jones. *The mediaeval mason; an economic history of English stone building in the later middle ages and early modern times*. 1967. See Gee (2299), and William Cunningham, *PBA*, VI, 1913, pp. 167–77.

1267   Kramer, Stella. *The English craft gilds and the government* (Colorado University Studies in History, Economics and Public Law, 23). New York, 1905. Also her monograph, publ. 1927; but see more accurate and profound analysis of Thrupp (1139). Another study by Erwin F. Meyer is in Colorado Studies, no. 16, 17, publ. 1929–30; also, William Cunningham, *TRHS*, n.s., III, 1886, pp. 371–92; for parochial, religious gilds (1621).

1268   Lipson, Ephraim. *An introduction to the economic history of England. I: the middle ages*. 1915 (and various rev. eds. to 1929).

1269   Lloyd, Terence H. *The movement of wool prices in mediaeval England* (EcHR, Supp. VI). Cambridge, 1973. See (1236).

1270   —— *Some aspects of the building industry in mediaeval Stratford-upon-Avon* (Dugdale Society, Occasional Papers, XIV). 1961.

1271   Lobel, Mary D. *The history of Dean and Chalford* (Oxfordshire Record Society, XVII). Oxford, 1935.

1272   McClenaghan, Barbara. *The Springs of Lavenham and the Suffolk cloth trade in the XV and XVI centuries*. Ipswich, 1924. See (1197).

1273   Morgan, Marjorie M. *The English lands of the Abbey of Bec*. Oxford, 1946. And see (1163).

1274   Platt, Colin. *Medieval Southampton: the port and trading community A.D. 1000–1600*. 1974. See (118) and *Excavations in medieval Southampton 1953–1969* by Platt and R. Coleman-Smith, 1975, 2 vols.

1275   Postan, Michael M. *Essays on medieval agriculture and general problems of the medieval economy*. 1973. But see A.R. Bridbury's critique, *EcHR*, 2nd ser., XXVI, 1973, pp. 518–24 (1237).

1276   —— *Medieval economy*. 1972.

1277   —— *Medieval trade and finance*. Cambridge, 1973. These three books bring together Postan's numerous articles, and mature reflections, that make him the most important and provocative English scholar of medieval economic history.

1278   Power, Eileen E. *The wool trade in English medieval history*. 1939. Now significant for its sweeping, clear and elegant exposition of the historical issues and evidence (1197).

1279   —— and Michael M. Postan (eds.). *Studies in English trade in the fifteenth century*. 1933. Reviewed in *Hansische Geschichts-Blätter*, LX, 1936, pp. 222–31; note particularly the articles by Power (wool trade), Postan (the Hansa), Sylvia L. Thrupp (on London Grocers), and Howard L. Gray (Yorkist foreign trade). This book remains the standard for modern scholarship in its field (1189, 1197, 1202, 1212).

1280   Putnam, Bertha A. *The enforcement of the statute of labourers* (Columbia University Studies in History, Economics, and Public Law, XXII). New York, 1908.

1281   Raftis, J. Ambrose. *The estates of Ramsey Abbey: a study in economic growth and organization*. Toronto, 1957. Completely replaces earlier monograph by Nellie Neilson; although the focus is more on the fourteenth century, as with his solid study of *Tenure and mobility*, Raftis continues to shape the analysis of local economic studies. More on monastic economy (1163), and see Hilton (1258, 1342–5).

1282 Rogers, J.E. Thorold. *History of agriculture and prices 1259–1793*. Oxford, 1866–1902, 8 vols. Esp. vols I–IV, considered pioneering effort, like Beveridge (1236).

1283 Ross, Charles D. *The estates and finances of Richard Beauchamp, earl of Warwick* (Dugdale Society, Occasional Papers XII). 1956. Also ed. of the mainly thirteenth century cartulary of Cirencester Abbey, 1964, and of St Mark's Hospital, Bristol, 1959; and see (1235).

1284 Ruddock, Alwyn A. *Italian merchants and shipping in Southampton 1270– 1600*. (Southampton Record Series, I). 1951. And (118, 1202, 1274); more on Italian trade (1309, 1332, 1341, 1346, 1361, 1384, 1390, 1396, 1397, 1411). For detailed descriptions of Italian sources for commercial history see Armando Sapori, *Le marchand Italien au moyen âge*, Paris, 1952.

1285 Ruinen, Jan. *De oudste handelsbetrekkingen van Holland en Zeeland met Engeland tot in het laatste kwartaal der XIV^{de} eeuw*. Amsterdam, 1919. See (1264, 858).

1286 Salzmann, Louis F. *English industries of the middle ages*. New ed., 1964. Also his monograph on English trade, re-issued 1964.

1287 Schanz, Georg. *Englische handelspolitik gegen ende des mittelalters*. Leipzig, 1881, 2 vols. Still a basic study of English commerce.

1288 Schulz, Friedrich. *Die Hanse und England von Eduards III bis auf Heinrichs VIII Zeit*. Berlin, 1911. And see (1189).

1289 Searle, Eleanor. *Lordship and Community*. Toronto, 1974. Definitive, detailed analysis of the economic and social context of Battle Abbey (1163, 1219).

1290 Sherborne, James W. *The port of Bristol in the middle ages* (Historical Association, no. 13, Bristol Branch). Bristol, 1965. Judicious and succinct analysis with important conclusions; also (1243, 134).

1291 Stein, Walter. *Beiträge zur Geschichte der deutschen Hanse bis um die Mitte des fünfzehnten Jahrhunderts*. Giessen, 1900. See (1189).

1292 —— *Die Hanse und England: ein hansisch-englischer Seekreig im 15. Jahrhundert*. Leipzig, 1905.

1293 Thrupp, Sylvia L. *A short history of the worshipful company of bakers of London*. 1933. See (130, 1080, 1279).

1294 Touchard, Henri. *Le commerce maritime Breton à la fin du moyen âge*. Paris, 1967. Magnificent study, inspired by Michel Mollat and his Dieppe researches, using diverse sources, esp. English customs records, both royal and local (1155, 1202).

1295 Veale, Elspeth M. *The English fur trade in the later middle ages*. Oxford, 1966. Comprehensive history of domestic uses, Baltic trade, and the London industry; also, her article on rabbits in *AgHR*, 1957, pp. 85–90; generally (1202).

1296 Wee, Herman van der. *The growth of the Antwerp market and the European economy (fourteenth–sixteenth centuries)*. The Hague, 1963, 3 vols. Definitive statistical reconstruction and analysis, but also see Oscar de Smedt's study, in Dutch, Antwerp, 1924; and (858).

1297 Williams, David H. *The Welsh Cistercians: aspects of their economic history*. Pontypool, 1969. Previewed in *ArchCamb*, CXIV, 1965, pp. 2–47; and (1163, 1321, 1423, 1636, 97).

1298 Wolff, Philippe. *Commerces et marchands de Toulouse vers 1350–1450*. Paris, 1954. Excellent and careful study, especially for English imports of wood and exports of cloth, for which see *EcHR*, 2nd ser., II, 1950, pp. 290–4; and (1202, 1197).

3 Articles

1299 Allmand, Christopher T. 'The Lancastrian land settlement in Normandy, 1417–50', *EcHR*, 2nd ser., XXI (1968), 461–79.

1300 Baker, Alan R.H. 'Open fields and partible inheritance on a Kent manor', *EcHR*, 2nd ser., XVII (1964), 1–23. See (1328).

1301   Bartlett, J.N. 'The expansion and decline of York in the later middle ages', *EcHR*, 2nd ser., XII (1959), 17—33. See (153).

1302   Bean, John M.W. 'Plague, population and economic decline in the later middle ages', *EcHR*, 2nd ser., XV (1963), 423—37. See (1140, 1401, 1466).

1303   Beaven, Alfred B. 'The grocer's company and the aldermen of London in the time of Richard II', *EHR*, XXII (1907), 523—5. See Sylvia L. Thrupp in *BIHR*, IX, 1932, pp. 193—6, and (1279, 130).

1304   Bennett, Richard. 'The king's mills of ancient Liverpool', *Lancs Historic*, XLVIII (1896), 29—78.

1305   Berry, Elizabeth K. 'The borough of Droitwich and its salt industry, 1215—1700', *UBHJ*, VI (1957—8), 39—61. See (1238).

1306   Beveridge, William H. 'Wages in the Winchester manors [1208—1453]', *EcHR*, VII (1936—7), 22—43; 2nd ser., VIII (1955), 18—35. Begins attempt to survey systematically, and the second article reports Westminster Abbey evidence; now see the more reliable Phelps-Brown and Hopkins (1375—7), and generally (1236).

1307   —— 'The yield and price of corn in the middle ages [Winchester 1200—1450]', *Economic History*, I (1927), 155—67; II (1930), 19—44. See (1236, 1427).

1308   Birrell, Jean R. 'The forest economy of the honour of Tutbury in the fourteenth and fifteenth centuries', *UBHJ*, VIII (1962), 114—34.

1309   Biscaro, Gerolamo. 'Il banco Filippo Borromei e campagni di Londra, 1436—1439', *Archivio Storico Lombardo*, XL (1913), 37—126. See (130, 1202, 1284).

1310   Blanchard, Ian S.W. 'The miner and the agricultural community in late medieval England', *AgHR*, XX (1972), 93—106; XXII (1974), 54—61, 62—74. The second article is John Hatcher's challenge to distinguish the tin from lead miners on the basis of the size and degree of concentration and organization, but this is convincingly refuted in Blanchard's rejoinder.

1311   Brenner, Y.S. 'Prices and wages in England, 1450—1550', *BIHR*, XXXIV (1961), 103—5. Esp. his article on early Tudor prices in *EcHR*, 2nd ser., XIV, 1961—2, pp. 225—39; generally (1236).

1312   Brent, Judith A. 'Alciston manor in the later middle ages', *SussexS*, CVI (1968), 89—102. See (1246, 120).

1313   Butler, R.M. 'The common lands of the borough of Nottingham [circa 1480]', *ThorotonS*, LIV (1950), 45—62. Also, Joseph Bramley on Plumptre Hospital in 1392 in *ibid.*, XLIV, 1940, pp. 46—50.

1314   Carus-Wilson, Eleanora M. 'Evidences of industrial growth on some fifteenth-century manors', *EcHR*, 2nd ser., XII (1959), 190—205. Numerous other articles available in repr. vol. (1242).

1315   Clark, Andrew. 'Great Waltham five centuries ago', *Essex Review*, XIII (1904), 1—19, 65—80, 129—49, 197—214. Thorough analysis for manorial history (120, 1246).

1316   Cobb, Henry S. 'Local port customs accounts prior to 1550', in Felicity Ranger (ed.), *Prisca munimenta: studies in archival and administrative history presented to Dr. A.E.J. Hollaender*. 1973, pp. 215—28. Thorough survey of extant evidence revising his article of the same title in *Journal of the Society of Archivists*, I, 1958; see (1155).

1317   Dale, Marian, K. 'London silkwomen of the 15th century', *EcHR*, IV (1932—4), 324—35. More on women (1097).

1318   Davies, R.R. 'Baronial accounts, incomes, and arrears in the later middle ages', *EcHR*, 2nd ser., XXI (1968), 211—29. See (1235, 1386—7, 1394).

1319   Dilks, Thomas B. 'Bridgwater Castle and demesne towards the end of the fourteenth-century', *SomersetP*, LXXXVI (1941), 86—113. And (159).

1320   Dobson, Richard B. 'Admissions to the freedom of the city of York in the later middle ages', *EcHR*, 2nd ser., XXVI (1973), 1—22. See (153).

1321   Donnelly, James S. 'Changes in the grange economy of English and Welsh Cistercian abbeys, 1300—1540', *Traditio*, X (1954), 399—458. See (1297, 1423, 97).

1322   Drinkwater, Charles H. 'The drapers' company charter, 12 Jan., 1461—2', *ShropsT*, 2nd ser., VIII (1896), 175—90. See (162).

1323   Du Boulay, Francis R.H. 'A rentier economy in the later middle ages: the archbishopric of Canterbury', *EcHR*, 2nd ser., XVI (1964), 427–38. See (1235, 1249).

1324   Dyer, Christopher. 'Population and agriculture on a Warwickshire manor in the later middle ages', *UBHJ*, XI (1967–8), 113–27. See (1246).

1325   —— 'A redistribution of incomes in the fifteenth century', *Past and Present*, XXXIX (1968), 11–33. With support from Barbara J. Harris, *ibid.* XLIII, 1969, pp. 146–50.

1326   —— 'A small landowner in the fifteenth century', *Midland History*, I (1972), 1–14.

1327   Engel, Karl. 'Die Organisation der deutschhansischen Kaufleute in England im 14. und 15. Jahrhundert bis zum Utrechter Frieden von 1474', *Hansische Geschichts-Blätter*, XIX (1913), 445–517; XX (1914), 173–225. See (1189).

1328   Faith, Rosamund J. 'Peasant families and inheritance customs in medieval England', *AgHR*, XIV (1966), 77–95. See (1300, 1064).

1329   Firth, Catherine B. 'Village gilds of Norfolk in the fifteenth century', *NA*, XVIII (1914), 161–203.

1330   Flenley, Ralph. 'London and foreign merchants in the reign of Henry VI', *EHR*, XXV (1910), 644–55. And (130, 1202).

1331   Fox, Levi. 'The Coventry guilds and trading companies, with special reference to the position of women', *Transactions of the Birmingham Archaeological Society*, LXXVIII (1960), 13–26. See (190, 1097).

1332   Fryde, Edmund B. 'Anglo-Italian commerce in the fifteenth-century: some evidence about profits and the balance of trade', *Revue belge de philologie et d'histoire*, L (1972), 345–55. See (1202, 1284).

1333   Genet, Jean-Philippe. 'Économie et société rurale en Angleterre au XVe siècle d'après les comptes de l'hôpital d'Ewelme', *Annales, Économies, Sociétés, Civilisations*, XXVII (1972), 1449–74. And (1246, 2014).

1334   Giuseppi, Montague S. 'Alien merchants in England in the fifteenth century', *TRHS*, n.s., IX (1895), 75–98. Finds that the majority are Italian, see Thrupp (1143); and (1202, 1284).

1335   Gray, Howard L' 'Incomes from land in England in 1436', *EHR*, XLIX (1934), 607–39.

1336   Harvey, Barbara. 'The leasing of the abbot of Westminster's demesnes in the later middle ages', *EcHR*, 2nd ser., XXII (1969), 17–27. See (1235, 1405).

1337   Harvey, John H. 'The king's chief carpenters', *JBAA*, 3rd ser., XI (1948), 13–34. See (2298, 2230, 2263).

1338   Haward, Winifred I. 'Economic aspects of the wars of the roses in East Anglia', *EHR*, XLI (1926), 170–89.

1339   —— 'The trade of Boston in the fifteenth-century', *Reports and Papers of the Architectural and Archaeological Societies*, XLI (1933), 169–78. And see (1155, 1197).

1340   Heath, Peter. 'North sea fishing in the fifteenth century: the Scarborough fleet', *Northern History*, III (1968), 53–69. Using unique parish tithe booklets, showing individual incomes and techniques.

1341   Heers, Jacques. 'Les Génois en Angleterre: la crise de 1458–1466', in *Studi in onore di Armando Sapori*, II. Milan, 1958, pp. 807–32. See (1202, 1284).

1342   Hilton, Rodney, H. 'Winchcombe Abbey and the manor of Sherborne', in Herbert P.R. Finberg (ed.), *Gloucestershire Studies*. Leicester, 1957, pp. 89–113. Reprinted from *UBHJ*, II, 1949, pp. 32–52; also (1246).

1343   —— 'Rent and capital formation in feudal society', *Second International Conference of Economic History*, II (1962), 33–68. Argues that profit was invested in urban rents and that re-investment is missing in later, fifteenth century economics (1358).

1344   —— 'A study in the pre-history of English enclosure in the fifteenth century', in *Studi in onore di Armando Sapori*, I. Milan, 1958, pp. 673–85.

1345   —— 'Old enclosure in the West Midlands: a hypothesis about their late medieval development', *Géographie et Histoire Agraires, Annales de l'Est*, Memoire no. 21 (Nancy, 1959), 272–83.

1346 Holmes, George A. 'Florentine merchants in England, 1346–1436', *EcHR*, 2nd ser., XIII (1960), 193–208. And (1202, 1284, 1361).

1347 —— 'The libel of English policy', *EHR*, LXXVI (1961), 193–216. Emphasizes propaganda element in this literary attack on economic practices *c.* 1437; see Warner (1522), and (1212, 1226).

1348 Hoskins, William G. 'The wealth of medieval Devon', in his *Old Devon*. Newton Abbot, 1966, pp. 154–85.

1349 Johnston, Francis R. 'The Lancashire lands of Syon Abbey', *Lancs Historic*, CVII (1955), 41–53.

1350 Jones, Andrew. 'Land and people at Leighton Buzzard in the later fifteenth century', *EcHR*, 2nd ser., XXV (1972), 18–27. Quantitatively analyses court rolls for landholding patterns, 1393–8 and 1464–1508; and (1246, 120).

1351 Jones-Pierce, T. 'A Caernarvonshire manorial borough', *Transactions of the Caernarvonshire History Society*, IV (1942–3), 35–50. Manor of Pwllheli, after 1355 (205, 1165, 1437, 97).

1352 Kerling, Nelly J.M. 'Relations of English merchants with Bergen op Zoom, 1480–1481', *BIHR*, XXXI (1958), 130–40. See (977, 1189).

1353 Knoop, Douglas and Gwilym P. Jones. 'The English medieval quarry', *EcHR*, IX (1939), 17–37. See (2299, 2311).

1354 —— 'The building of Eton College, 1442–1460. A study in the history of operative masonry', *Ars Quatuor Coronatorum*, XLVI (1937), 70–114.

1355 —— 'London Bridge and its builders. A study of the municipal employment of masons mainly in the fifteenth century', *Ars Quatuor Coronatorum*, XLVII (1938), 5–44; XLVIII (1939), 5–46. And (130, 2311).

1356 —— 'Masons and apprenticeship in medieval England', *EcHR*, III (1931–2), 346–66; VIII (1937–8), 57–67. And Gee (2299).

1357 —— 'Masons' wages in mediaeval England', *Economic History*, II (1933), 473–99. And (1236, 2299).

1358 Kosminsky, Evgeny. 'The evolution of feudal rent in England from the XIth to the XVth centuries', *Past and Present*, VII (1955), 12–36. Provides a modern Marxist summation; see (1343, 694, 1421).

1359 Mace, Frances A. 'Devonshire ports in the fourteenth and fifteenth centuries', *TRHS*, 4th ser., VIII (1925), 98–126; *BIHR*, III (1926), 180–3. See (1155, 1212).

1360 Maitland, Frederic W. 'The history of a Cambridgeshire manor', *EHR*, IX (1894), 417–39. Excellent introduction to potentialities in manorial muniments, here for Wilburton, Edward I to Henry VIII (120).

1361 Mallett, Michael E. 'Anglo-Florentine commercial relations, 1465–1491', *EcHR*, 2nd ser., XV (1962), 250–65. See (1202, 1284, 1346).

1362 Martin, Geoffrey H. 'Shipments of wool from Ipswich to Calais, 1399–1402', *Journal of Transport History*, II (1956), 177–81. See (1197, 1202).

1363 McFarlane, Kenneth B. 'A business partnership in war and administration, 1421–1445', *EHR*, LXXVIII (1963), 290–310.

1364 —— 'The investment of sir John Fastolf's profits of war', *TRHS*, 5th ser., VII (1957), 91–116; *Medium Aevum*, XXX (1961), 176–80. —

1365 Miskimin, Harry A. 'Monetary movements and market structure – forces for contraction in fourteenth- and fifteenth-century England', *Journal of Economic History*, XXIV (1964), 470–90. With commentary by Richard Ware, pp. 491–5, all of which is weak on the fifteenth century.

1366 Mollat, Michel. 'Anglo-Norman trade in the fifteenth century', *EcHR*, XVII (1947), 143–50. Historian of fifteenth century Norman trade, the port of Dieppe, and biographer of Jacques Coeur; see (1202) and his survey of maritime commerce, including England, 1952.

1367 Mumford, W.F. 'The manor of Oxted, 1360–1420', *Surrey Archaeological Collections*, LXII (1966), 66–94. See (1246, 120).

1368 Munro, John H. 'Bruges and the abortive staple in English cloth: an incident in the shift of commerce from Bruges to Antwerp in the late fifteenth century', *Revue Belge de philologie et d'histoire*, XLIV (1966), 1137–59.

See (1197, 1202). Now see his fundamental study of *Wool, cloth and gold: the struggle for bullion in the Anglo-Burgundian trade 1340–1478.* Toronto, 1974.

1369 —— 'The costs of Anglo-Burgundian interdependence', *Revue belge de philologie et d'histoire*, XLVI (1968), 1228–38. Critical review of Thielemans (940); also (919).

1370 —— 'An economic aspect of the collapse of the Anglo-Burgundian alliance, 1428–1442', *EHR*, LXXXV (1970), 225–44.

1371 North, Douglas C. and Robert P. Thomas. 'The rise and fall of the manorial system: a theoretical model', *Journal of Economic History*, XXXI (1971), 777–803; XXXII (1972), 938–44. Extraordinarily naïve application of social science approach, criticized by Andrew Jones in the second article.

1372 Palais, Hyman. 'England's first attempt to break the commercial monopoly of the Hanseatic League, 1377–1380', *AHR*, LXIV (1959), 852–65. See (1189).

1373 Pelham, Reginald A. 'The cloth markets of Warwickshire during the later middle ages', *Transactions of the Birmingham Archaeological Society*, LXVI (1945–6), 131–41. See (1197, 1112).

1374 Perry, R. 'The Gloucestershire woollen industry, 1100–1690', *Bristol-Gloucs*, LXVI (1945), 49–137.

1375 Phelps-Brown, Ernest H. and Sheila V. Hopkins. 'Seven centuries of wages and prices: some earlier estimates', *Economica*, n.s., XXVIII (1961), 30–6. See (1236).

1376 —— 'Seven centuries of the prices of consumables, compared with builders' wage-rates', *Economica*, n.s., XXIII (1956), 293–314. Using 1453–1460 as the base, this is the index used by most historians (1236).

1377 —— 'Seven centuries of building wages', *Economica*, n.s., XXII (1955), 195–206. Uses J.E. Thorold Rogers' data for pre-1700 figures (1236, 1282, 1357).

1378 Pollard, A.J. 'Estate management in the later middle ages: the Talbots and Whitchurch, 1383–1525', *EcHR*, 2nd ser., XXV (1972), 553–66. See (1235).

1379 Postan, Michael M. 'The costs of the Hundred Years' War', *Past and Present*, XXVII (1964), 34–53. Discounts the war by itself as an economic impetus. Numerous articles of Postan's now collected in (1275–7), and (539, 1120).

1380 —— 'Credit in medieval trade', *EcHR*, I (1927–8), 234–61.

1381 —— 'Partnership in English medieval commerce', in *Studi in onore di Armando Sapori*, I. Milan, 1958, pp. 521–49.

1382 —— 'Some economic evidence of declining population in the later middle ages', *EcHR*, 2nd ser., II (1950), 221–46. Presents persuasive evidence especially for the movements in wages that indicate demographic contractions. Basic statement of Postan's neo-Malthusian views; see Schreiner (1404), and (93, 1235, 1237, 1392).

1383 —— 'The fifteenth-century', *EcHR*, IX (1939), 160–7.

1384 —— 'Spread of techniques: Italy and the economic development of England in the middle ages', *Journal of Economic History*, XI (1951), 339–46. And (1284).

1385 Prior, W.H. 'Notes on the weights and measures of medieval England', *Bulletin du Cange*, I (1925), 77–141. See (60, 1173).

1386 Pugh, Thomas B. and Charles D. Ross. 'The English baronage and the income tax of 1436', *BIHR*, XXVI (1953), 1–28. And (1235, 1318, 1394).

1387 —— 'Some materials for the study of baronial incomes in the fifteenth century', *EcHR*, 2nd ser., VI (1953), 185–94. See (691, 1235).

1388 Putnam, Bertha H. 'Records of courts of common law, especially of the sessions of the justices of the peace: sources for the economic history of England in the fourteenth and fifteenth centuries', *Proceedings of the American Philosophical Society*, XCI (1947), 258–73.

1389 Raftis, J. Ambrose. 'Rent and capital at St Ives', *Medieval Studies*, XX (1958), 79–92.

1390 Rawlinson, Hugh G. (ed.). 'The Flanders gallery: some notes on seaborne trade between Venice and England, 1327—1532', *Mariner's Mirror*, XII (1926), 145—68. And see (1202, 1212, 1284, 1396).

1391   Rich, Edwin E. 'Mayors of the staples', *CHJ*, IV (1934), 120—42.

1392   Robinson, W.C. 'Money, population and economic change in late medieval Europe', *EcHR*, 2nd ser., XII (1959), 63—76. With Postan's reply, pp. 77—82, to attack on Postan's economic theory and emphasis on population.

1393   Rosenthal, Joel T. 'The estates and finances of Richard, duke of York (1411—60)', *Studies in Medieval and Renaissance History*, II, ed. by William Bowsky. Nebraska, 1965. Reviewed critically by Charles D. Ross, *WHR*, III, 1966—7, pp. 299—302.

1394   —— 'Fifteenth-century baronial incomes and Richard, duke of York', *BIHR*, XXXVII (1964), 233—9. See (1235, 1318, 1386, 691).

1395   Rose-Troup, Frances. 'The kalendars and the Exeter trade-gilds before the Reformation', *DevonA*, XLIV (1912), 406—30. See (314, 1139, 1412).

1396   Ruddock, Alwyn A. 'The Flanders galleys', *History*, n.s., XXIV (1940), 311—17. Venetian trade into England (1202, 1212, 1284, 1390).

1397   —— 'The merchants of Venice and their shipping in Southampton in the fifteenth and sixteenth centuries', *Proceedings of the Hants. Field Club and Archaeological Society*, XV (1943), 274—91. See (1202, 118, 1274, 1284).

1398   —— 'The method of handling the cargoes of mediaeval merchant galleys', *BIHR*, XIX (1944), 140—8.

1399   Salter, Frank R. 'The Hanse, Cologne, and the crisis of 1468'. *EcHR*, III (1931—2), 93—101. See (1189).

1400   Saltmarsh, John. 'A college home-farm in the fifteenth century', *Economic History*, III (1936), 157—72.

1401   —— 'Plague and economic decline in England in the later middle ages', *CHJ*, VII (1941), 23—41. Fundamental correlations that inform more recent work of Postan, Russell, Thrupp, and others (1140, 1302, 1466).

1402   Scammell, Geoffrey V. 'English merchant shipping at the end of the middle ages: some east coast evidence', *EcHR*, 2nd ser., XIII (1961), 327—41. And Burwash (1524), also (1212, 1202).

1403   Schofield, Roger S. 'The geographical distribution of wealth in England, 1334—1649', *EcHR*, 2nd ser., XVIII (1965), 483—510. Brilliant reconstruction from parliamentary lay taxation records showing shifts from East Anglia, and see Cooper (1095); also, the survey of wealth's distribution made by E.J. Buckatzsch, *EcHR*, 2nd ser., III, 1950, which Schofield revises.

1404   Schreiner, Johann. 'Wages and prices in England in the later middle ages', *Scandinavian Economic History Review*, II (1954), 61—73. Author of *Pest og prisfall-i senmiddelalderen*, Oslo, 1948; here he reviews Postan (1382), challenging him on prices while emphasizing fifteenth-century declines in supplies of precious metals; and see (1236).

1405   Slack, W.J. 'The Condover extents, 1283—1580. A study in ancient demesne tenure', *ShropsT*, L (1940—1), 105—42. Particularly for 1430; also edits extents and rentals for Oswestry, 1393—1607; and see (1235, 1336, 1431).

1406   Smith, Reginald A.L. 'The history of Pershore Abbey and its estates', *BIHR*, XVI (1938), 119—20. See (1163, 1605).

1407   Stein, Walter. 'Die Hanse und England beim Ausgang des hundertjährigen Krieges', *Hansische Geschichte-Blätter*, XXVI (1921), 27—126. See (1189).

1408   Stewart-Brown, Ronald. 'The hospital of St John at Chester', *Lancs Historic*, LXXVIII (1926), 66—106.

1409   Thrupp, Sylvia L. 'Economy and society in medieval England', *Journal of British Studies*, II (1962), 1—13. Excellent historiographical summary (11, 1436).

1410   Von Brandt, Ahasver. 'Recent trends in research on Hanseatic history', *History*, n.s., XLI (1956), 25—37. Particularly emphasizing Fritz Rörig's work on Lubeck and the Hansa (1189).

1411   Watson, W.B. 'The structure of the Florentine galley trade with Flanders and
        England in the fifteenth century', *Revue Belge de Philologie et d'Histoire*,
        XXXIX (1961), 1073—91; XL (1962), 317—47. See (1202, 1212, 1284,
        1346).
1412   Whitley, Henry M. 'The maritime trade of Exeter in mediaeval times',
        DevonA, XLIV (1912), 530—46. Compares data for 1398—9 with that for
        1493—4 (314, 1395).
1413   Wilson, Keven P. 'The port of Chester in the fifteenth century', *Lancs
        Historic*, CXVII (1965), 1—15. Also ed. Chester's customs accounts
        (1234); and (132, 1155).

IX. AGRICULTURAL HISTORY

1 Printed sources

1414   Amherst, Alicia M.T. (ed.). 'A fifteenth-century treatise on gardening. By
        mayster Jon Gardener', *Arch*, LIV (1894), 157—72. Poem, 1440—1450,
        now ms. in Trinity College, Cambridge (2235).
1415   Hollis, Edwin (ed.). 'Farm accounts — late 14th century', *Records of Buck-
        inghamshire*, XII (1928), 165—92. At Water Eaton, 1394—5, in great
        detail.
1416   Lodge, Barton and Sidney J.H. Herrtage (eds.). *Palladius on husbondrie.
        From the unique ms. of about 1420 A.D. in Colchester Castle* (EETS,
        XXXIX, LXXII). 1872—9, 2 vols.

2 Monographs

1417   Ault, Warren O. *Open-field farming in medieval England; a study of village
        by-laws.* 1972. Argues common pastures under communal control, with
        range of documents; also his more specialized (296); see (120, 360, 1426).
1418   Cromarty, Dorothy. *The fields of Saffron Walden in 1400.* Chelmsford, 1966.
1419   Ernle, Lord. *English farming past and present* [New intro. by George E.
        Fussell and C.R. McGregor]. 6th ed., 1936.
1420   Hodgett, Gerald A.J. *Agrarian England in the later middle ages* (Historical
        Association, Aids for Teachers, XIII). 1966.
1421   Kosminsky, Evgeny A. *Studies in the agrarian history of England*, ed. by
        Rodney H. Hilton. Oxford, 1956. See (1358).
1422   Lambert, Joyce M. *et alii. The making of the Broads: a reconsideration of
        their origin in the light of new evidence.* 1960. Wide-ranging detection by
        diverse specialists in geology and stratigraphy (76, 78, 83).
1423   Platt, Colin. *The monastic grange in medieval England: a reassessment.* 1969.
        Clear reconstruction of Cistercian exploitation of agricultural lands, to
        1540; for Wales (1297).
1424   Rees, William. *South Wales and the March, 1284—1415: a social and agrarian
        study.* Oxford, 1924. See (97, 242, 1297).
1425   Trow-Smith, Robert. *A history of British livestock husbandry*, Vol. I: *to
        1700.* 1957.

3 Articles

1426   Ault, Warren O. 'By-laws of gleaning and the problems of harvest', *EcHR*,
        2nd ser., XIV (1961), 210—17. See (296).
1427   Bennett, Merrill K. 'British wheat yield per acre for seven centuries', *Econ-
        omic History*, III (1935), 12—29. And (1307, 1429).
1428   Brandon, P.F. 'Arable farming in a Sussex scarp-foot parish during the late
        middle ages', *SussexS*, C (1962), 60—72.
1429   —— 'Cereal yields on the Sussex estates of Battle Abbey during the later
        middle ages', *EcHR*, 2nd ser., XXV (1972), 403—20. Showing notable
        high productivity and efficiency (1307, 1427).

1430   Du Boulay, Francis R.H. 'Late-continued demesne farming at Otford', *Arch-Cant*, LXXIII (1959), 116—24. Lands completely leased in 1444.

1431   —— 'Who were farming the English demesnes at the end of the middle ages?' *EcHR*, 2nd ser., XVII (1965), 443—55. See (1235, 1336, 1405).

1432   Field, R.K. 'Worcestershire peasant buildings, household goods and farming equipment in the later middle ages', *Medieval Archaeology*, IX (1965), 105—45. Only work on the subject for the fifteenth century.

1433   Galpin, Francis W. 'Pigs and pannage — a short chapter on mediaeval stock-rearing', *EssexT*, n.s., XVII (1923), 1—9.

1434   Hallam, Herbert E. 'The agrarian economy of south Lincolnshire in the mid-fifteenth century', *Nottingham Mediaeval Studies*, XI (1967), 86—95. Emphasizes depressed population and economy in Spalding, Holbeach, and Gedney areas; and see (1235, 1383, 1439).

1435   —— 'The Postan thesis', *Historical Studies*, XV (1972), 203—22. Challenges Postan and Titow on declines in husbandry and grain yields, arguing from published sources (1275).

1436   Hilton, Rodney H. 'The content and sources of English agrarian history before 1500', *AgHR*, III (1955), 3—19. Excellent bibliographical introduction to the evidence (11, 1409).

1437   Jones-Pierce, T. 'Some tendencies in the agrarian history of Caernarvonshire during the later middle ages', *Transactions of the Caernarvonshire History Society*, I. 1939, pp. 18—36. See (205, 1165, 1235, 1351).

1438   Pelham, Reginald A. 'The agricultural geography of the Chichester estates in 1388', *SussexS*, LXXVIII (1937), 195—210.

1439   Postan, Michael M 'Medieval agrarian society in its prime: England', in Michael M. Postan (ed.). *The Cambridge economic history of Europe*, I. Cambridge, 1966, 2nd ed., pp. 548—632. The first three volumes are of basic, general value (1239—40, 1275).

1440   —— 'Investment in medieval agriculture', *Journal of Economic History*, XXVII (1967), 576—87.

1441   Price, Derek J. 'Medieval land surveying', *Geographical Journal*, CXXXI (1955), 1—10.

1442   Spufford, Margaret. 'A Cambridgeshire community: Chippenham from settlement to enclosure', *University of Leicester, Dept. of English Local History, Occasional Papers*, XX (1965). See (1246, 120).

X. SCIENCE AND TECHNOLOGY

1 Printed sources

1443   Asmole, Elias (ed.). *Theatrum chemicum britannicum*. 1652. Prints diverse medical and alchemical tracts from the fifteenth century and after; for alchemy see (1459, 1464, 1468, 1470, 1471); for medical mss. (1457, 1461, 1474) and generally (1447); for disease (1466).

1444   Craig, Hardin (ed.). *The works of John Metham*, (EETS, CXXXII). 1916. Dated 1448—1449, including treatises on palmistry, physiognomy, and lunar reckonings; similar science in (1446, 1455, 1456, 1458, 1460, 1468, 1471, 1473, 1480).

1445   Dawson, Warren R. (ed.). *A leechbook or collection of medical recipes of the fifteenth century, by Archippus (pseud.)*. 1934. See (1447).

1446   Evans, Joan and Mary S. Serjeantson (eds.). *English mediaeval lapidaries* (EETS, CXC). 1932. Five of seven mss. date from fifteenth century (1046, 1444).

1447   Fleischhacker, Robert von (ed.). *Lanfrank's 'Science of cirurgie'* (EETS, CII). 1894. *Circa* 1400, providing a full medical dictionary; more on medicine and surgery in (1443, 1445, 1449—53, 1457, 1461, 1472, 1474—80, 1483, 1487—9, 1491, 1492).

1448   Gunther, Robert W.T. (ed.). *Chaucer and Messahalla on the astrolabe. Now printed in full for the first time with the original illustrations.* Oxford,

1929. [Vol. V of 'Early Science in Oxford' in 9 vols., 1920–32.] Other eds. are by Walter W. Skeat in *EETS*, e.s., XVI, 1872, and at Antwerp, 1940, for Bibliothèque royale de Belgique, LXXXIX; see (1454, 1465, 1485, 1490, 1528).

1449 Nichols, Robert E., Jr. (ed.). 'Procreation, pregnancy, and parturition: extracts from a middle English metrical encyclopedia', *Medical History*, XI (1967), 175–81. See (1447).

1450 Ogden, Margaret S. (ed.). *The liber de diversis medicinis* (EETS, CCVII). 1938.

1451 Osler, William. *Incunabula medica . . . 1467–1480* (Bibliographical Society, XIX). Oxford, 1923.

1452 Pettigrew, Thomas J. (ed.). *An historiall expostulation against the beastlye abusers, both of chyrurgerie and physyke . . . by J. Halle* (Percy Society, XI). 1844.

1453 Power, D'Arcy (ed.). *Treatises of fistula in ano, haemorrhoids, and clysters, By John Arderne* (EETS, CXXXIX). 1910. And (1447).

1454 Price, Derek J. (ed.). *The equatorie of the planetis.* Cambridge, 1955. Ascribed here to Geoffrey Chaucer, not Simon Bredon (1444, 1448).

1455 —— (ed.). *An old palmistry, being the earliest known book of palmistry in English.* Cambridge, 1953. And see (1444).

1456 Raine, James [the elder] (ed.). 'Divination in the fifteenth century by aid of a magical crystal', *AJ*, XIII (1856), 372–4. Magician's confession under the threat of heresy prosecution, 1465; see (1444).

1457 Robbins, Rossell H. (ed.). 'Medical manuscripts in middle English', *Speculum*, XLV (1970), 393–415. Includes exhaustive mss. list (1443, 1461).

1458 Seymour, M.C. (ed.). 'More of a middle English abstract of Bartholomaeus, *De proprietatibus rerum*', *Anglia*, LXXXVII (1969), 1–25; XCI (1973), 18–34. Follows Trevisa's English translation, printed *c.* 1495, and now ed. by Seymour, Oxford, 1975, 2 vols. For the broad topic of herbals consult A. Arber, 1938, or E.S. Rohde, 1922, also C.R. Eaven's study of naturalists, 1947; and (1444, 2348).

1459 Singer, Dorothea W. (ed.). *Catalogue of Latin and vernacular alchemical manuscripts in Great Britain and Ireland dating from before the XVI century.* Brussels, 1928–31, 3 vols. See (1443).

1460 —— (ed.). 'Handlist of scientific mss. in the British Isles dating from before the sixteenth century', *Transactions of the Bibliographical Society*, XV (1917–19), 185–99. See (1444).

1461 —— (ed.). 'Survey of medical manuscripts in the British Isles dating from before the sixteenth century', *Proceedings of the Royal Society of Medicine*, XII (1918), 96–107. See (1443).

1462 Steele, Robert (ed.). *The earliest arithmetics in English* (EETS, e.s., CXVIII). 1916. See (1486, 2462).

2 Monographs

1463 Creighton, Charles. *History of epidemics in Britain: from A.D. 664 to the extinction of the plague.* Cambridge, 1891, 2 vols. Still a good survey, as is A.H. Gale, *Epidemic diseases*, 1959; see (1466), and the general *Medieval English medicine*, 1974, by Stanley Rubin.

1464 Crombie, Alastair C. *Augustine to Galileo; the history of science. A.D. 400–1650.* 1952. Several chapters revised and published as *Medieval and early modern science*, Cambridge, Mass., 1963, 2nd ed., 2 vols.; and (1443).

1465 Edwardes, Ernest L. *Weight-driven chamber clocks of the middle ages and renaissance.* Altrincham, Cheshire, 1965. And see Bernard Mason's 1969 survey of clockmaking in Colchester; also (1444).

1466 Hirst, Louis F. *Conquest of the plague: a study of the evolution of epidemiology.* 1953. And see Charles F. Mullett, *The bubonic plague and England*, 1956, or the recently popular synthesis by Philip Ziegler, *The black death*, 1969; see (988, 1121, 1122, 1140, 1302, 1401, 1463, 1467, 1520).

1467 Mode, P.G. *Influence of black death on English monasteries.* 1960.

1468   Sarton, George. *Science and learning in the fourteenth century*. Baltimore, 1948. See (1443, 1444).

1469   Shrewsbury, John F.D. *A History of bubonic plague in the British Isles*. 1969. And (1466).

1470   Taylor, Frank S. *The alchemists: founders of modern chemistry*. New York, 1949. Broad but succinct account, similar to E.J. Holmyard, *Alchemy*, 1957; also (1443).

1471   Thorndike, Lynn. *A history of magic and experimental science [vols. III and IV]*. New York, 1929. See (1444, 1464).

3 Articles

1472   Barnet, Margaret C. 'The barber-surgeons of York', *Medical History*, XII (1968), 19–30. See (1447, 153).

1473   Bennett, Henry S. 'Science and information in English writings of the fifteenth-century', *Modern Language Review*, XXXIX (1944), 1–8. See (1443, 1444).

1474   Bullough, Vern L. 'Duke Humphrey and His medical collections', *Renaissance News*, XIV (1961), 87–91. And (724, 1447).

1475   —— 'Medical study at mediaeval Oxford', *Speculum*, XXXVI (1961), 600–12; *Medieval Studies*, XXIV (1962), 161–8. And at Cambridge (2394, 2457).

1476   —— 'Medieval medical and scientific views of women', *Viator*, IV (1973), 485–501. And (1097, 1489).

1477   Flemming, Percy. 'The medical aspect of the mediaeval monastery in England', *Proceedings of the Royal Society of Medicine*, XXII (1928), 771–82.

1478   Garbaty, Thomas J. 'The Summoner's occupational disease', *Medical History*, VII (1963), 348–58. See (2066, 2131, 2191).

1479   Gask, George E. 'The medical services of Henry V's campaign of the Somme in 1415', *Proceedings of the Royal Society of Medicine*, XVI (1922), 1–10. See (1447).

1480   Harland, John and William E.A. Axon. 'Some account of a curious astronomical, astrological, and medical ms. in the Chetham Library, Manchester', *Lancs Historic*, XXIX (1876–7), 1–8. Written between 1461 and 1483, with illuminations (1444, 1447, 1448).

1481   Harvey, John H. 'Four fifteenth-century London plans', *London Topographical Society*, XX (1952), 1–8. And (87, 1483–4, 1493, 130, 626, 1546, 2276, 2336–7) about London's topography.

1482   Holand, H.R. 'An English scientist in America 130 years before Columbus', *Transactions of the Wisconsin Academy*, XLVIII (1959), 205–19. See (1584–5, 1590).

1483   Honeybourne, Marjorie B. 'The leper hospitals of the London area: with an appendix on some other medieval hospitals of Middlesex', *London-Midd*, n.s., XXI (1967), 1–61. Mapped and catalogued; see Thomas J. Pettigrew, *JBAA*, XI, 1855, pp. 9–34, 95–117 for house lists; on hospital administration, see Margaret A. Seymour, BIHR, XXI, 1948, pp. 249–50; also (2276, 2074).

1484   —— 'The reconstructed map of London under Richard II', *London Topographical Society*, XXII (1965), 29–76. See (87, 1481, 1493, 2074).

1485   Howgrave-Graham, Robert P. 'Some clocks and jacks, with notes on the history of horology', *Arch*, LXXVII (1928), 257–312. See (1448).

1486   Karpinski, Louis C. 'The algorism of John Killingworth', *EHR*, XXIX (1914), 707–17. See (1462).

1487   Merke, F. 'The history of endemic goitre and cretinism in the thirteenth to fifteenth centuries', *Proceedings of the Royal Society of Medicine*, LIII (1960), 995–1002. Based on continental mss. now in the Wellcome Historical Medical Library, London; and see (1447).

1488   Mustain, James K. 'A rural medical practitioner in fifteenth-century England', *Bulletin of the History of Medicine*, XLVI (1972), 469–76.

1489   Power, Eileen E. 'Some women practitioners of medicine in the middle ages',

Proceedings of the Royal Society of Medicine, XV (1921—2), 20—3. See (1097, 1497).

1490 Smyser, Hamilton M. 'A view of Chaucer's astronomy', Speculum, XLV (1970), 359—73. Also, J.D. North in Review of English Studies, n.s., XX, 1969, pp. 129—54, 257—83, and 418—44; and (1448).

1491 Talbert, Ernest W. 'The notebook of a fifteenth-century practising physician (John Crophill)', Studies in English, University of Texas, (1942), 5—30. See (1447, 1488).

1492 Thompson, Charles J.S. 'The apothecary in England from the thirteenth to the close of the sixteenth century', Proceedings of the Royal Society of Medicine, VIII, Part II (1914), 36—44. Also wrote The witchery of Jane Shore, Edward IV's mistress, 1933 (687).

1493 Walker, Violet W. 'Mediaeval Nottingham: a topographical study', ThorotonS, LXVII (1963), 28—45. And (87, 1481, 1484).

XI. MILITARY AND NAVAL HISTORY

1 Printed sources

1494 Anon. (ed.). 'A fifteenth-century book of arms', Ancestor, III (1902), 185—213; IV (1903), 225—50; V (1903), 175—90; VII (1903), 184—215; IX (1904), 159—80. From the 1450's, now B.M., Harleian ms. 2169; for heraldry (899, 1045, 1104, 1495, 1544, 1560, 1570) and chivalry (1500) and the law of arms (1535).

1495 Barnard, Francis P. (ed.). Edward IV's French expedition of 1475. The leaders and their badges: being ms. 2 M. 16 College of Arms. Oxford, 1925. See (648, 687, 1118).

1496 —— (ed.). The essential portions of Nicholas Upton's 'De studio militari', before 1446, translated by John Blount, fellow of All Souls (c. 1500). Oxford, 1931. See (1500, 1045, 1060).

1497 Bayley, John (ed.). 'Account of the first battle of St Albans, from a contemporary manuscript', Arch, XX (1824), 519—23. See (1563).

1498 Beaucourt, Gaston du Fresne de (ed.). Chronique de Mathieu d'Escouchy (Société de l'Histoire de France). Paris, 1863—4, 3 vols. Last phases of Hundred Years' War, 1444—50; other French sources are (1499, 1502—3, 1512, 1515, 1527) and here in Section VI, p. 44; also (1523).

1499 Bellaguet, Louis F. (ed.). Chronique du religieux de St Denis, 1380—1422. Paris, 1839—52, 6 vols.

1500 Byles, Alfred T.P. (ed.). The book of the ordre of chyvalry, translated and printed by William Caxton from a French version of Ramon Lull's 'Le libre del orde de cavayleria . . . '. (EETS, CLXVIII). 1925. Earlier ed. by Beriah Botfield, 1847; more on chivalry (1501, 1504—6, 572, 648, 719) and jousts (889, 993, 1010, 1028, 1071) and heraldry (1045, 1494).

1501 —— (ed.). The book of fayttes of armes and of chyvalrye (EETS, CLXXXIX). 1932; 2nd ed. enlarged, 1937. See Bentley (993).

1502 Courteault, Henri (ed.). Histoire de Gaston IV, comte de Foix, par Guillaume Leseur, (Société de l'Histoire de France). Paris, 1893—6, 2 vols. See (1498).

1503 Delachanel, Roland (ed.). Chroniques des règnes de Jean II et de Charles V. Paris, 1910—1920, 4 vols.

1504 Dillon, Harold A.L. (ed.). 'A ms. collection of ordinances of chivalry of the fifteenth century belonging to Lord Hastings', Arch, LVII (1900), 29—70. See (1071, 1500, 2237).

1505 Dugdale, William (ed.). The manner of ordenaunce withinne lists. 1666. Attributed to Thomas of Woodstock, duke of Gloucester, 1355—97; also, the edition for the Roxburghe Club, no. 56, 1840; and see (623, 1500).

1506 Dyboski, Roman and Zygmund M. Arend (eds.). Knyghthode and bataile, A XVth century verse paraphrase of Flavius Vegetius Renatus' treatise 'De re militari' (EETS, CCI). 1936. Time of Henry VI, see (1500).

1507   Fletcher, William G.D. (ed.). 'Some documents [1403] relative to the battle of Shrewsbury', *ShropsT*, 2nd ser., X (1898), 227–250; XII (1900), 39–44. See (1549, 162).

1508   Hudson, William (ed.). 'A commission to arm and array the clergy in 1400', *SussexS*, LI (1908), 153–62. See (1539).

1509   Hull, Felix (ed.). 'An early Kentish militia roll [*circa* 1415]', *ArchCant*, LXVIII (1954), 159–66.

1510   Huscher, Herbert (ed.). *John Page's 'Siege of Rouen'.* Leipzig, 1927.

1511   Jarry, Louis (ed.). *Le compte de l'armée anglaise au siège d'Orleans, 1428–1429.* Orleans, 1892. Contemporary list of captains, troops, pay and other details (1539); a more readable study of the event is by Régine Pernoud, Paris, 1969; also, the immensely detailed work of R. Boucher de Molandon and Adalbert de Beaucorps, Orleans, 1892.

1512   Lecestre, Léon (ed.). *Le jouvencel par Jean de Bueil, suivi du commentaire de Guillaume Tringaut* (Société de l'Histoire de France). Paris, 1887–9, 2 vols. Last phases of Hundred Years' War (1498).

1513   Lewis, Norman B. (ed.). 'Indentures of retinue with John of Gaunt, duke of Lancaster, enrolled in chancery, 1367–1399', *Camden Miscellany XXII* (Camden Society, 4th ser., I). 1964, pp. 77–112. See (151, 510, 1539).

1514   Marsden, Reginald G. (ed.). *Select pleas in the court of admiralty [of the West]* (Selden Society, VI). 1892. Particularly 1390–1404; more materials on the navy and admiralty in (1524, 1532, 1536, 1545, 1548, 1561, 1585–7, 1591–3, 1602).

1515   Moranvillé, Henri (ed.). *Chroniques de Perceval de Cagny* (Société de l'Histoire de France). Paris, 1902. Hundred Years' War during the time of Joan of Arc (911, 1498).

1516   Nicolas, Nicholas H. (ed.). *The Scrope and Grosvenor controversy: de controversia in curia militari inter Ricardum le Scrope et Robertum Grosvenor, 1385–90.* 1832, 2 vols. See (1535, 836).

1517   —— (ed.). 'An account of the army with which Richard II. invaded Scotland in 1385', *Arch*, XXII (1829), 13–19. From Harleian mss. 1309 and 369, and Ashmole ms. 865 (1539).

1518   Quicherat, Jules E.J. (ed.). *Procès de condamnation et de rèhabilitation de Jeanne d'Arc, dite La Pucelle d'Orléans* (Société de l'Histoire de France). Paris, 1841–9, 5 vols. See (882, 911, 932, 1535); there is a new, well-annotated ed. by Pierre Tisset and Yvonne Lanhers, 1960; the best English translations are by W.P. Barrett, 1931, and W.S. Scott, 1956; important memoirs of fifteen assessors are ed. by P. Lanéry d'Arc, Paris, 1889; and see Régine Pernoud's account, Paris, 1962.

1519   Rogers, Alan (ed.). 'Hoton *versus* Shakell: a ransom case in the court of chivalry, 1390–5', *Nottingham Mediaeval Studies*, VI (1962), 74–108; VII (1963), 53–78. See (1535, 1543).

1520   Skene, Felix J.H. (ed.). *Book of Pluscarden.* Edinburgh. 1800. Good source for northern border conflicts and plague, *c.* 1461; see (735, 1264, 1466), and for Scotland (629, 856, 863, 1).

1521   Twiss, Travers (ed.). *Monumenta juridica: the black book of the admiralty* (Rolls Series, LV). 1871–6, 4 vols. Major source for maritime law; see also, (1226, 1514, 1522).

1522   Warner, George F. (ed.). *'The libelle of englysche polycye': a poem on the use of sea power, 1436.* Oxford, 1926. Also available in Richard Hakluyt, *Principal Navigations . . .* , I, 1599, pp. 187–208; Thomas Wright, *Political Poems . . .* , II, 1861, pp. 157–205; William Hertzberg, publ. in Leipzig, 1878; and (1347).

2 Monographs

1523   Burne, Alfred H. *The Agincourt war: a military history of the latter part of the Hundred Years' War from 1369 to 1453.* 1956. And (1498, 1527, 1530, 1532, 1538, 1539, 1572, 1583, 1588, 1594). Also see his two immensely useful volumes on *Battlefields of England*, 1950–2.

1524   Burwash, Dorothy H. *English merchant shipping 1460–1540.* 1947. Emphasis early Tudor, describing size, type and science of shipping and the sea-man's work; see (1514, 1448).

1525 Clephan, Robert C. *The defensive armour and the weapons and engines of war* . . . . 1900. Also his monograph on pre-1500 firearms, 1906, and see Guy Laking's authoritative *European armour and arms*. On the crossbow, see Ralph Payne-Gallwey, 1958; and (1528).

1526 Contamine, Philippe. *Guerre, état et société à la fin du moyen âge: études sur les armées des rois de France, 1337–1494* (École pratique des hautes études – Sorbonne, VIe section: sciences économiques et sociales, Centre de recherches historiques. Civilisations et Sociétés, 24). Paris, 1972. Def-initive and massive analysis of military and social context (1048, 1542), and now his article in *BIHR*, XLVII, 1974, pp. 125–49.

1527 De Flamare, Henri. *Le Nivernais pendant la guerre de cent ans [1404–50]*. Nevers, 1913–25, 2 vols. More on England's occupation in France (911, 1523, 1529, 1531, 1532, 1534, 1537, 1542, 1553, 1554, 1556, 1564, 1565, 1567, 1571, 1573, 1574, 1578–81, 1599–1601).

1528 ffoulkes, Charles J. *The armourer and his craft from the XIth to the XVIth century*. 1912. More recently see monographs of Samuel E. Ellacott, 1962, James G. Mann, 1962, Paul Martin, 1967, and Ronald E. Oakeshott, 1964; for military technology (1525, 1540, 1541, 1557, 1566, 1595–8, 2344), also (1448).

1529 Finot, Jules. *Recherches sur les incursions des Anglais et des grandes com-pagnies dans la duché et le comté de Bourgogne à la fin du XIVe siècle*. Vesoul, 1874. See (919, 1527).

1530 Fowler, Kenneth (ed.). *The Hundred Years' War*. 1971. Most recent and sound survey available in the form of these eight original essays by various scholars, with (1048, 1526, 1542).

1531 Guillon, Felix. *Étude historique sur le journal du siège qui fût mis devant Orleans par les anglais en 1428–1429*. Paris, 1913.

1532 Huguet, Adrien. *Aspects de la guerre de cent ans en Picardie maritime, 1400–1450* (Mémoires de la Société des Antiquaires de Picardie, XLVIII, I). Amiens and Paris, 1941–4, 2 vols. See (1514, 1527).

1533 Jacob, Ernest F. *Henry V and the invasion of France*. 1947. And (579, 689).

1534 Jouet, M.R. *La résistance à l'occupation anglaise en Basse-Normandie (1418–1450)* (Cahier des Annales de Normandie, V). Caen, 1969.

1535 Keen, Maurice H. *The laws of war in the later middle ages*. Oxford, 1965. Excellent analysis and synthesis of the enforcement of the chivalric code in the Hundred Years' War, also (1494, 1496, 1516, 1519, 1543, 1552, 1560).

1536 Lloyd, Christopher. *The British seamen, 1200–1860: a social survey*. 1968. And Nicholas H. Nicolas, *History of the royal navy*, 1847, 2 vols.; and Michael Oppenheim, *The administration of the royal navy*, 1896; also, generally (1514).

1537 Monicat, Jacques. *Histoire du Velay pendant la guerre de cent ans; les grandes compagnies en Velay (1358–1392)*. Paris, 1928. See *École Nationale des Chartes: position des thèses*, LXXIX (1927), pp. 95–113; and (1527).

1538 Newhall, Richard A. *The English conquest of Normandy, 1416–1424: a study in fifteenth-century warfare*. New Haven, Conn., 1924.

1539 —— *Muster and review: a problem of English military administration 1420–1440*. Cambridge, Mass., 1940. And (952, 1508, 1509, 1511, 1513, 1517, 1568, 1582, 1589, 1603, 1604).

1540 O'Neil, Bryan H. St John. *Castles: an introduction to the castles of England and Wales*. 1953. And see Charles W. Oman, 1926, and an excellent study by Reginald A. Brown, *English medieval castles*, 1954; and see (1595–7, 1528).

1541 —— *Castles and cannon. A study of early fortifications in England*. Oxford, 1960. An important survey, reviewed by Claude Gaier in *Revue Belge de philologie et d'histoire*, XL (1962), pp. 1220–7.

1542 Perroy, Edouard. *The Hundred Years' War*. 1951. Best general survey avail-able, first publ. in Paris, 1945; and see (1523, 1526, 1527, 1530).

1543 Squibb, George D. *The high court of chivalry: a study of the civil law in England*. Oxford, 1959. Mainly post 1485, but the only survey available, detailed and interesting (1519, 1535, 1496).

1544   Woodward, John and George Burnett. *A treatise on heraldry, British and foreign*. Edinburgh, 1892—6, 2 vols. Exhaustive treatment, now partly replaced in works of Anthony R. Wagner (1045).

3 Articles

1545   Anderson, Roger C. 'The *Grace de Dieu* of 1446—86', *EHR*, XXXIV (1919), 584—6. See (1602, 1514).

1546   Andrews, Michael C. 'The British Isles in the nautical charts of the XIVth and XVth centuries', *Geographical Journal*, LXVIII (1926), 474—81. See (1591) or generally (87, 1481).

1547   Blyth, J.D. 'The battle of Tewkesbury', *Bristol-Gloucs*, LXXX (1961), 99—120. Also, William Bazeley, *ibid*. XXVI, 1903, pp. 173—93.

1548   Brindley, Harold H. 'Mediaeval ships in painted glass and on seals', *Mariner's Mirror*, I (1911), 43—7, 71—5, 129—34, 193—200; II (1912), 1—6, 44—52, 129—34, 166—73, 239—43; III (1913), 14—17, 337—40; IV (1914), 44—9, 110—14, 129—33. Similarly, *Proceedings of the Cambridge Antiquarian Society*, XVII, 1913, pp. 139—45; on ship models, Henry B. Culver, *Mariner's Mirror*, XV, 1929, pp. 213—21; Alfred B. Emden, *ibid*. VIII, 1922, pp. 167—73; Alan H. Moore, *ibid*. V, 1917, pp. 15—20; Robert Nance, *ibid*. 1911, pp. 65—7, and *ibid*. XLI, 1955, pp. 180—92; and J.W. Van Nouhuys, *ibid*. XVIII, 1931, pp. 327—46; and generally (1514).

1549   Burne, Alfred H. 'The battle of Shrewsbury: a military reconstruction', *ShropsT*, LII (1947—8), 141—52. Earlier study of same by James H. Wylie *et alii*, *ibid*. III, 1903, pp. 139—266; and (1507, 162).

1550   Cass, Frederick C. 'The battle of Barnet', *London-Midd*, VI (1890), 1—52. With full pedigree, 14 April 1471.

1551   Charlesworth, Dorothy. 'The battle of Hexham, 1464', *ArchAel*, 4th ser., XXX (1952), 57—68. And Jasper Gibson, *ibid*., n.s., IV, 1860, pp. 6—7.

1552   Dumas, Auguste. 'Deux procès de prises maritimes a l'epoque de la guerre de cent ans', *Revue Générale de Droit International Public*, XVI (1909), 5—45. On fifteenth century international law concerning war and prizes, see Keen (1535), and (1521).

1553   Endrès, André. 'Situation économique au Nord de Meaux pendant la guerre de cent ans (1422—1426)', *Bulletin Philologique et Historique (Jusqu'a 1610) du Comité des Travaux Historiques et Scientifiques*, (1964), 559—68. See (1526, 1527).

1554   Fourquin, Guy. 'La batellerie à Paris au temps des Anglo-Bourguignons (1418—1436)', *Le Moyen Âge*, LXIX (1963), 707—25. See (1527, 919, 1556).

1555   Gaupp, Fritz. 'The condottiere John Hawkwood', *History*, n.s., XXIII (1939), 305—21. Indicates one Englishman active in Italy, died 1394 (990).

1556   Grassoreille, Georges. 'Histoire politique du chapitre de Notre-Dame de Paris pendant la domination anglaise', *Mémoires de la Société de l'histoire de Paris et de l'Ile-de-France*, IX (1882), 109—92. See (1527, 1554).

1557   Gregory, F.W.C. 'The plan of the mediaeval castle at Nottingham', *ThorotonS*, XLVIII (1944), 1—31. And, Herbert Green on Greasley Castle, *ibid*. XXXVIII, 1934, pp. 34—53; and (1528, 1540, 1595, 2322).

1558   Huard, Robert. 'La régence du duc de Bedford à Paris, de 1422 à 1435', *École Nationale des Chartes: Positions des thèses*, LIII (1902), 43—55. See (726).

1559   Jack, R. Ian. 'A quincentenary: the battle of Northampton, July 10th, 1460', *Northamptonshire Past & Present*, III (1960); 21—5.

1560   Keen, Maurice. 'Brotherhood in arms', *History*, XLVII (1962), 1—17. Describes nature of personal military and chivalric relationships (1535).

1561   Kingsford, Charles L. 'The beginnings of English maritime enterprise', *History*, n.s., XIII (1928), 97—106, 193—203. See (1514).

1562   Lander, Jack R. 'The Hundred Years' War and Edward IV's 1475 campaign in France', in Arthur J. Slavin (ed.)., *Tudor men and institutions*. Baton Rouge, Louisiana, 1972, pp. 70—100. See (687).

1563   Lane, Hilda, M.M. ' "The male journey" of St Albans, Thursday, May 22nd,

1455', *Transactions of the St Albans and Hertfordshire Architectural and Archaeological Society*, (1931), 109–21. That is, the Battle of St Albans (1497, 722).

1564   Lauriot-Prévost, Catherine. 'La guerre de course en Bretagne pendant la guerre de cent ans', *Bulletin Philologique et Historique (Jusqu'a 1610) de Comité des Travaux Historiques et Scientifiques* (1966), 61–79. See (1527, 1574).

1565   Lefèvre-Pontalis, Germain. 'Episodes de l'invasion anglaise: la guerre de partisans dans la haute Normandie, 1424–29', *Bibliothèque de l'École des Chartes*, LIV (1893), 475–521; LV (1894), 259–305; LVI (1895), 433–508; LVII (1896), 5–54; XCVII (1936), 102–30; *Le Moyen Âge*, VII (1894), 81–91. See (1527).

1566   Legg, Leopold G.W. 'Windsor Castle, New College, Oxford, and Winchester College: a study in the development of planning by William of Wykeham', *JBAA*, 3rd ser., III (1939), 83–95. See (1528, 1540, 1595, 1966).

1567   Leroux, Alfred. 'Le sac de la cité de Limoges et son relèvement 1370–1464', *Bulletin des Société archéologique et historique du Limousin*, LVI (1906), 155–203. See (1527).

1568   Lewis, Norman B. 'The last medieval summons of the English feudal levy, 13 June 1385', *EHR*, LXXIII (1958), 1–26. See (1577, 1539).

1569   Lewis, Peter S. 'War propaganda and historiography in fifteenth-century France and England', *TRHS*, 5th ser., XV (1965), 1–21. See (2478, 2483).

1570   London, Hugh S. 'Some medieval treatises on English heraldry', *AntiqJ*, XXXIII (1953), 169–83. Convenient list and discussion of extant mss., with (1045, 1069).

1571   Lorière, Edouard de. 'Le chateau de l'Isle pendant l'occupation anglaise', *Revue Historique et Archeologique du Maine*, LXXVII (1921), 56–82. See (1527, 1579).

1572   Malden, Arthur R. 'An official account of the battle of Agincourt', *Ancestor*, XI (1904), 26–31. Found in Leger Book A, f. 55, in the town of Salisbury's muniments, dated 1415; and (1523).

1573   Mirot,.Lucien. 'Une tentative d'invasion en Angleterre pendant la guerre de cent ans (1385–1386)', *Revue des Études historiques*, LXXXI (1915), 250–87, 416–66.

1574   Mollat, Guillaume. 'Les désastres de la guerre de cent-ans en Bretagne', *Annals de Bretagne*, XXVI (1911), 168–201. See (1527, 1564).

1575   Myres, John N.L. 'The campaign of Radcot Bridge in December 1387', *EHR*, XLII (1927), 20–33.

1576   Newhall, Richard A. 'Bedford's ordinance on the watch of September, 1428', *EHR*, L (1935), 36–60.

1577   Palmer, J.J.N. 'The last summons of the feudal army in England (1385)', *EHR*, LXXXIII (1968), 771–5. See (1568, 1539).

1578   Planchenault, René. 'La bataille de Baugé', in *Mémoires de la Société nationale d'agriculture, sciences et arts d'Angers*, 5th ser., XXVIII (1925), 5–30; 6th ser., V (1930), 90–107. See (1527).

1579   —— 'La conquête de Maine par les anglais. I. La campagne de 1414–1425', *Revue Historique et Archeologique du Maine*, LXXXI (1925), 3–31; LXXXIX (1933), 125–52; 2nd ser., XVII (1937), 24–34, 160–72. The second and third articles continue the study through 1429.

1580   —— 'La déliverance du Mans (Janvier–Mars 1448)', *Revue Historique et Archeologique du Maine*, LXXIX (1923), 185–202.

1581   —— 'Le lutte contre les anglais en Anjou pendant la première moitié du XVe siècle', *École Nationale des Chartes: Positions des thèses*, LXXV (1923), 75–82. See (1527).

1582   Powicke, Michael R. 'Lancastrian captains', in T.A. Sandquist and Michael R. Powicke (eds.), *Essays in medieval history presented to Bertie Wilkinson*. Toronto, 1969, pp. 371–82. See (1539).

1583   Probert, Ynyr. 'Mathew Gough 1390–1450', *Transactions of the Honourable Society of Cymmrodorion*, (1961), 34–44. Aspects of his career in the Hundred Years' War, and discussion of the battle of Cravant, 1423.

1584   Quinn, David B. 'The argument for the English discovery of America between 1480 and 1494', *Geographical Journal*, CXXVII (1961), 277–85. See (1590, 1482).

1585   —— 'Edward IV and exploration', *Mariner's Mirror*, XXI (1935), 275–84.

1586   Richmond, Colin F. 'English naval power in the fifteenth century', *History*, LII (1967), 1–15. See (1514).

1587   —— 'The keeping of the seas during the Hundred Years' War', *History*, XLIX (1964), 283–98.

1588   Rowe, Benedicta J.H. 'A contemporary account of the Hundred Years' War from 1415 to 1429', *EHR*, XLI (1926), 504–13.

1589   —— 'Discipline in the Norman garrisons under Bedford, 1422–35', *EHR*, XLVI (1931), 194–208. See (1539).

1590   Ruddock, Alwyn A. 'John Day of Bristol and the English voyages across the Atlantic before 1497', *Geographical Journal*, CXXXII (1966), 225–33. See (1482, 1584–5).

1591   Rylands, Thomas G. 'The map-history of the coast from the Dee to the Duddon. A search for the Belisama of Horsley', *Lancs Historic*, XXXI (1878–9), 83–96. Examines portulanes, or books of harbor directions for coastal navigation (1514, 1546).

1592   Senior, William. 'Admiralty matters in the fifteenth century', *LQR*, XXXV (1919), 73–83, 290–9. See (1514).

1593   Sherborne, James W. 'The English navy. Shipping and manpower 1369–1389', *Past and Present*, XXXVII (1967), 163–75. See (1514).

1594   Simpson, Martin A. 'The campaign of Verneuil [1424]', *EHR*, XLIX (1934), 93–100.

1595   Simpson, William D. ' "Bastard feudalism" and the later castles', *AntiqJ*, XXVI (1946), 145–71. Controversial study of how castle construction mirrored social changes, with (1540, 1557, 1566, 1528, 2322); on building (2189).

1596   —— 'Castles of "livery and maintenance" ', *JBAA*, 3rd ser., IV (1939), 39–54; 3rd ser., V (1940), 63–72. Good background information, mainly thirteenth and fourteenth centuries; the second article, on Tonbridge Castle, describes fifteenth-century modifications for mercenary warfare.

1597   —— 'Warkworth: a castle of livery and maintenance', *ArchAel*, 4th ser., XV (1938), 115–36. See (1540).

1598   Smith, Terence P. 'The medieval town defences of King's Lynn', *JBAA*, 3rd ser., XXXIII (1970), 57–88.

1599   Soyer, Jacques. 'La bataille de Patay (samedi 18 juin 1429)', *Bulletin des Société archéologique et historique de l'Orleannais*, XVI (1916), 416–24. See (1527).

1600   Tattegrain, Anne-Marie. 'Le Vexin français sous la domination anglaise (1419–1449)', *École Nationale des Chartes: Positions des Thèses*, LXXXIX (1937), 157–65.

1601   Triger, Robert. 'Le chateau et la ville de Beaumont-le-Vicomte pendant l'invasion anglaise (1417–50)', *Revue Historique et Archeologique du Maine*, XLIX (1901), 241–84; L (1901), 52–70. See (1527).

1602   Turner, (Mrs) W.J.C. 'The building of the *Gracedieu*, *Valentine*, and *Falconer* at Southampton, 1416–1420', *Mariner's Mirror*, XL (1954), 55–72, 270–81. Also, the *Holy Ghost of the Tower* (1545, 1514).

1603   Wrottesley, George (ed.). 'Military service performed by Staffordshire tenants during the reign of Richard II', *SaltS*, XIV (1893), 221–64. See (1539); for some of Humphrey Stafford's indentures, 1402–60, see A.C. Reeves in *Nottingham Mediaeval Studies*, XVI, 1972.

1604   Wylie, James H. 'Notes on the Agincourt roll', *TRHS*, 3rd ser., V (1911), 105–40. Military muster records (1523, 1572, 1539).

XII. RELIGIOUS HISTORY

1 Printed sources

1605 Andrews, Francis B. (ed.). 'The *compotus* rolls of the monastery of Pershore', *Transactions of the Birmingham Archaeological Society*, LVII (1933), 1– 94. Early fifteenth century records of the sacrists; more monastic obedientiary accounts are (1622, 1643, 1644, 1656, 1671, 1672, 1688, 1693, 1724, 1735, 1736, 1742, 1764, 1789, 1791–3, 1797–9, 1802, 1837, 1848, 2051, 2158, 2421).

1606 Anon. (ed.). 'The last ancress of Whalley', *Lancs Historic*, LXIV (1912), 268–72. Female hermit named Isolda Heton, 1437 (1867).

1607 Archer, Margaret (ed.). *The register of bishop Philip Repingdon 1405–1419* (Lincolnshire Record Society, LVII, LVIII). 1963, 2 vols. See (1613, 1699, 1928, 1977).

1608 Arnold, Thomas (ed.). *Memorials of St Edmund's abbey* (Rolls Series, XCVI). 1890–6, 3 vols. Particularly vol. III for fifteenth century materials; more monastic muniments are (1605, 1624, 1630, 1636, 1639–40, 1650, 1659–61, 1682, 1692, 1699, 1705, 1709, 1732, 1749, 1755, 1772–3, 1779, 1790, 1802–3, 1805, 1809, 1813–14, 1818, 1829, 1832–3, 1836, 1843), and (1917).

1609 Atchley, Edward G.C.F. (ed.). 'Mediaeval parish clerks in Bristol', *StPaulS*, n.s., V (1905), 107–16; VI (1910), 35–67; and V (1905), 163–9. Order book from 1481 and other parish records from St Nicholas, Bristol; the last article identified the 'Jesus Mass and Anthem'; more parochial materials in (1759, 1655, 1701, 1706, 1725, 1743–4, 1747, 1769, 1777, 1796, 1842, 1845, 1859, 1871, 1875, 1876, 1878, 1900, 1902, 1914, 1949) and (1982).

1610 Axon, William E.A. (ed.). 'A fifteenth-century devotion: the "Golden litany of the holy Magdalen" ', *Transactions of the Royal Society of Literature*, 2nd ser., XXVII (1907), 123–37. See Jolliffe (1625) and for more popular devotional materials (1620, 1627, 1628, 1631, 1646, 1649, 1652, 1666, 1670, 1675, 1679, 1680, 1684, 1685, 1708, 1719, 1723, 1726, 1727, 1731, 1748, 1763, 1765, 1767, 1774, 1780, 1781, 1785, 1804, 1811, 1816, 1817, 1821, 1824, 1834, 1839, 1840, 1905, 1994, 2131, 2482).

1611 —— (ed.). 'On a plenary indulgence granted at Manchester in 1477 to Adam de Chetham', *Lancs Antiq*, XXIV (1906), 133–8. See (1716, 1853).

1612 Babington, Churchill (ed.). *The repressor of overmuch blaming of the clergy. By Reginald Pecock* (Rolls Series, XIX). 1860, 2 vols. More of Pecock in (1690, 1714, 1715, 1766, 1965, 1969, 2478).

1613 Bannister, Arthur T. (ed.). *Registrum Edmundi Lacy, episcopi Herefordensis, 1417–20: Registrum Thome Poltone, episcopi Herefordensis, 1420–22* (Canterbury and York Society, XXII). 1918. Other episcopal registers are (1607, 1614–16, 1618, 1638, 1651, 1657, 1663, 1695, 1697, 1704, 1710–12, 1720–2, 1728, 1729, 1734, 1757, 1758, 1761, 1775, 1776, 1786, 1838, 1844, 1846, 1866) and (1977).

1614 —— (ed.). *Registrum Thome Spofford, episcopi Herefordensis, 1422–48* (Canterbury and York Society, XXIII). 1918.

1615 —— (ed.). *Registrum Ricardi Beauchamp, episcopi Herefordensis, 1449–50; Registrum Reginaldi Boulers, episcopi Herefordensis, 1450–53; Registrum Johannis Stanbury, episcopi Herefordensis, 1453–74* (Canterbury and York Society, XXV). 1919.

1616 —— (ed.). *Registrum Thome Myllyng, episcopi Herefordensis, 1474–92* (Canterbury and York Society, XXVI). 1920.

1617 —— (ed.). 'Visitation returns of the diocese of Hereford in 1397', *EHR*, XLIV (1929), 279–89, 444–53; XLV (1930), 92–101, 444–63. More visitation and disciplinary materials are (1660, 1667, 1668, 1687, 1691, 1694, 1699, 1738, 1787, 1806, 1819, 1879, 1922, 1954, 2002, 2010, 2021, 2032, 2062, 2066, 2071, 2109, 2117, 2124, 2148).

1618   Barnes, Ralph (ed.). *Liber pontificalis of Edmund Lacy, bishop of Exeter, a ms. of the fourteenth century.* Exeter, 1847. Contains episcopal offices performed; see (1613, 1663, 1710, 1991, 2022, 2027) and (314).

1619   Bateson, Mary (ed.). 'The register of Crabhouse nunnery', *NA*, XI (1892), 1—71. More materials on nunneries are (1625, 1639, 1688, 1737, 1749, 1797, 1798, 1832, 1861, 1935, 2123), and for women generally (1097).

1620   Bazire, Joyce (ed.). *The metrical life of St Robert of Knaresborough* (EETS, CCXXVIII). 1947. These holy legends, like (1726, 1767), have now been collected and studied by Klaus Sperk, 1970. The *Legenda aurea* provided most of the saints' lives, from which Osbern Bokenham selected the females (1811); see generally (1610).

1621   Bickley, William B. (ed.). *Register of the guild of Knowle, 1451—1535* Walsall, 1894. Other religious, parochial gilds are (1623, 1647, 1676, 1686, 1703, 1718, 1822, 1823, 1952, 2030, 2179); for secular, craft gilds (1139, 1267).

1622   Bloom, James H. (ed.). *Liber elemosinarii: the almoner's book of the priory of Worcester.* 1911. See (1605).

1623   ——— (ed.). *Register of the gild of the Holy Cross, the Blessed Mary, and St John the Baptist of Stratford-upon-Avon [1406—1535].* 1907.

1624   Blore, William P. (ed.). 'A monastic register of the fifteenth century. Register S.', *Canterbury Cathedral Chronicle*, XXVI (1937), 18—26. And (1608, 1866)

1625   Blunt, John H. (ed.). *The myroure of oure ladye, containing a devotional treatise on divine service, with a translation of the offices used by the sisters of the Brigittine Monastery of Sion* (EETS, e.s., XIX). 1873. See (1610, 1619, 1646). There is *A check-list of middle English prose writings of spiritual guidance*, Toronto, 1974, compiled by P.S. Jolliffe.

1626   Bond, Maurice F. (ed.). *The inventories of St George's Chapel, Windsor Castle, 1348—1667.* Windsor, 1947. And Edmund H. Fellowes' monograph on the vicars of minor canons there (1770, 1939, 1987, 2241, 591); for collegiate churches generally (1673, 1696, 1795, 1820, 1827, 1899, 1936, 1937, 2052, 2118).

1627   Borgström, Eduard (ed.). 'The complaint of God to sinful man and the answer of man. By William Lichfield', *Anglia*, XXXIV (1911), 498—525.

1628   Brandeis, Arthur (ed.). *Jacob's well, an English treatise on the cleansing of man's conscience* (EETS, CXV). 1900. And (1610).

1629   Breck, Allen D. (ed.). *Wyclif's Tractatus de trinitate.* Boulder, Colorado, 1962. See (1750).

1630   Brewer, John S. and Richard Howlett (eds.). *Monumenta franciscana* (Rolls Series, IV). 1858—1882, 2 vols. More on Franciscans in (1732, 1745, 1812, 1873, 1906, 1920, 1921, 2180, 2218) and (1917).

1631   Brown, Carleton F. (ed.). *Religious lyrics of the XVth century.* Oxford, 1939; 2nd ed. enlarged, 1952. Or Frances M.M. Comper's collection, 1936 (1781, 2453).

1632   Brown, James E. (ed.). 'Clerical subsidies in the archdeaconry of Bedford, 1390—2 and 1400—1', *Bedfordshire Historical Record Society*, I (1913), 27—61. More on clerical taxation in (1733, 2018, 116).

1633   Buddensieg, Rudolf (ed.). *John Wyclif's De veritate sacrae scripturae.* 1905—7, 3 vols. See Loserth (1750—4); also, Buddensieg's ed. of *John Wiclif's Polemical works in Latin*, English ed., 1883.

1634   Bühler, Curt F. (ed.). 'A Lollard tract: on translating the Bible into English (circa 1407)', *Medium Aevum*, VII (1938), 167—83. More on Lollards in (1645, 1669, 1674, 1681, 1707, 1762, 1800, 1806, 1815, 1824, 1828, 1831, 1835, 1857, 1881—3, 1948, 1950, 1979, 1992, 1995, 2000, 2001, 2004, 2009, 2029, 2050, 2065, 2076, 2134, 2142, 2151—2, 2154, 2159).

1635   Calvert, Edward (ed.). 'Manuscript sermon', *ShropsT*, 2nd ser., VI (1894), 99—106; XII (1900), 57—63. Other sermons are in (1653, 1666, 1780, 1860, 1929—31, 2159), and the *Middle English Sermons*, ed. by Woodburn O. Ross, for *EETS*, CCIX, 1940.

1636   Canivez, Joseph M. (ed.). *Statuta capitulorum generalium ordinis Cisterciensis.* Louvain, 1933—41, 6 vols. And (1297, 1608, 1829, 1927, 2016, 2034, 2040, 2141).

1637   Capes, William W. (ed.). *Charters and records of Hereford Cathedral.* 1908.
More on diocesan administration (1641, 1689, 1826, 1854, 1866, 1879,
1896, 1910, 1943, 1947, 1951, 1954) and for Hereford (1613).

1638   —— (ed.). *Registrum Johannis Trefnant, episcopi Herefordensis, 1389–
1404* (Canterbury and York Society, XX). 1916. See (1613).

1639   Clark, Andrew (ed.). *The English register of Godstow nunnery, near Oxford,
written about 1450* (EETS, CXXIX, CXXX, CXLII). 1905–11, 3 vols.
See (1619).

1640   —— (ed.). *The English register of Oseney Abbey, by Oxford, written about
1460* (EETS, CXXXIII, CXLIV). 1907–12, 2 vols.

1641   —— (ed.). *Lincoln diocese documents, 1450–1544* (EETS, CXLIX).
1914. Includes wills, confessions, presentations, prosecutions (1607,
1637).

1642   Collins, Arthur J. (ed.). *Manuale ad usum percelebris ecclesie Sarisburiensis*
(Henry Bradshaw Society, XCI). 1960. More Mass books and liturgical
manuals in (1654, 1700, 1702, 1740, 1741, 1746, 1748, 1777, 1784,
1785, 1816, 1817, 1841, 1849–52, 1863, 1887, 1914, 1938, 2024–6,
2101, 2134, 2137, 2176).

1643   Cotton, Charles (ed.). 'A contemporary list of the benefactions of Thomas
Ikham, sacrist to St Austin's Abbey, Canterbury, *circa* 1415', *ArchCant*,
XXXVII (1925), 152–9. See (1605, 1866).

1644   —— (ed.). 'St Austin's Abbey, Canterbury. Treasurer's accounts, 1468–9,
and others', *ArchCant*, LI (1940), 66–107.

1645   Cronin, Harry S. (ed.). *Rogeri Dymmok liber contra XII errores et hereses
Lollardorum.* 1922. See (1634).

1646   Cumming, William P. (ed.). *The revelations of Saint Birgitta* (EETS,
CLXXVIII). 1928. See (1610, 1625).

1647   Curling, Thomas H. (ed.). 'Gild of All Saints', *EssexT*, n.s., XI (1911), 223–
9. Publishes the statutes and prayers, 1473 (1621).

1648   Davis, Alfred H. (ed.). *William Thorne's Chronicle of Saint Augustine's
Abbey, Canterbury [to 1397].* Oxford, 1934. See (1866).

1649   Day, Mabel K. (ed.). *The Wheatley manuscript* (EETS, CLV). 1917. Fifteenth-
century religious prose and verse (1610, 1631, 2453).

1650   Deedes, Cecil (ed.). *Register of memorial of Ewell [1408–1423].* 1913. And
(1608).

1651   —— (ed.). 'The episcopal register of Robert Rede, ordinis predicatorum,
lord bishop of Chichester 1397–1415', *Sussex Record Society*, VIII
(1908), 1–205; XI (1910), 209–444; and IV (1905), 85–214. The last is
extracts from Richard Praty's register, Chichester, for 1438–45; generally
(1613).

1652   D'Evelyn, Charlotte (ed.). *Meditations on the life and passion of Christ*
(EETS, CLVIII). 1921. Late fourteenth century, after Richard Rolle
(1905, 1916), and generally (1610).

1653   Devlin (Sister) Mary Aquinas (ed.). *The sermons of Thomas Brinton, bishop
of Rochester (1373–1389)* (Camden Society, 3rd ser., LXXXV,
LXXXVI). 1954, 2 vols. See (1635, 1988).

1654   Dewick, Edward S. (ed.). 'On a ms. psalter formerly belonging to the abbey
of Bury St Edmund's', *Arch*, LIV (1895), 399–410. An early fifteenth-
century litany (1642).

1655   —— (ed.). 'On an inventory of church goods belonging to the parish of St.
Martin Ludgate', *StPaulS*, n.s., V (1905), 117–28. And (1609).

1656   Dickins, Bruce (ed.). 'Premonstratensian itineraries from a Titchfield Abbey
ms. at Welbeck [1400–5]', *LeedsS*, IV (1938), 349–61. See (1605, 1682,
1898, 1981, 2035).

1657   Du Boulay, Francis R.H. (ed.). *Registrum Thome Bourgchier Cantuariensis
archiepiscopi A.D. 1454–1486* (Canterbury and York Society, LIV).
Oxford, 1957. And (1613, 1866).

1658   —— (ed.). 'The quarrel between the Carmelite friars and the secular clergy
of London, 1464–1468', *JEH*, VI (1955), 156–74.

1659   Duckett, George F. (ed.). *Charters and records of Cluny, II.* Lewes, 1888.
And (1608).

1660   —— (ed.). *Visitations of English Cluniac foundations [1390, 1405, etc.]*. 1890. See (1617, 2041).

1661   Dugdale, William. *Monasticon Anglicanum*. 1655—73, 3 vols.; 1817—30, 6 vols. Still a basic starting point, particularly for cartulary evidence (1608).

1662   Duncan, Leland L. (ed.). 'The will of William Courtenay, archbishop of Canterbury, 1396', *ArchCant*, XXIII (1898), 55—67; XXIV (1900), 244—52. The second is for Cardinal Bourgchier, 1486; and (1866, 1961).

1663   Dunstan, Gordon R. (ed.). *The register of Edmund Lacy, bishop of Exeter, 1420—1455: Registrum commune*. 1963—1968, 3 vols. This edition replaces the 1909—1915 edition by C.G. Browne and O.J. Reichel; and Dunstan continues ed. in *Canterbury and York Society*, CXXXIX, 1972; see (1613, 1618, 1710).

1664   Dziewicki, Michael H. (ed.). *Johannis Wyclif miscellanea philosophica*. Vol. I: *De actibus anime, Replicacio de universalibus, De materia forma . . .* Vol. II: *De universalibus, Fragmenta, Notae et quaestiones variae, De materia*. 1902—5, 2 vols. Also edited Wycliffe on apostasy, on simony, on blasphemy, on logic; see Loserth (1750).

1665   —— (ed.). *Johannis Wyclif De ente librorum duorum excerpta. Libri I: Tractatus tertius et quartus; Libri II: Tractatus primus et tertius; et fragmentum de annihilatione*. 1909.

1666   Erbe, Theodor (ed.). *Mirk's Festial: a collection of homilies by Johannes Mirkus* (EETS, e.s., XCVI). 1905. See (1777), plus Lillian L. Steckman, *Studies in Philology*, XXXIV, 1937, pp. 36—48; see (1610, 1635).

1667   Evans, Seiriol J.A. (ed.). 'Ely chapter ordinances and visitation records: 1241—1515', *Camden Miscellany XVII* (Camden Society, 3rd ser., LXIV). 1940, pp. 1—74. See (1617).

1668   Feltoe, Charles L. and E.H. Minns (eds.). *Vetus liber archidiaconi Eliensis* (Cambridge Antiquarian Society, Octavo Series, XLVIII). 1917.

1669   Forshall, Josiah (ed.). *Remonstrance against Romish corruptions in the Church, addressed to the people and parliament of England in 1395. By John Purvey*. 1851. Purvey was parish assistant to Wycliffe (1750), and generally (1634).

1670   Foster, Frances A. (ed.). *A stanzaic life of Christ, compiled from Higden's Polychronicon and the Legenda aurea* (EETS, CLXVI). 1924. See (568, 1610, 1620).

1671   Fowler, Joseph T. (ed.). *Extracts from the account rolls of the abbey of Durham [1303—1541]* (Surtees Society, XCIX, C, CIII). 1898—1901, 3 vols. See (1605, 1247).

1672   —— (ed.). *Memorials of the abbey of St Mary of Fountains. Bursars book 1456—9, and memorandum book of Thomas Swynton, 1446—58* (Surtees Society, CXXX). 1918.

1673   —— (ed.). *Memorials of the Church of Ss. Peter and Wilfrid, Ripon* (Surtees Society, LXIV, LXXIV, LXXVIII, LXXXI, CXV). 1875—1908. 5 vols. Begins with acts of the chapter 1452—1506, and then publishes the accounts and registers to 1542 (1626).

1674   Foxe, John. *Acts and monuments*, ed. by S.R. Cattley and G. Townsend. 1870, 8 vols. Though a century later, especially valuable for Lollards (1634).

1675   Furnivall, Frederick J. (ed.). *The book of quinte essence or the fifth being; that is to say, man's heaven* (EETS, IV). 1866. And (1610).

1676   —— (ed.). *The gild of St Mary, Lichfield; being ordinances of the gild of St Mary, and other documents* (EETS, e.s., CXIV). 1920. See (1621).

1677   —— (ed.). *Hymns to the Virgin and Christ, the Parliament of Devils, and other religious poems* (EETS, XXIV). 1867.

1678   —— (ed.). *The pilgrimage of the life of man. Englisht by John Lydgate, 1426* (EETS, e.s., LXXVII, LXXXIII, XCII). 1899—1904, 3 vols.

1679   —— (ed.). *Robert of Brunne's Handlyng sinne* (*EETS*, LXXIII). 1901. See (1610).

1680   —— (ed.). *The Stacions of Rome, the Pilgrims' sea voyage, with Clene maydenhod* (EETS, XXV). 1867. See (1610, 1765).

1681   Gage, John (ed.). 'Letters from king Henry VI to the abbot of St Edmundsbury, and to the alderman and bailiffs of the town, for the suppression of the Lollards', *Arch*, XXIII (1831), 339—43. From *Registrum Curteys, c.* 1431 (1634).

1682 Gasquet, Francis A. (ed.). *Collectanea Anglo-Premonstratensia, documents drawn from the original register of the order* . . . (Camden Society, 3rd ser., VI, X, XII). 1904—6, 3 vols. Includes visitations, correspondence, elections, membership lists, but see Colvin for corrections (1869); and generally (1608, 1656).

1683 Gibson, Edmund (ed.). *Codex juris ecclesiastici anglicani.* 1713. 2 vols. Important for church law, with Wilkins (1844) and Lyndwood (1756); also, from diocese of London after 1475, see William H. Hale's 1847 collection of precedents.

1684 Goates, Margery (ed.). *The Pepysian gospel harmony* (EETS, CLVII). 1919. Popular gloss on the stories of the Gospels, *c.* 1400; see (1610).

1685 Gollancz, Israel and Magdalene M. Weale (eds.). *The quatrefoil of love; an alliterative religious lyric* (EETS, CXCV). 1934.

1686 Grace, Mary (ed.). 'Records of the gild of St George in Norwich, 1389—1547', *Norfolk Record Society Publications*, IX (1937), 3—157. See (1621).

1687 Gray, Andrew (ed.). '*A Carthusian carta visitationis of the fifteenth century*', *BIHR*, XL (1967), 91—101. See (1617).

1688 Gray, Arthur (ed.). *The priory of Saint Radegund, Cambridge* (Cambridge Antiquarian Society, Octavo Series, XXXI). 1898. Charters and accounts, 1449—51 and 1481—2; and see (1605, 1619).

1689 Greenwell, William (ed.). *Bishop Hatfield's survey: a record of the possessions of the see of Durham [1377—1382]* (Surtees Society, XXXII). 1857. See (1247, 1671, 1692).

1690 Greet, William C. (ed.). *The reule of crysten religioun, by Reginald Pecock, D.D., bishop of St Asaph and Chichester* (EETS, CLXXI). 1926. See (1612, 1714, 1715).

1691 Haines, Roy M. (ed.). 'Bishop Carpenter's injunctions to the diocese of Worcester in 1451', *BIHR*, XL (1967), 203—7. And (1617), also (2048).

1692 Halcrow, Elizabeth M. (ed.). 'The social position and influence of the priors of Durham, as illustrated by their correspondence', *ArchAel*, 4th ser., XXXIII (1955), 70—86. Index of the letters, mainly fifteenth century, see Dobson (1247); more on Durham generally (1689, 1986, 2015, 2051, 2152, 2398, 2434).

1693 Hamilton, Sidney G. (ed.). *Compotus rolls of the priory of Worcester of XIVth and XVth centuries* (Worcestershire Historical Society). 1910. In the same series, 1907, Hamilton gives a full list of obedientiary accounts (1605).

1694 Hamilton Thompson, Alexander (ed.). 'Documents relating to diocesan and provincial visitations from the registers of Henry Bowet, 1407—23, and John Kempe, 1425—52', *Miscellanea II* (Surtees Society, CXXVII). 1916, pp. 131—302. See (1617).

1695 ——— (ed.). 'Lambeth institutions to benefices . . . 1279—1532', *Reports and Papers of the Architectural and Archaelogical Societies*, XL (1930), 33—110. For the *sede vacante* periods in Lincoln diocese (1607, 1613).

1696 ——— (ed.). 'Notes on colleges of secular canons in England. Appendix: the statutes of the new collegiate church of St. Mary, Leicester, 1355—6 and 1490—1', *AJ*, LXXIV (1917), 139—239. See (1626).

1697 ——— (ed.). 'The registers of the archdeaconry of Richmond, 1361—1442 [and 1442—7]', *YorksJ*, XXV (1920), 129—268; XXX (1931), 1—132; XXXII (1936), 111—45.

1698 ——— (ed.). 'The statutes of the college of St Mary and All Saints, Fothering-hay', *AJ*, LXXV (1918), 241—309. Yorkist chantry foundation (1955).

1699 ——— (ed.). *Visitations of religious houses . . . 1420 [1449 in Lincoln diocese]* (Lincolnshire Record Society, VII, XIV, XXI). 1914—29. 3 vols. Published also for the *Canterbury and York Society*, XVII, XXIV, XXXIII, 1915—27, 2 vols. in 3; and see (1607, 1608, 1617, 1854, 1928, 2062).

1700 —— (ed.). 'On a ms. book of devotions in the collection of Professor H.A. Ormerod, with some notes on a fragment of a mortuary roll bound up with it', *LeedsS*, II (1932), 129—48. Rare mortuary roll from Newstead monastery, Sherwood Forest, 1424—55; and (1642).

1701 —— and Charles T. Clay, *et al.* (eds.). *Fasti parochiales* (YorksRS, LXXXV, CVII, CXXIX). 1933—1966, 3 vols. See (1609, 1743—4, 153).

1702 Hampson, Robert T. (ed.). *Medii aevi kalendarium or Dates, charters and customs of the middle ages, with kalendars from the tenth to the fifteenth-century*. 1841, 2 vols. in 1. See (24, 1075, 1855, 1934, 1642).

1703 Haskins, Charles H. (ed.). 'The original bederoll of the Salisbury tailors' gild [*circa* 1444]', *WiltsMag*, XXXIX (1915—17), 375—9. See (1621).

1704 Haslop, G.S. (ed.). 'Two entries from the register of John de Shirburn, abbot of Selby, 1369—1408', *YorksJ*, XLI (1963—6), 287—96.

1705 Hearne, Thomas (ed.). *The history and antiquities of Glastonbury*. Oxford, 1722. And (1608, 1917).

1706 Heath, Peter (ed.). *Medieval clerical accounts* (St Anthony's Hall Publication, no. 26). York, 1964. Detailed parish priests' accounts for vicarage and rectory of Hornsea, 1481—1493; generally (1609).

1707 Heyworth, Peter L. (ed.). *Jack Upland, Friar Daw's reply, and Upland's re-joinder*. 1968. Fascinating Lollard polemic (1634).

1708 Hill, Betty (ed.). 'The fifteenth-century prose *Legend of the cross before Christ*', *Medium Aevum*, XXXIV (1965), 203—22. And (1610).

1709 Hilton, Rodney H. (ed.). *The Stoneleigh leger book* (Dugdale Society, XXIV). 1960. Cartulary with extensive historical notes, to 1494 (1149, 1608).

1710 Hingeston-Randolph, Francis C. (ed.). *The register of Edmund Lacy, bishop of Exeter (A.D. 1420—1455)*. 1909—15, 2 vols. See (1613, 1618, 1663, 314).

1711 —— (ed.). *Register of Edmund Stafford, bishop of Exeter, 1395—1419*. 1886.

1712 —— (ed.). *The register of Thomas de Brantyngham, bishop of Exeter, (A.D. 1370—1394)*. 1901—6, 2 vols.

1713 Hirsche, K. (ed.). *Thomae Kempensis De Imitatione Christi*, Berlin, 1891, 2nd ed. The *opera omnia* edited by M.J. Pohl, Freiburg, 1902—18, 8 vols., were translated after 1904; but see the fifteenth-century translations in EETS, e.s., LXIII, 1893; numerous editions are now available, preferably Betty I. Knott's translation, 1963; and (2108).

1714 Hitchcock, Elsie V. (ed.). *The Donet by Reginald Pecock, D.D., bishop of St Asaph and Chichester . . . Collated with the Poore Mennis Myrrour* (EETS, CLVI). 1918. See (1612).

1715 —— (ed.). *The Folewer to the Donet, by Reginald Pecock, D.D., bishop of St Asaph and Chichester* (EETS, CLXIV). 1923.

1716 HMSO. *Calendar of the entries in the papal registers relating to Great Britain and Ireland, papal letters* [1362—1492, vols. IV—XIV], ed. by William H. Bliss and J.A. Twemlow. 1902—61, 11 vols. Records of papal activities for indulgences, benefices, licenses, dispensations and diverse other administrative instruments, see (2002) for an index; and for Anglo-papal matters (1858, 1895, 1918, 1924, 1933, 1974, 2041, 2044, 2073, 2084, 2122, 2169).

1717 —— *Calendar of petitions to the Pope [1342—1419]*, ed. by William H. Bliss. 1896.

1718 Hodgkinson, Robert F.B. (ed.). 'The account books of the gilds of St George and of St Mary in the church of St Peter Nottingham [1459—1546]', *Thoroton Society, Record Series*, VII (1939), 7—123. See (1621).

1719 Hodgson, Phyllis, and Gabriel M. Liegey (eds.). *The orcherd of Syon* (EETS, CCLVIII). 1966. Being an early fifteenth century translation of *The dialogues* of St Catherine of Siena; also (1610, 1916).

1720 Holmes, Thomas S. (ed.). *Register of Henry Bowet, bishop of Bath and Wells, 1401—07* (Somerset Record Society, XIII). 1899. And (1613, 1757).

1721 —— (ed.). *The register of John Stafford, bishop of Bath and Wells, 1425—1443* (Somerset Record Society, XXXI, XXXII). 1915—16, 2 vols.

1722 ——— (ed.). *The register of Nicholas Bubwith, bishop of Bath and Wells,
1407–1424* (Somerset Record Society, XXIX, XXX). 1914, 2 vols.

1723 Holmstedt, Gustaf (ed.). *Speculum Christiani* (EETS, CLXXXII). 1929. And
(1610, 1916).

1724 Holt, Beryl (ed.). 'Two obedientiary rolls of Selby Abbey', *Miscellanea IV*
(YorksRS, XCVIII, 1951, pp. 31–52. Accounts of the cellarer 1411–
1412 and of the abbot's proctor 1420–1421; and generally (1605, 1789).

1725 Hope, William H. St John (ed.). 'The colour-rule of Pleshy College, 1394–5',
StPaulS, n.s., VIII (1917–20), 41–8; II (1886–90), 233–72; *Arch*, LX
(1907), 465–92. Details rules for liturgical vestments; the second article
lists eds. of parish inventories, 1220–1556; and the third describes
episcopal ornamentations; see (1609, 1904, 2102).

1726 Horstmann, Carl (ed.). *The life of St Katherine of Alexandria by John
Capgrave* (EETS, C). 1893. See (620, 1610, 1620, 1765); also, Horstmann's
ed. of *Yorkshire writers*, 1895–6, 2 vols., which includes works of
Richard Rolle (1905).

1727 Hulme, William H. (ed.). *The harrowing of hell, and The gospel of Nicodemus*
(EETS, e.s., C). 1908.

1728 Isaacson, Robert F. (ed.). *The episcopal registers of the diocese of St. David's
1397 to 1518* (Cymmrodorion Record Series, VI). 1917–20, 3 vols. See
(2044, 97, 1613).

1729 Jacob, Ernest F. (ed.). *The register of Henry Chichele, archbishop of
Canterbury, 1414–1443* (Canterbury and York Society, XLII, XLVII,
CXII, CXIII). Oxford, 1938–1947, 4 vols. See (1613, 1967, 2078, 2169,
1866); the second vol. ed. with Harold C. Johnson.

1730 ——— (ed.). 'Some English documents of the conciliar movement', *BJRL*, XV
(1931), 358–94. See (1909).

1731 Jones, Dorothy (ed.). *The minor works of Walter Hylton.* 1929. For the
major works of this English mystic see Sitwell (1821); and generally
(1610, 1916).

1732 Kingsford, Charles L. (ed.). *The Grey Friars of London: their history with
the register of their convent and an appendix of documents* (British
Society of Franciscan Studies, VI). Aberdeen, 1915. See (1608, 1630,
1745, 1873, 1921, 1926, 2038, 2092).

1733 Kirby, John L. (ed.). 'Clerical poll-taxes in the diocese of Salisbury', *Collectanea* (Wiltshire Archaeological and Natural History Society, Record
Branch, XII). 1956, pp. 157–67. See (2156, 116, 135).

1734 Kirby, Thomas F. (ed.). *Wykeham's register [1366–1404]* (Hampshire Record Society, XI, XIII). 1896–9, 2 vols. And (1613, 1966).

1735 Kirk, Richard E.G. (ed.). *Accounts of the obedientiars of Abingdon Abbey
[1322–1532]* (Camden Society, n.s., LI). 1892. And (1605).

1736 Kitchin, George W. (ed.). *Compotus rolls of the obedientiaries of St
Swithun's Priory, Winchester [1308–1537]* (Hampshire Record Society,
VII). 1892.

1737 Kock, Ernst A. (ed.). *Three middle-English versions of the rule of St Benet
and two contemporary rituals for the ordination of nuns* (EETS, CXX).
1902. See (1619).

1738 Leach, Arthur F. (ed.). *Visitations and memorials of Southwell Minster*
(Camden Society, n.s., XLVIII). 1891. See (1617).

1739 ——— (ed.). 'A fifteenth-century fabric roll of Beverley minster [1445–6]',
Transactions of the East Riding Antiquarian Society, VI (1898), 56–103;
VII (1899), 50–83.

1740 Legg, John W. (ed.). *Missale ad usum Ecclesie Westmonasteriensis* (Henry
Bradshaw Society, I, V, XII). 1891–7, 3 vols. See (1642); this missal was
in use between 1388 and 1540; more for Westminster Abbey in (1742,
1802, 1837, 1932, 2032, 2036, 2075, 2311, 2352).

1741 ——— (ed.). *Tracts on the Mass* (Henry Bradshaw Society, XXVII). 1904.
Pre-Reformation English, mainly during Henry VII's reign (1642).

1742 ——— (ed.). 'Inventory of the vestry in Westminster Abbey in 1388', *Arch*,
LII (1890), 195–286. See (1605).

1743   Le Neve, John and Thomas D. Hardy. *Fasti Ecclesiae Anglicanae, or A calendar of the principal ecclesiastical dignitaries in England and Wales, and of the chief officers in the universities of Oxford and Cambridge*. 2nd ed., Oxford, 1854, 3 vols. This and the following *fasti* are chronological registers of diocesan officials and members of cathedral chapters. Also (1702, 1796, 1609, 2177).

1744   —— *John Le Neve: Fasti Ecclesiae Anglicanae 1300—1541*. I: *Lincoln diocese*, ed. H.P.F. King. 1962. There are at least eleven additional volumes now available like this one, edited by either Joyce M. Horn or B. Jones, covering many of the dioceses in both provinces, completing and revising Le Neve (1743).

1745   Little, Andrew G. (ed.). 'An illuminated letter of fraternity', *PBA*, XXVII (1941), 269—73. From John Zouch, provincial minister of Friars Minor, to William, lord Ferrers, 1406—7, and (1630).

1746   Littlehales, Henry (ed.). *English fragments from Latin medieval service books* (EETS, e.s., XC). 1903. See (1642).

1747   —— (ed.). *The Medieval records of a London city church (St Mary at Hill) 1420—1559* (EETS, CXXV, CXXVIII). 1904—5, 2 vols. And (1609).

1748   —— (ed.). *The prymer, or Lay folks' prayer book* (EETS, CV). 1895. See (1610, 1642, 1741, 1816).

1749   Liveing, Henry G.D. (ed.). *Records of Romsey Abbey: an account of the Benedictine house of nuns ... (A.D. 907—1558)*. Winchester, 1906. And (1608, 1619).

1750   Loserth, Johann (ed.). *Johannis Wyclif opera minora*. 1913. Best editions; for Wycliffe's attack on transubstantiation see *EHR*, V, 1890, pp. 328—30; the other Wycliffe materials are (1629, 1633, 1664, 1665, 1669, 1782, 1783, 1815, 1825, 1830, 1831, 1857, 1877, 1880, 1919, 1923, 1925, 1973) and (397, 2107); the ed. of *de officio regis* is (652).

1751   —— (ed.). *Johannis Wyclif de civili dominio, liber secundus*. 1900. For *liber primus*, see (1782).

1752   —— (ed.). *Johannis Wyclif de civili dominio, liber tertius*. 1903—4, 2 vols.

1753   —— (ed.). *Johannis Wyclif tractatus de mendatis divinis, accedit tractatus de statu innocencie [and] De differentia inter peccatum mortale et veniale*. 1922.

1754   —— (ed.). *Johannis Wyclif tractatus de potestate pape*. 1907. See Loserth's 1924 ed. of *Shirley's Catalogue* of Wycliffe's Latin writings, and (1633); there is a recent general survey of scholarship on Wyclif's political theories by Lowrie J. Daly, *Medievalia et Humanistica*, n.s., IV, 1973, pp. 177—87.

1755   Luard, Henry R. (ed.). *Annales monastici: annales monasterii de Bermundeseia (A.D. 1042—1432)* (Rolls Series, XXXVI, no. 3). 1866. And (1608).

1756   Lyndwood, William. *Provinciale (seu constitutiones Angliae) continens constitutiones provinciales quatuordecim archiepiscoporum Cant' a Stephano Langtono ad Henricum Chichleium*. 1679. Best ed. of the fundamental source on church law in Canterbury province, *circa* 1430; an English outline by J.V. Bullard and H.C. Bell, 1929; see (357, 1617, 1683, 1844, 1858, 1866, 1888, 1922, 1954, 2067, 2086, 2091, 2111, 2136, 2146, 2148, 2149) for more about church law; and C.R. Cheney's critical essay on Lyndwood in his *Medieval texts and studies*, 1973.

1757   Lyte, Henry C. Maxwell (ed.). *The registers of Robert Stillington, bishop of Bath and Wells, 1466—1491, and Richard Fox, bishop of Bath and Wells, 1492—1494* (Somerset Record Society, LII). 1938. See (1613, 1720).

1758   —— and M.C.B. Dawes (eds.). *The Register of Thomas Bekynton, bishop of Bath and Wells, 1443—1465* (Somerset Record Society, XLIX, L). 1934—5, 2 vols.

1759   Maclean, John (ed.). 'Notes on the accounts of the churchwardens of the parish of St Ewen's, Bristol', *Bristol-Glouc*, XV (1891), 139—82, 254—96. Other churchwardens' accounts publ. in single volumes can be found under the editors' names and dates publ., as follows: J.L. Glasscock, 1882 (St Michael's, Bishops Stortford); Alison Hanham, 1970 (Ashburton, Devon); Edmund Hobhouse, 1890 (Croscombe, Pilton, Yatton, Tintinhull, Morebath, and St Michael's, Bath); Robert W.M. Lewis, 1947 (Walberswick,

Suffolk); William T. Mellows, 1939 (Peterborough, Northamptonshire); William H. Overall, 1871 (St Michael, Cornhill, London); Arthur D. Stallard, 1922 (Tilney All Saints, Norfolk); Henry J.F. Swayne, 1896 (St Edmund and St Thomas, Salisbury); Charles Welch, 1912 (All hallows, London Wall); and (1760, 1768, 1771, 1778, 1801, 1808, 1875, 1609, 2023).

1760 Mander, Gerald P. (ed.). 'Church-wardens' accounts of All Saints' church Walsall, 1462—1531', *SaltS*, (1928), 175—267.

1761 Marett, Warwick P. (ed.). *A calendar of the register of Henry Wakefield, bishop of Worcester 1375—95* (Worcestershire Historical Society, n.s., VII). 1973. And (750, 1613).

1762 Mathew, F.D. (ed.). 'The trial of Richard Wyche', *EHR*, V (1890), 530—44. Text of heresy trial, *c.* 1401 (1634).

1763 Meech, Sanford B. (ed.). *The book of Margery Kempe* (EETS, CCXII). 1940. Also, the W. Butler-Bowdon edition of 1936, repr. Oxford, 1954; the most recent biography is by Louise Collis; and see (1051, 1610, 1916).

1764 Mellows, William T. (ed.). *The book of William Morton, almoner of Peterborough Monastery 1448—1467* (Northamptonshire Record Society, XVI). 1954. And (1605).

1765 Mills, C.A. (ed.). *Ye solace of Pilgrimes. A description of Rome, circa A.D. 1450 by John Capgrave, an Austin friar of King's Lynn.* 1911. Capgrave also considered the author of *Nova legenda Angliae*, relied on the *Sanctilogium* of John of Tinmouth for some of his hagiography but this remains a most important source (1610, 1620, 1680, 1726).

1766 Morison, John L. (ed.). *A book of faith. By Reginald Pecock.* Glasgow, 1909. See (1612).

1767 Munro, John J. (ed.). *John Capgrave's Lives of St Augustine and St Gilbert of Sempringham, and a sermon* (EETS, CXL). 1910. See Horstmann (1726) and (1610, 1620).

1768 Mylne, Robert S. (ed.). 'Churchwardens' accounts of the parish of St Peter-in-the-East, city of Oxford, 1444', *Proceedings of the Society of Antiquaries of London*, 2nd ser., X (1884), 25—8. See (1759).

1769 Newcourt, Richard (ed.). *Reportorium ecclesiasticum parochiale Londinense.* 1708—10, 2 vols. Lists of London parish clergy (1609, 1743—4).

1770 Ollard, Sidney L. (ed.). *Fasti Wyndesorienses: the deans and canons of Windsor.* Windsor, 1950. See (1626).

1771 Otter, William B. (ed.). 'Churchwardens' accounts of the parish of Cowfold [1460—85]', *SussexS*, II (1849), 316—25. See (1759).

1772 Pantin, William A. (ed.). *Documents illustrating the activities of the general and provincial chapters of the English Black Monks, 1215—1540* (Camden Society, 3rd ser., XLV, LXVII, LIV). 1931—1937, 3 vols.

1773 —— 'English monastic letter-books', in John G. Edwards, Vivian H. Galbraith, and Ernest E. Jacob (eds.), *Historical essays in honour of James Tait.* Manchester, 1933, pp. 201—22.

1774 Parker, Roscoe E. (ed.). *The middle English stanzaic versions of the life of St Anne* (EETS, CLXXIV). 1927. And (1610).

1775 Parry, Joseph H. (ed.). *Registrum Johannis Gilbert. episcopi Herefordensis, 1375—89* (Canterbury and York Society, XVIII). 1915. See (1613).

1776 —— (ed.). *Registrum Roberti Mascall, episcopi Herefordensis, 1404—16.* (Canterbury and York Society, XXI). 1917.

1777 Peacock, Edward (ed.). *Instructions for parish priests [c. 1450]. By John Myrc* (EETS, XXXI). 1902, rev. ed. See (1666), also excerpts publ. by Karl Young in *Speculum*, XI, 1936, pp. 224—31; generally (1609, 1642).

1778 Pearson, Charles B. (ed.). 'The churchwardens' accounts of the church and parish of St. Michael without the North Gate, Bath, 1349—1575', *SomersetP*, XXII (1876), 1—28; XXIV (1878); XXV (1879), 29—100. Oldest extant churchwardens' accounts known (1759).

1779 Peckham, Walter D. (ed.). *The acts of the dean and chapter of the cathedral church of Chichester, 1472—1544 (the white act book)* (Sussex Record Society, LII). 1952. And (1608).

1780 Perry, Aaron J. (ed.). *Trevisa's Dialogus inter militem et clericum, sermon by fitzRalph, and Ye bygynnyng of ye world* (EETS, CLXVII). 1924. See Trevisa's translation of Bartholomaeus (1458); and generally (1610, 1635, 1929).

1781 Perry, George G. (ed.). *Religious pieces in prose and verse* (EETS, XVII). 1867. From Lincoln Cathedral mss., *c*. 1440 (1631, 2453).

1782 Poole, Reginald L. (ed.). *Johannis Wyclif De civili dominio, liber primus.* 1885. See Loserth (1750, 1751).

1783 —— (ed.). *Johannis Wycliffe De dominio divino, libri tres.* 1890.

1784 Powell, Margaret J. (ed.). *The Pauline epistles, contained in ms. Parker 32, Corpus Christi College, Cambridge* (EETS, e.s., CXVI). 1915. See (1642).

1785 Procter, Francis and Edward S. Dewick (eds.). *The martiloge in Englysshe after the use of the chirche of Salisbury and as it is redde in Syon with addicyons* (Henry Bradshaw Society, III). 1893. And (1610).

1786 Pryce, Arthur I. (ed.). 'The register of Benedict, bishop of Bangor 1408–17', *ArchCamb*, 7th ser., II (1922), 80–107. And (1613, 97).

1787 Purvis, John S. (ed.). *A mediaeval act book, with some account of ecclesiastical jurisdiction at York.* York, 1943. See (1617).

1788 —— (ed.). 'Obituary kalendar of the Dominican friary of Guildford', *Surrey Archaeological Collections*, XLII (1934), 90–9.

1789 —— (ed.). 'Two fifteenth-century lists of Yorkshire religious', *YorksJ*, XXIX (1929), 386–9. From Guisborough in 1425 and Selby Abbey in 1436 (1724, 1605).

1790 Raine, James [the younger] (ed.). *Historical papers and letters from the northern registers.* (Rolls Series, LXI). 1873. Scattered selections from Carlisle and Durham, to 1415; and (1608, 1613).

1791 —— (ed.). *The inventories and account rolls of the Benedictine houses or cells of Jarrow and Monk-Wearmouth* (Surtees Society, XXIX). 1854. And (1605, 1606).

1792 Raine, James [the elder] (ed.). *Obituary roll [1446–8] of William Ebchester and John Burnby, priors of Durham* (Surtees Society, XXX). 1856. See (1700, 1788, 1818, 2434).

1793 —— (ed.). *The priory of Finchale* (Surtees Society, VI). 1837. Includes diverse account rolls and inventories, like (2197).

1794 —— (ed.). *Sanctuarium Dunelmense et Sanctuarium Beverlacense* (Surtees Society, IV). 1837. Unique sanctuary lists, 1464–1524 and 1478–1539, respectively; but see important chronological corrections by Samuel H. Thomson, *EHR*, XXXIV, 1919, pp. 393–7.

1795 —— (ed.). 'The statutes ordained by Richard duke of Gloucester, for the college of Middleham. Dated July 4, 18 Edw. IV., (1478)', *AJ*, XIV (1857), 160–70. Collegiate church founded by Richard III, giving clear example of organization; the original, complete edition is by William Atthill, in the *Camden Society*, XXXVIII, 1847, for the Middleham muniments; and (1626).

1796 Reaney, Percy H. 'Early Essex clergy', *Essex Review*, XLVI (1937), 6–11; XLVII (1938), 8–12, 82–6, 130–7, 186–91; XLVIII (1939), 92–6, 128–31, 176–84; XLIX (1940), 75–84, 136–41, 206–15; L (1941), 32–8, 113–17, 144–51, 234–9; LI (1942), 43–53, 101–9, 159–65, 211–16; LII (1943), 40–4, 96–9, 145–8, 196–201; LIII (1944), 26–31, 60–5, 96–100, 128–33; LIV (1945), 33–6, 77–81, 123–6, 166–9. See other *fasti* (1743–4), and generally (1609).

1797 Redstone, Lilian J. (ed.). 'The cellarer's account for Bromholme Priory, Norfolk, 1415–1416', *Norfolk Record Society Publications*, XVII (1944), 45–91. And (1605).

1798 —— (ed.). 'Three Carrow account rolls', *NA*, XXIX (1946), 41–88. Cellarer of the nunnery for 1456, 1485, 1528; for Blackbergh nunnery, see *NA*, XXII, 1926, pp. 83–5; also (1619).

1799 Rees, William (ed.). 'The possessions of the abbey of Tewkesbury in Glamorgan — accounts of the ministers for the year 1449–1450', *South Wales and Monmouthshire Record Society*, II (1950), 129–86. See (97, 340, 1605).

1800   Richardson, Henry G. (ed.). 'John Oldcastle in hiding, August—October
        1417', *EHR*, LV (1940), 432—8. And William T. Waugh, *EHR*, XX, 1905,
        pp. 434—56 and 637—58; on Lollards (1634), and Oldcastle (1824, 700).
1801   Robertson, William A.S. (ed.). 'Hythe churchwardens' accounts in the time
        of Henry IV [1412—13]', *ArchCant*, X (1876), 242—9. See (1759).
1802   Robinson, Joseph A. (ed.). *The history of Westminster Abbey by John Flete
        [to 1386]*. Cambridge, 1909. Flete was a monk at Westminster 1420—65
        (656, 1932); see also (1608, 1740, 1837).
1803   Royce, David (ed.). *Landboc sive registrum monasterii beatae Mariae virginis
        et sancti Cenhelmi de Winchelcumba . . . A.D. 1422*. Exeter, 1903. And
        (1608).
1804   Royster, James F. (ed.). 'A middle English treatise on the ten commandments
        (from St John's College Oxford ms. 94, *temp*. 1420—34)', *Studies in
        Philology*, VI (1910), 5—39. See (1610).
1805   Salter, Herbert E. (ed.). *Chapters of the Augustinian Canons* (Oxford His-
        torical Society, LXXIV). 1922. See (1608).
1806   —— (ed.). *Snappe's Formulary and other records* (Oxford Historical
        Society, LXXX). 1924. John Snappe, doctor of decrees, flourished 1397—
        1404, includes record of Archbishop Arundel's assaults against Lollardy in
        1411 (1617, 1634).
1807   —— (ed.). 'The annals of the abbots of Oseney [notes written 1454—60]',
        EHR, XXXIII (1918), 498—500.
1808   Salzmann, Louis F. (ed.). 'Early churchwardens' accounts, Arlington [1455—
        1479]', *SussexS*, LIV (1911), 85—112. See (1759).
1809   Schofield, Bertram (ed.). *Muchelney memoranda edited from a breviary of
        the abbey* (Somerset Record Society, XLII). 1927. Including an *ordo*, a
        local calendar of offices and feasts (1075, 1792).
1810   Searle, William G. (ed.). 'The chronicle of John Stone, 1415—1471', in
        Christ Church, Canterbury (Cambridge Antiquarian Society Publications,
        Octavo Series, XXXIV). 1902, pp. 1—152. Mainly a monastic necrology
        but contains descriptions of political events of importance.
1811   Serjeantson, Mary S. (ed.). *Legendys of hooly wummen, by Osbern
        Bokenham* (EETS, CCVI). 1938. Original ed. for Roxburghe Club, no. 50,
        in 1835; and (1610, 1620).
1812   Seton, Walter W. (ed.). *Two fifteenth-century Franciscan rules* (EETS,
        CXLVIII). 1914. And (1630).
1813   Sheppard, Joseph B. (ed.). *Christ Church letters; a volume of medieval letters
        relating to the affairs of the priory of Christ Church, Canterbury* (Camden
        Society, n.s., XIX). 1877. And (1608).
1814   —— (ed.). *Literae Cantuarienses: the letter-books of the monastery of
        Christ Church, Canterbury* (Rolls Series, LXXXV). 1887—9, 3 vols. Multi-
        tude of monastic mss. exemplifying detail and form, especially vol. III,
        including political comments (1866).
1815   Shirley, Walter W. (ed.). *Fasciculi Zizaniorum magistri Johannis Wyclif cum
        tritico, ascribed to Thomas Netter of Walden* (Rolls Series, V). 1858. Con-
        temporary account of the rise of Lollardy, to Henry V's reign, compiled
        by two Carmelite friars (1634); see J. Crompton, *JEH*, XII, 1962.
1816   Simmons, Thomas F. (ed.). *The lay folk's Mass book or The manner of hear-
        ing Mass . . . and offices in English according to the use of York* (EETS,
        XLVI, XLVII). 1879, 2 vols. See Littlehales (1748); generally (1610,
        1642).
1817   —— and Henry E. Nolloth (eds.). *The lay folks' catechism, or the English
        and Latin versions of archbishop Theresby's Instruction for the people*
        (EETS, CXVIII). 1901. See (1642).
1818   Simpson, William S. (ed.). *Documents illustrating the history of St. Paul's
        Cathedral* (Camden Society, n.s., XXVI). 1880. Especially the obituaries
        and calendar from Richard II's reign, pp. 61—107; and generally (1608,
        1990).
1819   —— (ed.). *Visitations of churches belonging to St Paul's Cathedral in 1297
        and in 1458* (Camden Society, n.s., LV). 1895. See (1617).

1820 ——— (ed.). 'Charter and statutes of the college of the Minor Canons in St Paul's Cathedral [1394–1395]', *Arch*, XLIII (1871), 165–200. See (1626).

1821 Sitwell, Francis G. (ed.). *Walter Hylton's The scale of perfection*. 1953. See (1731, 1916, 2033, 2144).

1822 Skaife, Robert H. (ed.). *Register of the guild of Corpus Christi in the city of York, with an appendix of illustrative documents [1408–1437]* (Surtees Society, LVII). 1872. See (1621).

1823 Smith, Joshua T. (ed.). *English gilds* (EETS, XL). 1870. Especially for religious and social parish activities, with introduction by Lucy T. Smith (1621).

1824 Smith, Lucy T. (ed.). 'Ballad by Thomas Occleve addressed to sir John Oldcastle, A.D. 1415', *Anglia*, V (1882), 9–42. See (1610, 1634, 1800).

1825 Stein, I.H. (ed.). 'The Latin text of Wyclif's "Complaint" ', *Speculum*, VII (1932), 87–94; VIII (1933), 254–5, 503–10; *EHR*, XLVII (1932), 95–103. Also fragments of the *Summa de ente* and *Confessio* (1750), while the final article gives the text of Vatican ms., Borghese 29, attributed to Wycliffe.

1826 Storey, Robin L. (ed.). *The register of Thomas Langley, bishop of Durham, 1406–1437*. 1956–71, 6 vols. Particularly valuable for its long and detailed focus on episcopal administration (1947), and for northern history (735, 1247).

1827 Styles, Dorothy (ed.). *Ministers' accounts of the collegiate church of St. Mary, Warwick 1432–85* (Dugdale Society, XXVI). 1969. See (1626).

1828 Swinburn, Lilian M. (ed.). *The lanterne of lizt* (EETS, CLI). 1915. Early fifteenth-century Lollard tract (1634).

1829 Talbot, Charles H. (ed.). *Letters from the English abbots to the chapter at Citeaux 1442–1521* (Camden Society, 4th ser., IV). 1967. See (1608, 1636, 1299, 1927).

1830 Thomson, Samuel H. (ed.). *Johannis Wyclif Summa de ente, libri primi, tractatus primus et secundus*. 1930. See (1750).

1831 Todd, James H. (ed.). *An apology for Lollard doctrines, attributed to Wicliffe* (Camden Society, XX). 1842. See (1634, 1750).

1832 Tolhurst, John B.L. (ed.). *The ordinale and customary of the Benedictine nuns of Barking Abbey* (Henry Bradshaw Society, LXV, LXVI). 1927–8, 2 vols. Written between 1394 and 1404, containing regulations and schedules; also (1608, 1619).

1833 ——— and the Abbess of Stanbrook (eds.). *The ordinale and customary of the abbey of saint Mary York* (Henry Bradshaw Society, LXXIII, LXXV, LXXXIV). 1936–51, 3 vols.

1834 Triggs, Oscar L. (ed.). *The assembly of gods: or The accord of reason and sensuality in the fear of death* (EETS, e.s., LXIX). 1896. And (1610).

1835 Tyndale, William (ed.). 'The examinations of the constant servant of God, William Thorpe, before Archbishop Arundel, written by himself, A.D. 1407', *Religious Tract Society*, (1831?), 39–102. See (1634, 1958).

1836 Venables, Edmund (ed.). *Chronicon abbatiae de Parco Ludae: the chronicle of Louth Park Abbey [to 1413]* (Lincolnshire Record Society, I). 1891. See (1608).

1837 Walcott, MacKenzie E.C. (ed.). 'Notes on an inventory of Westminster Abbey, A.D. 1388. Now in the library of Canterbury', *London-Midd*, V (1881), 425–32, 439–40. See (1608, 1740).

1838 ——— (ed.). 'Medieval registers of the bishops of Chichester', *Transactions of the Royal Society of Literature*, 2nd ser., IX (1870), 215–55. Abstracts only, 1396–1502; see generally (1613).

1839 Warrack, Grace (ed.). *Dame Julian of Norwich's Revelations of divine love*. 1950, 13th ed. And (1610, 1916).

1840 Warren, Florence (ed.). *The dance of death* (EETS, CLXXXI). 1929.

1841 Warren, Frederick E. (ed.). *The Sarum missal, in English* (Alcuin Club, XI). 1913, 2 vols. See (1642, 1850).

1842 Watkin, Aelred (ed.). *Archdeaconry of Norwich: inventory of church goods* (Norfolk Record Society, XIX). 1947–8, 1 vol. in 2 parts. See (1609).

1843 Watkin, Hugh R. (ed.). *The history of Totnes priory and medieval town, Devonshire.* Torquay, 1914—17, 3 vols. Complete translations of records, charters, lists of officials; generally (1608).

1844 Wilkins, David. *Concilia Magnae Britanniae et Hiberniae, A.D. 446—1718.* 1737, 4 vols. Monumental gathering of materials relating to church assemblies, found in various episcopal registers, see (2086, 1613).

1845 Wilkinson, John J. (ed.). 'Receipts and expenses in the building of Bodmin Church, 1469 to 1472', *Camden Miscellany VII* (Camden Society, n.s., XIV). 1875, pp. 1—49. And (1609).

1846 Willis-Bund, John W. (ed.). *Register of the diocese of Worcester during the vacancy of the see, usually called 'Registrum sede vacante', 1301—1435* (Worcestershire Historical Society). 1897.

1847 Wood-Legh, Kathleen L. (ed.). *A small household of the XVth century.* Manchester, 1956. Recording chantry expenditures by two chaplains, 1453—60, for Munden's chantry, Bridport (1955).

1848 Woodruff, Charles E. (ed.). 'The sacrist's roll of Christ Church, Canterbury [1341—1533]', *ArchCant*, XLVIII (1937), 38—80. And (1605, 1866).

1849 Wordsworth, Christopher (ed.). *Ceremonies and processions of the cathedral church of Salisbury. Edited from the fifteenth-century ms. no. 148 . . . .* Cambridge, 1901. See (1642).

1850 —— (ed.). *Ordinale Sarum sive directorium sacerdotum, auctore Clemente Maydeston* (Henry Bradshaw Society, XX, XXII). 1901—2, 2 vols. See (1642, 1841).

1851 —— (ed.). *The tracts of Clement Maydeston, with the remains of Caxton's Ordinale* (Henry Bradshaw Society, VII). 1894. Includes the *Directorium sacerdotum, crede michi* [A.D. 1495], with notes on weekly commemorations in England.

1852 —— (ed.). *Horae Eboracenses: the prymer or hours of the Blessed Virgin Mary, according to the use of the illustrious church of York, with other devotions as they were used by the lay-folk in the northern province in the 15th and 16th centuries* (Surtees Society, CXXXII). 1920. See (1642).

1853 —— (ed.). 'Some pardons or indulgences preserved in Yorkshire, 1412—1527', *YorksJ,* XVI (1901), 367—423; XIX (1907), 61—72. See (1611, 1716).

1854 —— and Henry Bradshaw (eds.). *Statutes of Lincoln Cathedral.* Cambridge, 1892—7, 3 vols. See (1607, 1637).

1855 Wormald, Francis (ed.). *English Benedictine kalendars after A.D. 1100* (Henry Bradshaw Society, LXXVII, LXXXI). 1939—46, 2 vols. See (24, 1702, 1934).

2 Monographs

1856 Baildon, William P. *Notes on the religious and secular houses of Yorkshire* (YorksRS, XVII, LXXXI). 1894—1931, 2 vols. And see (1608, 1917).

1857 Baker, Derek (ed.). *Schism, heresy and religious protest.* Cambridge, 1972. Important articles by Joan C. Greatrex on Rudborne's critique of the Council of Florence, Margaret Harvey on John Luke's sermon on the Great Schism, Anne Hudson on Lollard books, Alison K. McHardy on Lincoln's Lollards, and Michael Wilks on defining Wycliffe's protest. (1634, 1750).

1858 Barraclough, Geoffrey. *Papal provision. Aspects of church history, constitutional, legal and administrative, in the later middle ages.* Oxford, 1935. Fundamental outline of papal procedure and policy, mainly background to the fifteenth century (1716, 1756).

1859 Bill, P.A. *The Warwickshire parish clergy in the later middle ages* (Dugdale Society, Occasional Papers, XVII). 1967. And generally (1609).

1860 Blench, John W. *Preaching in England in the late fifteenth and sixteenth centuries: a study of English sermons 1450 — c. 1600.* Oxford. 1964. See (1635, 1929).

1861 Bourdillon, Anne F.C. *The order of Minoresses in England* (British Society of Franciscan Studies, XII). Manchester, 1926. See (1619).

1862   Burne, Richard V.H. *The monks of Chester: the history of St Werburg's Abbey*. 1962. See (1605, 1608, 1917).

1863   Butterworth, Charles C. *The literary lineage of the King James Bible, 1340–1611*. Philadelphia, 1941. See (1642, 1881).

1864   Capes, William W. *The English church in the fourteenth and fifteenth centuries*. 1900. And see Eduard Fueter's monograph, 1904.

1865   Chambers, Edmund K. *Eynsham under the monks* (Oxfordshire Record Society, XVIII). Oxford, 1936. See (1917).

1866   Churchill, Irene J. *Canterbury administration: the administrative machinery of the archbishopric of Canterbury* (Church Historical Society, n.s., XV). 1933, 2 vols. Absolutely essential reference to the topic, with Woodcock (1954); and generally (1637); materials pertaining to Canterbury (1624, 1643–4, 1648, 1657, 1662, 1729, 1756, 1810, 1813–14, 1848, 1873, 1879, 1908, 1943, 1945, 2008, 2018, 2077–8, 2186, 2296, 2393).

1867   Clay, Rotha M. *The hermits and anchorites of England*. 1914. See (1606, 1976, 1998–2000, 2145).

1868   Colledge, Eric. *The medieval mystics of England*. 1951. And (1916).

1869   Colvin, Howard M. *The White Canons in England*. 1951. See (1917).

1870   Cook, George H. *English monasteries in the middle ages*. 1961. Good general survey, with Knowles (1917).

1871   —— *The English medieval parish church*. 1954. And generally (1609, 1759, 1875).

1872   —— *Medieval chantries and chantry chapels*. 1947. Or the more scholarly (1955).

1873   Cotton, Charles. *The Grey Friars of Canterbury 1224 to 1538* (British Society of Franciscan Studies, e.s., II). Manchester, 1924. See (1630, 1732, 1866).

1874   Coulton, George G. *Ten medieval studies*. Cambridge, 1930.

1875   Cox, John C. *Churchwardens' accounts from the fourteenth to the close of the seventeenth century*. 1913. See (1759, 1609).

1876   —— *The English parish church*. 1914. Classic account of parochial society, better than either Francis A. Gasquet's monograph, 1906, or Augustus Jessopp's, 1901; see (1871).

1877   Cuming, G.J. and Derek Baker (eds.). *Councils and assemblies*. Cambridge, 1971. Important articles by Roy M. Haines on synodal legislation for education, Margaret Harvey on Ryssheton's analysis of the Council of Pisa's legitimacy. A.N.E.D. Schofield on the English delegates at Basle, and Edith C. Tatnall on Wycliffe's condemnation at Constance.

1878   Cutts, Edward L. *Parish priests and their people in the middle ages in England*. 1898. See (1609).

1879   Dahmus, Joseph H. *Metropolitan visitations of William Courteney, archbishop of Canterbury, 1381–1396*. Urbana, Illinois, 1950. Shaky attempt at important topics and sources (1617, 1634, 1866, 1961).

1880   —— *The prosecution of John Wyclyf*. New Haven, Connecticut, 1952. Brings Workman's biography (1973) up to date but not as reliable or profound as MacFarlane (1925); see generally (1750).

1881   Deanesley, Margaret. *The Lollard bible and other medieval biblical versions*. Cambridge, 1920. Basic reference work for the topic, and *CQR*, XCI, 1921, pp. 59–77; but see (2134), and generally (1634, 1992); and the most important work by Anne Hudson in *EHR*, XC, 1975, pp. 1–18.

1882   Dickens, Arthur G. *Heresy and the origins of Protestantism*. 1962.

1883   —— *Lollards and Protestants in the diocese of York, 1509–1558*. 1959. Work of fundamental importance for its method and lucidity, although for the later period; more generally, James Gairdner's older survey of Lollardy, 1908–13 (1634, 1950).

1884   Dickinson, John C. *Monastic life in medieval England*. New York, 1962. Like Cook (1870), a reliable survey; see his earlier work on the Walsingham shrine, 1956; and see (1917).

1885   Edwards, Kathleen. *The English secular cathedrals in the middle ages*. Manchester, 1967, 2nd ed. Another good guide is by A. Hamilton Thompson for SPCK, 1925.

1886   *Folk-Lore Society Publications.* Over 100 vols., each ranging chronologically from medieval tales to modern oral tradition, emphasizing aspects of popular religion that include magic, calendar customs, local saints, healing waters, and supernatural phenomena; e.g. vol. CXIV, *Somerset folklore* by Ruth L. Tongue (ed. by Katharine M. Briggs), 1965.

1887   Frere, Walter H. *Pontifical services* (Alcuin Club, III, IV). 1901, 2 vols. See (1642).

1888   Gabel, Leona C. *Benefit of clergy in the later middle ages* (Smith College Studies in History, no. 14). Northampton, Mass., 1929. And (1756, 2028).

1889   Galbraith, Vivian H. *The abbey of St Albans from 1300 to the dissolution of the monasteries.* Oxford, 1911. And (1608, 1917).

1890   Gwynn, Aubrey O. *The English Austin Friars in the time of Wyclif.* 1940. For Franciscans see (1630).

1891   Hadcock, Richard N. and David [Michael Clive] Knowles. *Map of monastic Britain.* 2nd ed., 1954–1955, 2 vols. These Ordnance Survey maps and bibliographies make excellent reference materials, one for northern Britain and the other for the south (1917).

1892   —— *Medieval religious houses: England and Wales.* 1953. Also, their 'Additions and corrections . . .', in *EHR*, LXXII, 1957, pp. 60–87.

1893   Haines, Charles R. *Dover priory.* Cambridge, 1930.

1894   Hall, Donald J. *English mediaeval pilgrimage.* 1966. Chatty and general survey of limited scholarly value; generally (1610) and the pilgrim theme (1765).

1895   Haller, Johannes. *England und Rom unter Martin V.* Rome, 1905. Reprinted from *Quellen und Forschungen aus italienischen Archiven,* VIII, 1905, pp. 249–304; and see (1716).

1896   Hamilton Thompson, Alexander. *The English clergy and their organization in the later middle ages.* Oxford, 1947. Fundamental introduction to institutional structure of the English church, reprinted in 1966; also, *The historical growth of the English parish church,* 1911 (1609); on church administration (1637).

1897   —— *English monasteries.* Cambridge, 1913. Brief and reliable accounts of monastic buildings (1917).

1898   —— *The Premonstratensian abbey of Welbeck.* 1938. See (1656).

1899   Harrison, Frederick. *Life in a medieval college; the story of the vicars-choral of York Minster.* 1952. Includes numerous extracted documents (1626).

1900   Hartridge, Reginald A.R. *A history of vicarages in the middle ages.* Cambridge, 1930 (repr. 1968). See (1609).

1901   Hays, Rhŷs W. *The history of the abbey of Aberconway 1186–1537.* Cardiff, 1963. And (1917, 1163, 97).

1902   Heath, Peter. *English parish clergy on the eve of the Reformation.* 1969. Superbly organized and detailed institutional description; generally (1609).

1903   Hope, William H. St John. *The history of the London Charterhouse from its foundation until the suppression of the monastery.* 1925.

1904   —— and Edward G.C.F. Atchley. *English liturgical colours.* 1918. And (1725).

1905   Horstmann, Carl. *Richard Rolle of Hampole and his followers.* 1896. The *opera omnia* first ed. in Paris, 1618; see Richard Misyn's 1434–5 translation, ed. in EETS, 1896.

1906   Hutton, Edward. *The Franciscans in England, 1224–1538.* 1926. See (1630).

1907   Jacob, Ernest F. *Essays in later medieval history.* Manchester, 1968. A valuable collection of his more important work.

1908   —— *The medieval registers of Canterbury and York; some points of comparison* (St Anthony's Hall Publication, no. 4). 1953. Or an earlier pamphlet by Robert C. Fowler on episcopal registers, 1918; see (1613, 1866).

1909   —— *Studies in the conciliar epoch.* Manchester, 1953. For church councils, more materials (1730, 1857, 1877, 1933, 1957, 1989, 2046, 2080, 2106, 2147).

1910   Jones, Douglas H. *The church in Chester 1300–1540* (Chetham Society, 3rd ser., VII). 1957. See (1637).

1911   Jones, William A.R. *Saint George, the order of Saint George and the church of Saint George in Stamford ... 1349–1449.* 1937.

1912   Junghanns, Hermann. *Zur Geschichte der englischen Kirchenpolitik von 1399–1413.* Freiburg-im-Breisgau, 1915. Similarly, the monograph of Max Wagner, 1904.

1913   Kemp, Eric W. *Counsel and consent.* 1961. Wide-ranging chronological study particularly good for fifteenth century clergy and ecclesiastical institutions.

1914   Kingsford, Hugh S. *Illustrations of the occasional offices of the church in the middle ages from contemporary sources* (Alcuin Club, XXIV). 1921. Emphasis on burial, penance, marriage, and baptism; see (1609, 1642, 1904).

1915   Knowles, David [Michael Clive Knowles]. *The English mystics.* 1927.

1916   —— *The English mystical tradition.* 1961. More on mysticism (1652, 1719, 1723, 1731, 1763, 1821, 1839, 1868, 1905, 2033, 2144, 2174).

1917   —— *The religious orders in England,* Vol. II: *the end of the middle ages.* Cambridge, 1955. Fundamental study for this topic (1605, 1608); other monographs are (1163, 1705, 1856, 1862, 1865, 1869, 1870, 1884, 1889, 1891–3, 1897, 1898, 1901, 1903, 1932, 1945, 1946).

1918   Lawrence, Clifford H. (ed.). *The English church and the papacy in the middle ages.* 1965. Especially the excellent article by Du Boulay for fifteenth-century relations (1716).

1919   Lechler, Gotthard V. *Johann von Wiclif und die Vorgeschichte der Reformation.* Leipzig, 1873, 2 vols. Translated and abridged by Peter Lorimer, *John Wiclif and his English precursors,* 1878, 2 vols; also, see Arthur Dakin, Heidelberg, 1911 (1750).

1920   Little, Andrew G. *Franciscan papers, lists, and documents* (Publications of the University of Manchester, Historical Series, LXXXI). Manchester, 1943. Especially for lists of chapters and houses, and for a sermon (1630).

1921   —— *Grey Friars at Oxford* (Oxford Historical Society, XX). 1892. Detailed historical and biographical notations (1630, 1732, 1873, 1926).

1922   Logan, Francis D. *Excommunication and the secular arm in medieval England: a study in legal procedure from the thirteenth to the sixteenth century.* Toronto, 1968. Superb analysis and description of institutional practices (1617, 357, 1082, 1756).

1923   Loserth, Johann. *Huss and Wiclif. Zur Genesis der Hussitischen Lehre.* Munich, 1925, rev. ed. (orig. ed., 1884). See (1750).

1924   Lunt, William E. *The financial relations of the papacy with England, 1327–1534* (Mediaeval Academy of America Publications, LXXIV). Cambridge, Mass., 1962. Carefully detailed description of an important issue (1716).

1925   McFarlane, Kenneth B. *John Wycliffe and the beginnings of English nonconformity.* 1952 [1953]. But see his (700); also Reginald L. Poole's assessment, 1911, and Gustav A.G. Siebert's monograph, 1905, and (1750).

1926   Moorman, John R.H. *The Grey Friars in Cambridge 1225–1538.* Cambridge, 1952. See (1630, 1732, 1921).

1927   O'Sullivan, Jeremiah F. *Cistercian settlements in Wales and Monmouthshire 1140–1540* (Fordham University History Series, II). New York, 1947. See (1297, 1636, 97).

1928   Owen, Dorothy M. *Church and society in medieval Lincolnshire* (History of Lincolnshire, V). 1971. Authoritative survey, readable and detailed (1607).

1929   Owst, Gerald R. *Preaching in medieval England: an introduction to the sermon manuscripts of the period, c. 1350–1450.* Cambridge, 1926. And (1635, 1860).

1930   —— *Literature and pulpit in medieval England.* Cambridge, 1933.

1931   —— *The Destructorium Viciorum of Alexander Carpenter: a fifteenth-century sequel to literature and pulpit in medieval England.* 1952.

1932   Pearce, Ernest H. *The monks of Westminster; being a register of the brethren of the convent from the time of the Confessor to the Dissolution, with lists of the obedientiaries.* Cambridge, 1916. Biographical directory organized chronologically and drawing attention to a large, rich collection of evidence (1740).

1933   Perroy, Edouard. *L'Angleterre et le grand schisme d'occident. Étude sur la politique religieuse de l'Angleterre sous Richard II (1378—1399)*. Paris, 1933. Remains the basic work defining England's relationship with the continental church (1716).

1934   Pfaff, Richard W. *New liturgical feasts in later medieval England*. Oxford, 1970. See (24); Pfaff concentrates exclusively on feasts for Christ and Mary (1075, 1702, 1809, 1855, 2029, 2068).

1935   Power, Eileen E. *Medieval English nunneries, c. 1275 to 1535*. Cambridge, 1922. And generally (1619); also, the antiquarian effort of Thomas Hugo, *The mediaeval nunneries of the county of Somerset and diocese of Bath and Wells*, 1867.

1936   Raines, Francis R. *The fellows of the collegiate church of Manchester [1422— 1706]* (Chetham Society, n.s., XXI). 1891. See (1626).

1937   —— *The rectors of Manchester, and the wardens of the collegiate church of the town* (Chetham Society, n.s., V). 1885, 2 vols. Biographical sketches, 1194—1595 (2118).

1938   Rickert, Margaret J. *The reconstructed Carmelite missal*. 1952. See (1642, 1841, 2137).

1939   Roberts, Anne K.B. *St George's Chapel, Windsor Castle 1348—1416; a study in early collegiate administration*. Windsor, 1951. See (1626).

1940   Rosenthal, Joel T. *The purchase of paradise; gift-giving and the aristocracy, 1307—1485*. 1972. Disappointing attempt to clarify the realities of institutionalized, ecclesiastical charities, with a muddled definition of aristocracy.

1941   —— *The training of an elite group: English bishops in the fifteenth-century* (Transactions of the American Philosophical Society, LX). 1970. Also (2139, 1983).

1942   Roth, Francis. *The English Austin Friars, 1249—1538*. New York, 1961— 1966, 2 vols.

1943   [Sayers, Jane E. (ed.).] *Medieval records of the archbishops of Canterbury*. 1962. Enlightening introductions to ecclesiastical records by Irene J. Churchill, Eric W. Kemp, Ernest F. Jacob, and Francis R.H. Du Boulay (1613, 1637); Sayers has also published a useful catalogue of *Estate documents of Lambeth Palace Library*, Leicester, 1965.

1944   Smith, Herbert M. *Pre-Reformation England*. 1938. Reliable and intelligent survey, mainly for early-Tudor era.

1945   Smith, Reginald A.L. *Canterbury Cathedral priory; a study in monastic administration*. Cambridge, 1943. See (1866).

1946   Snape, Robert H. *English monastic finances in the later middle ages*. Cambridge, 1926 (repr. 1968). An institutional study of structure and social status (1163, 1917).

1947   Storey, Robin L. *Diocesan administration in fifteenth-century England* (St Anthony's Hall Publication, no. 16). York, 2nd ed. rev., 1972. Brief, learned exposition on ecclesiastical bureaucracy (1637, 1826, 1972).

1948   Sumner, William H. *The Lollards of the Chiltern Hills: glimpses of English dissent in the middle ages*. 1906. Solid study, now somewhat aided by Thomson (1950), and generally (1634).

1949   Tate, William E. *The parish chest*. Cambridge, 1946. See (1609, 1871, 1875).

1950   Thomson, John A.F. *The later Lollards, 1414—1520*. Oxford, 1965. For Lollards in Kent in the 1430s, see his article, *BIHR*, XXXVII, 1964, pp. 100—2; and (1634).

1951   Weske, Dorothy B. *Convocation of the clergy* (Church Historical Society, n.s., XXIII). 1937. See (1637).

1952   Westlake, Herbert F. *The parish gilds of mediaeval England*. 1919. Also his article, *StPaulS*, n.s., VIII, 1918, pp. 99—110; and (1621).

1953   Williams, Glanmor. *The Welsh church from Conquest to Reformation*. Cardiff, 1962. Comprehensive, readable synthesis for the history of Wales and the church, and see (97).

1954   Woodcock, Brian L. *Medieval ecclesiastical courts in the diocese of Canter-bury*. 1952. Essential, if somewhat sketchy, description of institutional structure (1617, 1637, 1756, 1866).

1955   Wood-Legh, Kathleen L. *Perpetual chantries in Britain*. Cambridge, 1965. See her article in *TRHS*, 4th ser., XXVIII, 1946, pp. 47–60; and (563, 1698, 1847, 1872, 2013, 2057, 2138, 2274, 2275, 2325).

1956   Wrong, George M. *The Crusade of 1383, known as that of the bishop of Norwich*. 1892. Henry Despencer's mini-crusade against supporters of Clement VII in Flanders, in support of Urban VI; see Gerhard Skalweit's book, Königsberg, 1898; also, biography in *CQR*, CLIX, 1958, pp. 26–38 by Rowland Edwards.

1957   Zellfelder, August. *England und das Basler Konzil. Mit einem Urkunderanhang*. Berlin, 1913. And generally (1909).

3 Biographies

1958   Aston, Margaret E. *Thomas Arundel; a study of church life in the reign of Richard II*. Oxford, 1967. Excellent reading, thorough on episcopal administration, but see (2008).

1959   Bennett, Henry L. *Archbishop Rotheram, lord high chancellor [1474–83] of England and chancellor of Cambridge University: a sketch of his life and environment*. Lincoln, 1901.

1960   Brabrook, Edward W. 'Robert de Braybroke, bishop of London 1381–1404, lord chancellor 1382–83', *London-Midd*, III (1870), 528–46.

1961   Dahmus, Joseph H. *William Courtenay, archbishop of Canterbury, 1381–1396*. Philadelphia, 1966. See (1662, 1879).

1962   Fletcher, James M.J. 'Bishop Richard Beauchamp, 1450–1481', *WiltsMag*, XLVIII (1938), 161–73.

1963   Godwin, Francis. *A catalogue of the bishops of England*. 1615. Remains a useful reference for episcopal biographies and studies.

1964   Gibson, Edgar C.S. 'Thomas Bekynton', *Bristol-Gloucs*, XXXVI (1913), 42–54. More recently, Arnold Judd, *JEH*, VIII, 1957, pp. 153–65.

1965   Green, Vivian H.H. *Bishop Reginald Pecock: a study in ecclesiastical history and thought*. Cambridge, 1945. Also, Ernest M. Blackie in *EHR*, XXVI, 1911, pp. 448–68; and Everett H. Emerson in *Speculum*, XXXI, 1956, pp. 235–42; Green previewed this book in *CQR*, CXXIX, 1940, pp. 281–95; and see (1967, 2478).

1966   Heseltine, George C. *William of Wykeham: a commentary*. 1932. Other biographers include Robert Lowth, G.H. Moberley, and MacKenzie E.C. Walcott (1566, 1734).

1967   Jacob, Ernest F. *Archbishop Henry Chichele*, 1967. See Arthur Duck's biography, 1716, and Jacob's article, *BJRL*, XVI, 1932, pp. 428–81 (1729).

1968   —— 'Archbishop John Stafford [died 1452]', *TRHS*, 5th ser., XII (1962), 1–23.

1969   —— 'Reynold Pecock, bishop of Chichester', *PBA*, XXXVII (1951), 121–53. See (1612, 1965).

1970   —— 'Thomas Brouns, bishop of Norwich, 1436–1445', in Hugh R. Trevor-Roper (ed.), *Essays in British history presented to sir Keith Feiling*. New York, 1965, pp. 61–83.

1971   Solloway, John. *Archbishop Scrope* (York Minster Historical Tracts, XV). York, 1927.

1972   Storey, Robin L. *Thomas Langley and the bishopric of Durham, 1406–1437* (Church Historical Society). 1961. Solid institutional biography on episcopacy and its responsibilities (1637, 1826).

1973   Workman, Herbert B. *John Wyclif: a study of the English medieval church*. Oxford, 1926, 2 vols. Standard biographical study, but see Rudolf Buddensieg's book, 1885, and especially (1750).

4 Articles

1974   Ady, Cecilia M. 'Pius II and his experiences of England, Scotland and the

English', *English Miscellany*, IX (1958), 39–49. Also, Constance Head details his response to the wars of the roses in *Archivum Historiae Pontificiae*, VIII, 1970, pp. 139–78. And (1716, 981).

1975 Allmand, Christopher J. 'L'évêché de Sées sous la domination anglaise au quinzième siècle', *Annales de Normandie*, XI (1961), 301–7. Also, his essay on maintenance of clergy in G.J. Cuming (ed.), *Studies in church history*, III, 1966, pp. 179–90; also (2081, 2110).

1976 Anon. 'Anchorites in Faversham churchyard', *ArchCant*, XI (1877), 24–39. See (1867).

1977 Archer, Margaret. 'Philip Repingdon, bishop of Lincoln, and his cathedral chapter [1405–19]', *UBHJ*, IV (1953–4), 81–97. See (1607); on bishops generally (1613, 1908, 1983, 1986, 2022, 2048, 2063, 2095, 2096, 2116, 2120, 2139, 2175).

1978 Aston, Margaret E. 'The impeachment of Bishop Despencer [1383]', *BIHR*, XXXVIII (1965), 127–48.

1979 ——— 'Lollardy and sedition, 1381–1431', *Past and Present*, XVII (1960), 1–44; *History*, XLIX (1964), 149–70. See (1634, 301).

1980 Axon, Ernest. 'The family of Bothe [Booth] and the church in the 15th and 16th centuries', *Lancs Antiq*, LIII (1938), 32–82. Huge numbers of ecclesiastics in the family.

1981 Beck, Egerton. 'The appropriated churches of the English White Canons', *Analecta Praemonstratensia*, V (1929), 97–108, 178–97, 289–305; VI (1930), 54–73. Excellent list, with important descriptions of primary sources (1656); and for monastic economy (1163).

1982 Bennett, M.J. 'The Lancashire and Cheshire clergy 1379', *Lancs Historic*, CXXIV (1973), 1–30. More materials on the parish and lower clergy (471, 2014, 2019, 2021, 2023, 2037, 2058, 2088, 2093, 2131, 2135, 2173, 2184, 2185), and (1609).

1983 Betcherman, L.R. 'The making of bishops in the Lancastrian period', *Speculum*, XLI (1966), 397–419. Also, Rosenthal (1941, 2139) and generally (1613, 1977).

1984 Betts, Reginald R. 'English and Čech influences on the Hussite movement', *TRHS*, 4th ser., XXI (1939), 71–102. See (2150, 2154, 1750).

1985 Bishop, Edmund. 'The method and degree of fasting and abstinence of the Black Monks in England before the Reformation', *Downside Review*, XLIII (1925), 184–237.

1986 Blair, Charles H.H. 'Medieval seals of the bishops of Durham', *Arch*, LXXII (1922), 1–24. See (1692, 1977), and generally (335).

1987 Bond, Maurice F. 'Chapter administration and archives at Windsor', *JEH*, VIII (1957), 166–81. Description of fifteenth century muniments plus good, general bibliography (1626).

1988 Brandt, William J. 'Church and society in the late fourteenth century: a contemporary view', *Medievalia et Humanistica*, XIII (1960), 56–67. From sermons of Thomas Brinton, bishop of Rochester 1373–89; see Devlin (1653).

1989 Breck, Allen D. 'The leadership of the English delegation at Constance', *University of Colorado Studies in Humanities*, I (1941), 289–99. See (2147, 1909).

1990 Brooke, Christopher N.L. 'The deans of St Paul's, *c.* 1090–1499', *BIHR*, XXIX (1956), 231–44. See (1818).

1991 Brushfield, Thomas N. 'The bishopric of Exeter, 1419–20', *DevonA*, XVIII (1886), 229–60. See (1618, 2022, 314).

1992 Chaplin, W.N. 'Lollardy and the Great Bible', *CQR*, CXXVIII (1939), 210–37. See (1634, 1881, 2031, 2064, 2094, 2134, 2160).

1993 Cheetham, Frank H. 'Burscough priory', *Lancs Antiq*, XXVI (1908), 133–48.

1994 Chesney, Kathleen. 'Notes on some treatises of devotion intended for Margaret of York', *Medium Aevum*, XX (1951), 11–39. See (1610).

1995 Cheyney, Edward P. 'The recantation of the early Lollards', *AHR*, IV (1899), 423–38. See (1634, 2076).

1996 Clapham, Alfred W. 'The history and remains of the Augustinian abbey of Lesnes', *StPaulS.*, n.s., VII (1911–1915), 1–13.

1997 Clark-Maxwell, W.G. 'Some letters of confraternity', *Arch*, LXXV (1926), 19—60; LXXIX (1929), 179—216. Includes an index to nearly 300, mainly from the fifteenth century.

1998 Clay, Rotha M. 'Some northern anchorites; with a note on enclosed Dominicans', *ArchAel*, 4th ser., XXXIII (1955), 202—17. See (1867).

1999 —— 'Further studies on medieval recluses', *JBAA*, 3rd ser., XVI (1953), 74—86.

2000 Colledge, Eric. 'The recluse. A Lollard interpolated version of the *Ancren Riwle*', *Review of English Studies*, XV (1939), 1—15, 129—45. See (1867, 1634).

2001 Compston, Herbert F.B. 'The thirty-seven conclusions of the Lollards', *EHR*, XXVI (1911), 738—49. See (1634, 2004).

2002 Coulton, George G. 'A sidelight on the medieval visitation system', *EHR*, XLVIII (1933), 89—91. Gives useful index to *Calendar of papal registers 1418—1462* for depositions of beneficed incumbents (1716); and (1617).

2003 Cox, John C. 'Benefactions of Thomas Heywood, dean (1457—92), to the cathedral church of Lichfield', *Arch*, LII (1890), 617—46.

2004 Cronin, Harry S. 'The twelve conclusions of the Lollards', *EHR*, XXII (1907), 292—304. See (1634, 2001).

2005 —— 'Wycliffe's canonry at Lincoln', *EHR*, XXXV (1920), 564—9. See (1750, 2107).

2006 Dahmus, Joseph H. 'Did Wyclif recant?', *CHR*, XXIX (1943), 155—68. No, but he did submit to authority (1750, 2107).

2007 —— 'Richard II and the church', *CHR*, XXXIX (1954), 408—33.

2008 Davies, Richard G. 'Thomas Arundel as archbishop of Canterbury, 1396—1414', *JEH*, XXIV (1973), 9—21. See (1866, 1958).

2009 Davis, J.F. 'Lollards, reformers and St Thomas of Canterbury', *UBHJ*, IX (1963—4), 1—16. See his contribution on Lollards and clothworkers in G.J. Cuming (ed.), *Studies in church history*, III, 1966, pp. 191—201; and (1634).

2010 Davis-Winstone, W.E. 'Hales Owen Abbey at the end of the fifteenth century', *Transactions of the Birmingham Archaeological Society*, XXXV (1909), 1—15. From episcopal visitation records (1617).

2011 Dickinson, John C. 'Early suppressions of English houses of Austin Canons', in Veronica Ruffer and A.J. Taylor (eds.), *Medieval studies presented to Rose Graham*. Oxford, 1950, pp. 54—77.

2012 Dobson, Richard B. 'The election of John Ousthorp as abbot of Selby in 1436', *YorksJ*, XLII (1967), 31—40.

2013 —— 'The foundation of perpetual chantries by the citizens of medieval York', in G.J. Cuming (ed.), *Studies in Church History*, IV (1967), pp. 22—38. And (1955).

2014 Dodd, Joseph A. 'Ewelme', *StPaulS*, n.s., VIII (1917—20), 194—206. Fifteenth-century parish church and its records, in Oxfordshire, see Genet (1333); and generally (1982).

2015 Donaldson, Robert. 'Sponsors, patrons and presentations to benefices — particularly those in the gift of the priors of Durham — during the later middle ages', *ArchAel*, 4th ser., XXXVIII (1960), 169—77. See Dobson (1247), and generally (1692).

2016 Donkin, Robert A. 'The urban property of the Cistercians in mediaeval England', *Analecta Sacri Ordinis Cisterciensis*, XV (1959), 104—31. Lists of property in towns and in cities (1163, 1636).

2017 Du Boulay, Francis R.H. 'A fifteenth-century memorandum book from the diocese of Canterbury', *BIHR*, XXXVIII (1965), 210—12.

2018 —— 'Charitable subsidies granted to the archbishop of Canterbury, 1300—1489', *BIHR*, XXIII (1950), 147—64. See (116, 1632, 1866).

2019 Duncan, Leland L. 'The parish churches of west Kent, their dedications, altars, images, and lights', *StPaulS*, n.s., III (1895), 241—98. For dedications in *Lancs Antiq*, IV, 1886, pp. 93—8, in those counties; and (1609, 1982).

2020 Dunning, Robert W. 'Rural deans in England in the fifteenth-century', *BIHR*, XL (1967), 207—13.

2021 —— 'The Wells consistory court in the fifteenth century', *SomersetP*, CVI (1961–2), 46–61; CX (1965–6), 24–39; CXIV (1970), 91–5. Work of fundamental value (1617); the second article describes households of the Bath and Wells bishops, and the third provides a list of Somerset's parochial clergy, 1373–1404; and (2177, 1609, 1982).

2022 Dunstan, Gordon R. 'Some aspects of the register of Edmund Lacy, bishop of Exeter, 1420–1455', *JEH*, VI (1955), 37–47. Also see Muriel E.H. Curtis in *EHR*, XLV, 1930, pp. 290–1 (1618, 1663).

2023 Dymond, Robert. 'The history of the parish of St Petrock, Exeter', *DevonA*, XIV (1882), 402–92. Includes churchwardens' accounts 1425–1590 (2059, 1759, 1609, 1982).

2024 Eeles, Francis C. 'On a fifteenth-century York missal formerly used at Broughton-in-Amounderness, Lancashire', *Miscellany VI* (Chetham Society, n.s., XCIV), 1935, pp. 1–11. See (1642).

2025 —— 'On a manuscript of Sarum missal of the fifteenth century, probably used in or near Canterbury', *StPaulS*, n.s., VIII (1917–20), 72–84.

2026 Egbert, Donald D. 'The "Tewkesbury" psalter', *Speculum*, X (1935), 376–86. Belonged to Beauchamp family in fifteenth century, here calendared (1642, 2237).

2027 Erskine, Audrey M. 'The medieval financial records of the cathedral church of Exeter', *Journal of the Society of Archivists*, II (1962), 254–66. See (1618).

2028 Firth, Catherine B. 'Benefit of clergy in the time of Edward IV', *EHR*, XXXII (1917), 175–91. See (1888).

2029 Foreville, Raymonde. 'Manifestations de Lollardisme à Exeter en 1421? D'après une lettre ≪extravagante≫ de Henri Chichele', *Le Moyen Âge*, LXIX (1963), 691–706. Also author of monograph on Thomas à Becket's feast day, 1958 (1934); and (1634).

2030 Fowler, Robert C. 'The religious gilds of Essex', *EssexT*, n.s., XII (1913), 280–90. See (1621).

2031 Gairdner, James. 'Bible study in the fifteenth century', *Fortnightly Review*, I (1865), 710–20; II (1865), 59–78. See (1881, 1992).

2032 Galbraith, Vivian H. 'A visitation of Westminster in 1444', *EHR*, XXXVII (1922), 83–8. See (1617, 1740).

2033 Gardner, Helen L. 'Walter Hilton and the mystical tradition in England', *Essays and Studies*, XXII (1937), 103–27. Interesting literary and social summary of late fourteenth-century themes (1821, 1916).

2034 Gautier, Pierre. 'De l'état des monastères cisterciens anglais à la fin du XVe siècle', in *Mélanges d'histoire offerts à M. Charles Bémont* . . . . Paris, 1913, pp. 423–35. See (1636).

2035 Gerits, Trudo. 'A propos de l'organisation des bibliothèques médiévales de l'Ordre de Prémontré en Angleterre et en Allemagne', *Analecta Praemonstratensia*, XXXVII (1961), 75–84. And (1656, 1682, 2419).

2036 Gibbons, J.H. 'The royal shrine at Westminster: as it may have been at the end of the fourteenth century', *Lancs Antiq*, XXIX (1911), 89–100. And (1740).

2037 Godfrey, Cuthbert J. 'Non-residence of parochial clergy in the fourteenth century', *CQR*, CLXII (1961), 434–7. Generally (1609, 1982).

2038 Goldthorp, L.M. 'The Franciscans and Dominicans in Yorkshire: Part I, the Grey Friars; Part II, the Black Friars', *YorksJ*, XXXII (1936), 264–320, 365–428. See (1630, 1732).

2039 Gooder [Eileen] A. 'Mortmain and the local historian', *The Local Historian*, IX (1971), 387–94. Useful introductory comments regarding land alienation and the church (357).

2040 Graham, Rose. 'The great schism and the English monasteries of the Cistercian order', *EHR*, XLIV (1929), 373–87. See (1636, 1716).

2041 —— 'The papal schism of 1378 and the English province of the order of Cluny', *EHR*, XXXVIII (1923), 481–95. See (1659, 1716).

2042 —— 'The English province of the order of Cluny in the fifteenth century', *TRHS*, 4th ser., VII (1924), 98–130.

2043 Green, Herbert. 'Lenton priory', *ThorotonS*, XL (1936), 29–90.

2044 Greenaway, William. 'The papacy and the diocese of St David's, 1305–1417',

CQR, CLXI (1960), 436—48; CLXII (1961), 33—49. See (1728, 1716, 97).

2045 Gumbley, Walter. 'A fragment of the acts of an English Dominican chapter of the early fifteenth century', *Dominican Studies*, VI (1953), 90—100.

2046 Gwynn, Aubrey O. 'Ireland and the English nation at the council of Constance', *Proceedings of the Royal Irish Academy*, XLV (1940), 183—233. See (1909, 133, 877).

2047 Hackett, M.B. 'William Flete and the *De remediis contra temptaciones*', in John A. Watt, John B. Morrall, and Francis X. Martin (eds.), *Medieval studies presented to Aubrey Gwynn, S.J.* Dublin, 1961, pp. 330—48.

2048 Haines, Roy M. 'Aspects of the episcopate of John Carpenter, bishop of Worcester 1444—1476', *JEH*, XIX (1968), 11—40. Also his study of bishop William Gray in *Medieval Studies*, XXXIV, 1972, pp. 435—61; and of Gray's network of patronage, *JEH*, XXV, 1974, pp. 225—47 (1691, 1613, 1977).

2049 —— 'The education of the English clergy during the later middle ages: some observations on the operation of Pope Boniface VIII's constitution *Cum ex eo* (1298)', *Canadian Journal of History*, IV (1969), 1—22. See (1877).

2050 —— ' "Wilde wittes and wilfulnes": John Swetstock's attack on those "Poyswunmongeres", the Lollards', in G.J. Cuming and Derek Baker (eds.), *Popular Belief and Practice*, Cambridge, 1972, pp. 143—53; and (1634).

2051 Halcrow, Elizabeth M. 'Obedientiaries and counsellors in monastic administration at Durham', *ArchAel*, 4th ser., XXXV (1957), 7—21. See (1692, 1605).

2052 Hamilton Thompson, Alexander. 'The collegiate churches of the bishoprick of Durham', *Durham University Journal*, n.s., V (1944), 33—42. See (1626).

2053 —— 'A corrody from Leicester abbey, 1393—4, with some notes on corrodies', *Transactions of the Leicestershire Architectural and Archaeological Society*, XIV (1926), 114—34. See (2089).

2054 —— 'The deans and canons of Bridgnorth', *AJ*, LXXXIV (1927), 24—87.

2055 —— 'Diocesan organization in the middle ages: archdeacons and rural deans', *PBA*, XXIX (1943), 153—94. See (2071).

2056 —— 'Ecclesiastical benefices and their incumbents', *Transactions of the Leicestershire Archaeological Society*, XXII (1942), 1—32.

2057 —— 'English colleges of chantry priests', *Ecclesiological Society Transactions*, n.s., I (1943), 92—108. See (1955).

2058 —— 'Gnosall church in the fourteenth century, in the light of a lawsuit of 1395', *SaltS*, (1927), 83—116. Generally (1609, 1982).

2059 —— 'The inventories of the treasures of the cathedral church of St Peter in Exeter', *DevonA*, LXXVI (1944), 27—37. See (2023).

2060 —— 'Monasteries of Leicestershire in the fifteenth century', *Transactions of the Leicestershire Archaeological Society*, XI (1913), 89—108.

2061 —— 'The priory of St Mary of Newstead in Sherwood Forest. With some notes on houses of regular canons', *ThorotonS*, XXIII (1919), 33—141.

2062 —— 'Visitations of religious houses by William Alnwick, bishop of Lincoln, 1436—1449', *Proceedings of the Society of Antiquaries of London*, 2nd ser., XXVI (1914), 189—203. See (1617, 1699, 2109).

2063 Hannam, Una C. 'The episcopal registers of Roger Walden and Nicholas Bubwith', *London-Midd*, n.s., XI (1954), 123—36, 214—26. Indexed and analysed here for bishops of London, 1405—6 and 1406—7, respectively (1613, 1977).

2064 Hargreaves, Henry. 'An intermediate version of the Wycliffite Old Testament', *Studia Neophilologica*, XXVIII (1956), 130—47; XXXIII (1961), 285—300. See (1881, 1992, 1750, 2107).

2065 —— 'Sir John Oldcastle and Wycliffite views on clerical marriage', *Medium Aevum*, XLII (1973), 141—6. See (1634, 1800, 1750).

2066 Haselmayer, Louis A. 'The apparitor and Chaucer's summoner', *Speculum*, XII (1937), 43—57. See (2131, 2191, 1478, 1617).

2067 Hay, Denys. 'The church of England in the later middle ages', *History*, LIII (1968), 35—50. See (1756).

2068   Hennig, John. 'The place of Irish saints in late mediaeval English hagiography', *Medieval Studies*, XVI (1954), 165—71. See (1934, 877).

2069   Hibbert, Francis A. 'Croxden Abbey: its buildings and history', *CQR*, LXXV (1912—13), 38—71.

2070   Hinnebusch, W.A. 'Foreign Dominican students and professors at the Oxford Blackfriars', in *Oxford studies presented to Daniel Callus* (Oxford Historical Society, n.s., XVI). 1964, pp. 101—34. See (2394).

2071   Hodge, C.E. 'Cases from a fifteenth-century archdeacon's court [at St Albans, 1433—5]', *LQR*, XLIX (1933), 268—74. See (1617, 2055).

2072   Hodgson, Phyllis. '*Ignorancia sacerdotum*: a fifteenth-century discourse on the Lambeth Constitutions', *Review of English Studies*, XXIV (1948), 1—11.

2073   Hofmann, Georg. 'Briefe eines päpstlichen Nuntius in London über das Konzil von Florenz', *Orientalia Christiana Periodica*, V (1939), 407—33. Nine letters from Pietro del Monte, 1435—40 (1716, 2400, 2445).

2074   Honeybourne, Marjorie B. 'The Fleet and its neighbourhood in early and medieval times', *London Topographical Society*, XIX (1947), 13—87. Establishes locations of diverse pre-Reformation monastic properties in London (368, 1484).

2075   —— 'The sanctuary boundaries and environs of Westminster Abbey and the college of St Martin-le-Grand', *JBAA*, n.s., XXXVIII (1932), 316—33. See (1740).

2076   Hudson, Anne. 'The examination of Lollards', *BIHR*, XLVI (1973), 145—59. See (1634, 1995).

2077   Jacob, Ernest F. 'The Canterbury convocation of 1406', in T.A. Sandquist and Michael R. Powicke (eds.), *Essays in medieval history presented to Bertie Wilkinson*. Toronto, 1969, pp. 345—53. See (1866).

2078   —— 'Chichele and Canterbury', in Richard W. Hunt, William A. Pantin, and Richard W. Southern (eds.), *Studies in medieval history presented to Frederick M. Powicke*. Oxford, 1948, pp. 386—404. See (1729).

2079   —— 'The disputed election at Fountains Abbey, 1410—16', in Veronica Ruffer and A.J. Taylor (eds.), *Medieval studies presented to Rose Graham*. Oxford, 1950, pp. 78—97.

2080   —— 'Englishmen and the general councils of the fifteenth century', *History*, n.s., XXIV (1939), 206—19. See (1909).

2081   —— 'English university clerks in the later middle ages: the problem of maintenance', *BJRL*, XXIX (1945—6), 304—25; *JEH*, I (1950), 172—86. See (1975, 2085, 2457).

2082   —— 'Founders and foundations in the later middle ages', *BIHR*, XXXV (1962), 29—46.

2083   —— 'The medieval chapter of Salisbury Cathedral', *WiltsMag*, LI (1947), 479—95. See (1626).

2084   —— 'A note on the English concordat of 1418', in John A. Watt, John B. Morrall, and Francis X. Martin (eds.), *Medieval studies presented to Aubrey Gwynn, S.J.* Dublin, 1961, pp. 349—58. See (1716).

2085   —— 'Petitions for benefices from English universities during the Great Schism', *TRHS*, 4th ser., XXVII (1945), 41—59. See (2457).

2086   —— 'Wilkins's *Concilia* and the fifteenth century', *TRHS*, 4th ser., XV (1932), 91—131. See (1844, 1756).

2087   Jarrett, Bede. 'Bequests to the Black Friars of London during the fifteenth century', *EHR*, XXV (1910), 309—14.

2088   Johnston, Francis R. 'St Mary of Eccles — a mediaeval parish', *Lancs Antiq*, LXVIII (1958), 12—23. See (1609, 1982).

2089   Keil, Ian. 'Corrodies of Glastonbury Abbey in the later middle ages', *SomersetP*, CVIII (1963—4), 113—31. Emphasizing fifteenth-century monastic patronage (2053).

2090   —— 'Impropriator and benefice in the later middle ages', *WiltsMag*, LVIII (1963), 351—61. Glastonbury Abbey's estate in Longbridge Deverill church, with important evidence for vicarage agriculture (1163).

2091   Kelly, H.A. 'Canonical implications of Richard III's plan to marry his niece', *Traditio*, XXIII (1967), 269—311. See (685, 791, 1756).

2092 Kingsford, Charles L. 'Additional material for the history of the Grey Friars, London', *Collectanea Franciscana II* (British Society of Franciscan Studies, X). Manchester, 1922, pp. 61—149. Lists of names, with wills and documents relating to persons associated with the Grey Friars (1732, 1630).

2093 Kingsford, Hamilton. 'Parish clerks and some duties of parish clerks and sextons in pre-Reformation times', *Reports and Papers Read at Meetings of Architectural Societies*, XXV (1899), 165—72. See (1609, 1982).

2094 Knapp. Peggy A. 'John Wyclif as Bible translator: the texts for the English sermons', *Speculum*, XLVI (1971), 713—20. See (1750, 2107, 1992).

2095 Knecht, R.J. 'The episcopate and the wars of the roses', *UBHJ*, VI (1957—8), 108—31. See (103, 1613, 1977).

2096 Knowles, David [Michael Clive Knowles]. 'The English bishops, 1070—1532', in John A. Watt, John B. Morrall, and Francis X. Martin (eds.), *Medieval studies presented to Aubrey Gwynn, S.J.* Dublin, 1961, pp. 283—96. See (1977).

2097 —— 'The religion of the Pastons', *Downside Review*, XLIII (1925), 143—63. See (1011, 1102).

2098 Langson, J.N. 'Priors of Lanthony by Gloucester', *Bristol-Gloucs*, LXIII (1942), 1—144.

2099 Leach, Arthur F. 'A clerical strike at Beverley Minster in the fourteenth century [1381—1389]', *Arch*, LV (1896), 1—20.

2100 Leff, Gordon. 'John Wyclif: the path to dissent', *PBA*, LII (1966), 143—80. See (1750, 2107).

2101 Legg, John W. 'Liturgical notes on the Sherborne missal [1396—1407]', *StPaulS*, n.s., IV (1900), 1—31, 234. See (1642, 2414).

2102 —— 'Notes on the history of liturgical colours', *StPaulS*, n.s., I (1885), 95—134. Exhaustive attempt to catalogue for all countries, emphasizing England (1725).

2103 Léotaud, Alban. 'The Benedictines at Oxford, 1283—1539', *Downside Review*, LVII (1939), 215—35. See (2394).

2104 Little, Andrew G. 'Personal tithes', *EHR*, LX (1945), 67—88. Proves that they were collected and enforced (357, 2164).

2105 Lloyd, Albert H. 'Notes on Cambridge clerks petitioning for benefices [to the papacy], 1370—1399', *BIHR*, XX (1943—5), 75—96, 192—211. See (1716, 2457).

2106 Loomis, Louise R. 'Nationality at the council of Constance. An Anglo-French dispute', *AHR*, XLIV (1939), 508—27. See (1909, 2046, 93).

2107 Loserth, Johann. In *Sitzungsberichte der kaiserlichen Akademie der Wissenschaften Wien, Philosophisch-historische klasse*, CLVI (1908), 1—118, CLX (1909), 1—74; CLXIV (1910), 1—96; CLXXX (1916), 1—101; CCXXXVI (1918), 1—83. Indispensable articles on Wyclif; with (2005, 2006, 2064, 2065, 2094, 2100, 2111, 2114, 2119, 2125, 2133, 2150, 2155, 2160—2, 2165—8, 2181, 2183) and (397, 1750).

2108 Lovatt, Roger. 'The *Imitation of Christ* in late medieval England', *TRHS*, 5th ser., XVIII (1968), 97—121. See (1713).

2109 Maddison, Arthur R. 'A visitation of Lincoln Cathedral, held by William Alnwick, bishop of London A.D. 1437', *JBAA*, XLVII (1891), 12—24. See (1617, 2062, 1699).

2110 Mahieu, Bernard. 'Étude sur les évêques et le diocèse de Bayeux au milieu du XVe siècle (1431—1479)', *École Nationale des Chartes: Positions des Thèses*, XCV (1943), 143—53. Then under English administration (1975).

2111 Maitland, Frederic W. 'Canon law in England. I: William Lyndwood. II: Church, state, and decretals', *EHR*, XI (1896), 446—78, 641—72; XVI (1901), 35—45. The latter is his famous, penetrating reply to Dr MacColl; both essays available in his *Collected papers*, as is an essay on Wycliffe and the Roman Law (285); also (357, 1756).

2112 Major, Kathleen. 'Fifteenth-century presentation deeds in the Lincoln Diocesan Record Office', in Richard W. Hunt, William A. Pantin, and Richard W. Southern (eds.), *Studies in medieval history presented to Frederick M. Powicke*. Oxford, 1948, pp. 455—64.

2113 —— 'The offices of chapter clerk at Lincoln in the middle ages', in Veronica Ruffer and A.J. Taylor (eds.), *Medieval studies presented to Rose Graham*. Oxford, 1950, pp. 163–88.

2114 Manning, Bernard L. 'Wyclif', in Joseph R. Tanner, Charles W. Previté-Orton and Z.N. Brooke (eds.), *The Cambridge medieval history, VII*. Cambridge, 1932, pp. 486–507. Brief summary raising diverse, interesting questions (1750, 2107).

2115 Morgan, Marjorie M. 'The suppression of the alien priories [in 1414]', *History*, n.s., XXVI (1942), 204–12.

2116 Morris, Colin. 'The commissary of the bishop in the diocese of Lincoln', *JEH*, X (1959), 50–65. See (1896, 1613, 1977).

2117 —— 'A consistory court in the middle ages [at Lincoln]', *JEH*, XIV (1963), 150–9. See (1617, 2021).

2118 Moyes, James. 'Collegiation of Manchester Church [1426]', *Lancs Antiq*, XXIV (1906), 11–20. See (1626, 1936).

2119 Mudroch, Vaclav. 'John Wyclif and Richard Flemyng, bishop of Lincoln: gleanings from German sources', *BIHR*, XXXVII (1964), 239–45. See (1750, 2107).

2120 Owen, Dorothy M. 'The records of the bishop's official at Ely: specialization in the English episcopal chancery of the later middle ages', in Donald A. Bullough and Robin L. Storey (eds.), *The study of medieval records: essays in honour of Kathleen Major*. Oxford, 1971, pp. 189–205. See (1896, 2116, 1613, 1977).

2121 Owst, Gerald R. 'A fifteenth-century manuscript in St Albans abbey', *Transactions of the St Albans and Hertfordshire Architectural and Archaeological Society*, (1924), 43–59. Pulpit discourses during Henry VI's reign (1929).

2122 Palmer, J.J.N. 'England and the great western schism, 1388–1399', *EHR*, LXXXIII (1968), 516–22. Generally (1716).

2123 Palmer, William M. 'The Benedictine nunnery of Swaffham Bulbeck', *Proceedings of the Cambridge Antiquarian Society*, XXXI (1929), 30–65. See (1619).

2124 —— 'Fifteenth-century visitation records of the deanery of Wisbech', *Proceedings of the Cambridge Antiquarian Society*, XXXIX (1939), 69–75. See (1617).

2125 Pantin, William A. 'A Benedictine opponent of John Wyclif', *EHR*, XLIII (1928), 73–7. See (1750, 2107).

2126 —— 'The *Defensorium* of Adam Easton', *EHR*, LI (1936), 675–80. Oxford theologian accused of conspiracy against Urban VI *c.* 1378.

2127 —— 'General and provincial chapters of the English Black Monks, 1215–1540', *TRHS*, 4th ser., X (1927), 195–263.

2128 —— 'Some medieval English treatises on the origins of monasticism', in Veronica Ruffer and A.J. Taylor (eds.), *Medieval studies presented to Rose Graham*. Oxford, 1950, pp. 189–215.

2129 Peckham, Walter D. 'Dean Croucher's book', *SussexS*, LXXXIV (1945), 11–32.

2130 —— 'The vicars choral of Chichester Cathedral', *SussexS*, LXXVIII (1937), 126–59.

2131 Pfancer, H.G. 'Some medieval manuals of religious instruction in England and observations on Chaucer's Parson's Tale', *Journal of English and Germanic Philology*, XXV (1936), 234–58. See (1610, 2066, 1982).

2132 Plucknett, Theodore F.T. 'The case of the miscreant Cardinal', *AHR*, XXX (1924), 1–15. Avignon pope Clement VII, victim of *quare impedit* to recover his benefice of Wearmouth parish, Durham diocese, 1382–1383 (1716).

2133 Poole, Reginald L. 'On the intercourse between English and Bohemian Wycliffites in the early years of the fifteenth century', *EHR*, VII (1892), 306–11. See (1750, 2107, 1984, 2150).

2134 Pope, Hugh. 'The Lollard Bible', *Dublin Review*, CLXVIII (1921), 60–72. Review of Deanesley (1881), attacking view that English bibles did not exist before Wycliffe; and (1634, 1642, 1992).

2135 Putnam, Bertha H. 'Maximum wage-laws for priests after the black death, 1348–1381', *AHR*, XXI (1915), 12–32. See (1609, 1982).

2136 Richardson, Henry G. 'Heresy and the lay power under Richard II', *EHR*, LI (1936), 1–28. See (692, 1958, 1756).

2137 Rickert, Margaret J. 'The reconstruction of an English Carmelite missal', *The Burlington Magazine*, LXVII (1935), 99–113. See (1642, 1938).

2138 Riley, Marjorie A. 'The foundation of chantries in the counties of Nottingham and York, 1350–1400', *YorksJ*, XXXIII (1938), 122–65, 237–85. And (1955, 2012).

2139 Rosenthal, Joel T. 'The fifteenth-century episcopate: careers and bequests', in Derek Baker (ed.), *Sanctity and Secularity: the church and the world*. Oxford, 1973, pp. 117–28.

2140 —— 'Richard, duke of York: a fifteenth-century layman and the church', *CHR*, L (1964), 171–87.

2141 Rowe, Joshua B. 'Cistercian houses of Devon', *DevonA*, VII (1875), 329–66; VIII (1876), 797–893; IX (1877), 361–91; X (1878), 349–76. Describes mss. and architecture for Buckland, Buckfast, Newenham, Dunkeswell and Ford (1636).

2142 Russell, Henry G. 'Lollard opposition to oaths by creatures', *AHR*, LI (1946), 668–84. See (1634).

2143 Russell, Josiah C. 'The clerical population of medieval England', *Traditio*, II (1944), 177–212. See (1076).

2144 Russell-Smith, Joy M. 'Walter Hilton and a tract in defence of the veneration of images', *Dominican Studies*, VII (1954), 180–214. See (1821, 2033, 1916).

2145 Sanderlin, George. 'John Capgrave speaks up for the hermits', *Speculum*, XVIII (1943), 358–62. See (1726, 1867).

2146 Schoeck, Richard J. 'Canon law in England on the eve of the Reformation', *Mediaeval Studies*, XXV (1963), 125–47. Focus on the early Tudor era but of general interest (1756).

2147 Schofield, A.N.E.D. 'The first English delegation to the council of Basel [1433]', *JEH*, XII (1961), 167–96; XVI (1966), 29–64; *Church History*, XXXIII (1964), 248–78. The second article describes the second delegation in 1434, while the third is an important, general study, as is (1877, 1909).

2148 Senior, William. 'The advocates of the court of arches', *LQR*, XXXIX (1923), 493–506. See (1617, 1756).

2149 Shorrocks, D.M.M. 'Probate jurisdiction within the diocese of Canterbury', *BIHR*, XXXI (1958), 186–95. See (1756).

2150 Šmahel, František. ' "Doctor evangelicus super omnes evangelistas": Wyclif's fortune in Hussite Bohemia', *BIHR*, XLIII (1970), 16–34. See (1750, 1984, 2107, 2154).

2151 Smith, Herbert M. 'Lollardy', *CQR*, CXIX (1934), 30–60. See (1634).

2152 Snape, M.G. 'Some evidence of Lollard activity in the diocese of Durham in the early fifteenth century', *ArchAel*, 4th ser., XXXIX (1961), 355–61. See (1634, 1692).

2153 Somerville, Robert. 'Duchy of Lancaster presentations, 1399–1485', *BIHR*, XVIII (1941), 52–76, 122–34.

2154 Spinka, Mathew. 'Paul Kravař and the Lollard–Hussite relations', *Church History*, XXV (1956), 16–26. See (1634, 1750, 1984, 2133, 2150).

2155 Stein, I.H. 'The Wyclif manuscript in Florence', *Speculum*, V (1930), 95–7; VI (1931), 465–8. See (1750, 2107).

2156 Street, Fanny. 'The relations of the bishops and citizens of Salisbury (New Sarum) between 1225 and 1612', *WiltsMag*, XXXIX (1915–17), 185–257, 319–67. See (1733).

2157 Swarbrick, John. 'The abbey of St Mary-of-the-March at Cockersand', *Lancs Historic*, XL (1922–3), 163–93. Includes the architectural design, illustrations, and a bibliography.

2158 Swift, Eleanor. 'Obedientiary and other accounts of Battle Abbey in the Huntington Library', *BIHR*, XII (1935), 83–101; *SussexS*, LXXVIII

(1937), 37—62. Complete listings, by year, with indices supplies in second article; see (1219, 1289), and generally (1605).

2159 Talbert, Ernest W. 'A fifteenth-century Lollard sermon cycle', *Studies in English, The University of Texas*, (1939), 5—30. See (1634, 1635).

2160 —— 'A note on the Wyclyfite Bible translation', *Studies in English, The University of Texas*, (1940), 29—38. See (1992, 1750, 2107).

2161 —— 'The composition of the English Wyclifite sermons', *Speculum*, XII (1937), 464—74.

2162 Tatnall, Edith C. 'John Wyclif and *Ecclesia Anglicana*', *JEH*, XX (1969), 19—43. See (1750, 2107).

2163 Thomson, John A.F. 'Piety and charity in late medieval London', *JEH*, XVI (1965), 178—95.

2164 —— 'Tithe disputes in later medieval London', *EHR*, LXXVIII (1963), 1—17. See (2104).

2165 Thomson, Samuel H. 'The order of writing of Wyclif's philosophical works', in *Ceskou minlosti. Prace venovane profesoru Karlovy university Vaclavu Novotneum jeho zaky k sedesatym narozeninam*. Prague, 1929, pp. 146—66. See (1750, 2107, 2133).

2166 —— 'Three unprinted *opuscula* of John Wyclif', *Speculum*, III (1928), 248—53, 382—91; IV (1929), 339—46.

2167 —— 'Unnoticed mss. and works of Wyclif', *Journal of Theological Studies*, XXXVIII (1937), 24—36, 139—48; *Medium Aevum*, XII (1943), 68—70. The second article notices *De veritate sacre scripture* (1633, 1750, 2107).

2168 —— 'Wyclif or Wyclyf?', *EHR*, LIII (1938), 675—8.

2169 Ullmann, Walter. 'Eugenius IV, Cardinal Kemp, and Archbishop Chichele', in John A. Watt, John B. Morrall, and Francis X. Martin (eds.), *Medieval studies presented to Aubrey Gwynn, S.J.* Dublin, 1961, pp. 359—83. See (1729, 1716).

2170 Utley, Francis L. 'The layman's complaint and the friar's answer', *Harvard Theological Review*, XXXVIII (1945), 141—7.

2171 Vallance, [W.H.] Aymer. 'A curious case at Cranbrook in 1437', *ArchCant*, XLIII (1931), 173—86. Of church robbery and murder of a sexton.

2172 Wade-Evans, Arthur W. 'Bonedd y Saint, E.', *ArchCamb*, 7th ser., LXXXVI (1931), 158—75. Descent of the Welsh saints, from a copy of 1485 (97).

2173 Wadsworth, Frederic A. 'The parish churches and houses of friars of Nottingham, their chapels, gilds, images and lights', *ThorotonS*, XXII (1918), 75—113. See (1609, 1982).

2174 Walsh, James and Eric Colledge. 'Of the knowledge of ourselves and of God; a fifteenth-century spiritual *Florilegium*', *The Month*, n.s., XXIV (1960), 365—76. See (1916).

2175 Warren, Wilfred L. 'A reappraisal of Simon Sudbury, bishop of London, (1361—75) and archbishop of Canterbury (1375—81)', *JEH*, X (1959), 139—52. See (1977).

2176 Watkin, Aelred. 'An English mediaeval instruction book for novices', *Downside Review*, LVII (1939), 477—88. Generally (1642).

2177 —— 'The precentors, chancellors and treasurers in Wells Cathedral', *Collectanea II* (Somerset Record Society, LVII). 1942, pp. 51—103. In effect, a *fasti*, 1136—1940, with introductory comments (2020, 2021).

2178 Weiss, Roberto. 'An English Augustinian in late fourteenth-century Florence [Thomas de Clifton]', *English Miscellany*, IX (1958), 13—22.

2179 Westlake, Herbert F. 'The parish gilds of the later fourteenth century', *StPaulS*, n.s., VIII (1917—20), 99—110. And (1621).

2180 Whitfield, Derek W. 'Conflicts of personality and principle. The political and religious crisis in the English Franciscan Province, 1400—1409', *Franciscan Studies*, XVII (1957), 321—62. See (1630).

2181 Whitney, James P. 'A note on the work of the Wyclif Society', in Henry W.C. Davis (ed.), *Essays in history presented to Reginald L. Poole*. Oxford, 1927, pp. 98—114. See (1750, 2107).

2182 Wickham, W.A. 'Some notes on chapter-houses', *Lancs Historic*, LXIV (1912), 143—248. Extensive list and detail for all cathedral and monastic chapters.

2183   Wilks, Michael. 'Predestination, property, and power: Wyclif's theory of dominion and grace', in G.J. Cuming (ed.), *Studies in Church History*, II (1965), 220—36.

2184   Williams, John F. 'The black book of Swaffham', *NA*, XXXIII (1965), 243—53. Compiled by John Botright, 1400—74, chaplain to Henry VI; dated after 1454 and includes parish accounts, full bede roll, and list of papal indulgences (1609, 1982, 1611, 2123).

2185   —— 'Ordination in the Norwich diocese during the fifteenth century', *NA*, XXXI (1957), 347—58. See (1613, 1982).

2186   Woodruff, Charles E. 'Notes on the inner life and domestic economy of the priory of Christ Church, Canterbury, in the fifteenth century', *ArchCant*, LIII (1941), 1—16. See (1866, 1163).

XIII. HISTORY OF THE FINE ARTS

1 Printed sources

2187   Anon. (ed.). *A collection of songs and madrigals by English composers of the close of the fifteenth century* (Plainsong and Medieval Music Society). 1891. Other songs and carols in (2193, 2196, 2199, 2203, 2265, 2307, 2347).

2188   Bannister, Henry M. (ed.). *Anglo-French sequelae* (Plainsong and Medieval Music Society). 1934. More materials on music (2190, 2195, 2198, 2200, 2202, 2204, 2214, 2217, 2219, 2227, 2255, 2257, 2260, 2265, 2271—3, 2283, 2289—91, 2302, 2306, 2307, 2330, 2334, 2335, 2342, 2346—8, 2360, 2361, 2376, 2377, 2388, 2390) and esp. (2305).

2189   Brooks, Frederick W. (ed.). 'A medieval brick-yard at Hull', *JBAA*, 3rd ser., IV (1939), 151—74. See (2292). More on building construction (1595, 2197, 2201, 2208, 2210, 2220, 2222, 2226, 2234, 2250, 2253, 2258, 2292, 2296, 2298—9, 2303—4, 2309, 2311—12, 2332—3, 2336—7, 2349, 2371, 2393).

2190   Bukofzer, Manfred F. (ed.). *John Dunstable's Complete works* (Musica Britannica, 8). 1953. See (2267, 2188).

2191   Crow, Martin M. and Clair C. Olson (eds.). *Chaucer life-records*. Oxford, 1966. See (1074, 1478, 2066, 2462).

2192   Dawson, Giles E. (ed.). *Records of plays and players in Kent, 1450—1642* (Malone Society, Collections VII). 1965. See (2454).

2193   Greene, Richard L. (ed.). *The early English carols*. Oxford, 1935. Also, Judith Ashley in *Music and Letters*, V, 1924, pp. 67—71 (2187).

2194   Greg, Walter W. (ed.). 'Robin Hood and the sheriff of Nottingham: a dramatic fragment, c. 1475', *Malone Society, Collections I, Part II* (1908), 117—25. See (697, 752, 2454).

2195   Hanham, Alison (ed.). 'The musical studies of a fifteenth-century wool merchant [for George Cely by Thomas Rede, harper at Calais]', *Review of English studies*, n.s., VIII (1957), 270—4. See (2188, 1026).

2196   Maitland, John A.F. (ed.). *English carols of the fifteenth century*. 1891. And Edward K. Chambers in *Modern Language Review*, V—VI, 1910—11; James Copley's monograph, 1940, is also useful (2187).

2197   Raine, James [the younger] (ed.). *Fabric rolls of York Minster [1360—1639]* (Surtees Society, XXXV). 1859. Important for details of construction and architecture (2189, 2206).

2198   Ramsbotham, Alexander (ed.). *The Old Hall manuscript*. 1933—8, 3 vols. Works composed for St George's chapel, Windsor, 1422—61 (2260, 2268, 2188).

2199   Schofield, Bertram (ed.). 'The adventures of an English minstrel and his varlet [executed at Paris, 1384]', *The Musical Quarterly*, XXXV (1949), 361—76. See (2187).

2200   —— (ed.). 'A newly discovered fifteenth-century manuscript of the English

Chapel Royal', *The Musical Quarterly*, XXXII (1946), 509–36; XXXIII (1947), 38–51. See (2289, 2290, 2188).

2201 Simpson, William D. (ed.). *The building accounts of Tattershall Castle 1434–1472* (Lincolnshire Record Society, LV). 1960. See (1595, 2189, 2206, 2372).

2202 Stainer, John F.R. (ed.). *Early Bodleian music; sacred and secular songs... 1185 to about A.D. 1505*. 1901. See (2188).

2203 Stevens, John E. (ed.). *Mediaeval carols* (Musica Britannica, 4). 1952. See (2187).

2204 Wooldridge, Harry E. and Anselm [Henry V.] Hughes (eds.). *Early English harmony from the 10th to the 15th century* (Plainsong and Medieval Music Society). 1897–1913, 2 vols. See (2188).

2 Surveys

2205 Birch, Walter de Gray and Henry Jenner. *Early drawings and illuminations: an introduction to the study of illustrated manuscripts, with a dictionary of subjects in the British Museum*. 1879. And see George G. Coulton on Froissart miniatures in *The chronicler of European chivalry*, 1930; see (889, 2223).

2206 Bond, Francis. *Gothic architecture in England*. 1905. See Harvey (2215) and Geoffrey Webb's book, 1951. Bond's fundamental contributions include *Dedications and patron saints of English churches*, 1914, and (2226). More on architecture in (2209, 2210, 2215, 2216, 2218, 2220, 2224, 2225, 2234, 2250, 2254, 2266, 2274, 2279, 2308, 2310, 2314, 2333, 2336, 2337, 2354–6, 2363, 2368, 2372–4); for castles (1595).

2207 Brooke, Iris. *English costume of the later middle ages, the fourteenth and fifteenth centuries, drawn and described*. 1935. Also, monograph of Dion C. Calthrop, 1906; and the general study of Francis M. Kelly and Randolph Schwabe, 2nd ed., 1929, 2 vols.; also, vol. II of Herbert Norris's interesting survey, 1933; and (1079, 1089, 1147, 2297).

2208 Clifton-Taylor, Alec. *The pattern of English building*. 1962. Traces geographical distribution of wood, limestone, granite, brick, and thatch; also Frederick H. Crossley, *Timber building in England*, 1951; see (2375); and J.A. Wight on brick building, 1972; and generally (2189, 2206).

2209 Cook, Olive. *English abbeys and priories*. 1960. See (2206).

2210 Crossley, Frederick H. *English church design, 1040–1540 A.D.* 1948, 2nd ed., rev. Also William R. Lethaby on Westminster Abbey, 1906; Crossley on *English Church Craftsmanship*, 1941; and Katherine W. Barnardiston, *Clare Priory*, 1962; generally (2189, 2206, 2224).

2211 —— *English church monuments, A.D. 1150–1550. An introduction to the study of tombs and effigies of the medieval period*. 1921. See earlier manual by Edward L. Cutts, 1849, and (2238); also, the *Illustrated catalogue of the exhibition of English medieval alabaster work held in the rooms of the Society of Antiquaries*, 1913.

2212 —— and Frank E. Howard. *English church woodwork... 1250–1550*. 1927. Also Francis Bond, *Wood carvings in English churches*, 1910, 2 vols.; and [W.H.] Aymer Vallance, *English church screens*, 1936; and (2230, 2263).

2213 Evans, Joan. *The Oxford history of English art*. Vol. V: *English art, 1307–1461*. Oxford, 1949. More generally, O. Elfrida Saunders, *A history of English art in the middle ages*, Oxford, 1932; and Roger S. and Laura H. Loomis, *Arthurian legend in medieval art*, New York, 1938; also, the survey of *English medieval painting*, Cambridge, 1927, by Ernest W. Tristram and Carl T. Borenius, and (2278).

2214 Harrison, Frank L. *Music in medieval Britain*. 1958. More generally, see Gustave Reese, rev. ed., New York, 1959; or Ernest Walker; or Manfred Bukofzer, New York, 1950; also, Hugo Riemann on polyphonic theory, 1962 (2188).

2215 Harvey, John H. *Gothic England, a survey of national culture, 1300–1550*.

1947. Also Francis Bond's survey, 1913, or (2206). And see now James Acland's 1973 survey, *Medieval structure: the gothic vault*.

2216 —— and Arthur Oswald. *English medieval architects, a biographical dictionary down to 1550* ... 1954. See Gee (2298, 2299); and Harvey's more general *The mediaeval architect*, 1972, and *The gothic world, 1100—1600*, 1950; also (2206).

2217 Hughes, Anselm [Henry V.] and Gerald Abraham (eds.). *New Oxford history of music*, III: *Ars nova and the Renaissance 1300—1540*. 1960. Particularly chapters III, IV, VI and IX; also, Hughes's book on polyphony, 1951 (2188).

2218 Martin, Alan R. *Franciscan architecture in England* (British Society of Franciscan Studies, XVIII). Manchester, 1937. See (1630, 2206).

2219 Meyer-Baer, Kathi. *Liturgical music incunabula; a descriptive catalogue*. 1962. And see (2188, 2305).

2220 Pevsner, Nikolaus. *The buildings of England*. 1951—74, 45 vols. Monumental county by county, parish by parish, visual directories for local architecture, sometimes unreliable for ignoring documentary evidence (2189, 2206).

2221 Remnant, George L. *A catalogue of misericords in Great Britain. With an essay on their iconography*, by Mary D. Anderson. Oxford, 1969. See (2230).

2222 Salzmann, Louis F. *Building in England, down to 1540; a documentary history*. 2nd ed., Oxford, 1967. Thorough, somewhat discursive, and rich in detail, with appended sources (2189, 2206).

2223 Saunders, O. Elfrida. *English illumination*. Paris, 1928, 2 vols. Also the important study by Eric G. Millar, *English illuminated manuscripts*, Paris, 1928; Edward M. Thompson's study, 1895; and Reinhold Pauli, *Bilder aus Alt-England [1066—1485]*, Gotha, 1860, English version, Cambridge, 1861. More illuminations in (2205, 2243, 2249, 2280, 2285, 2315, 2331, 2340, 2357, 2365).

3 Monographs

2224 Anderson, Mary D. *Design for a journey*. Cambridge, 1940. Superb study of medieval English church architecture (2206).

2225 —— *Drama and imagery in English medieval churches*. Cambridge, 1964. With a good bibliography; see her *The medieval carver*, Cambridge, 1954; and (2230, 2206).

2226 Bond, Francis. *The chancel of English churches; the altar, reredos, lenten veil, communion table, altar rails, houseling cloth, piscina, credence, sedilia, aumbry, etc.* 1916. Also John C. Cox, *Pulpits, lecterns, and organs in English churches*, 1915, and Percy Dearmer on *Gothic Altars*, Alcuin Club, X, 1910; generally (2189, 2206, 2263).

2227 Bukofzer, Manfred F. *Geschichte des englischen Diskants und des Fauxbourdons nach den theoretischen Quellen. Mit zahlreichen Notenbeispielen*. Strassburg, 1936. And the monograph by Thrasybulos Georgiades, 1937 (2307, 2335, 2377, 2383, 2188).

2228 Caiger-Smith, A. *English medieval mural paintings*. Oxford, 1963. See Charles E. Keyser's lists, 1883; and Edward T. Long, *The Burlington Magazine*, LVI, 1930, pp. 225—32; and (2278).

2229 Cave, Charles J.P. *Roof bosses in medieval churches, an aspect of Gothic sculpture*. Cambridge, 1948. And his similar studies in separate pamphlets for Exeter, Lincoln, and Winchester (2230).

2230 Cescinsky, Herbert and Ernest R. Gribble. *Early English furniture and woodwork*, 1922, 2 vols. Also Harold C. Smith's catalogue, 1929; Frederic G. Roe, *Ancient coffers and cupboards*, 1902, and *Old oak furniture*, 1905. More on woodwork in (2212, 2221, 2225, 2226, 2229, 2233, 2248, 2263, 2284, 2328, 2329, 2375, 2381, 2382).

2231 Chamot, Mary. *English mediaeval enamels* (Monographs on English Mediaeval Art, no. 2). 1930. See (2278).

2232 Christie, A.G.I. *English medieval embroidery.* Oxford, 1938. Also, Betty Kurth, *AntiqJ*, XXIII, 1943, pp. 31–3; also, the Burlington Fine Arts Club, *Exhibition of English embroidery*, 1905; and (2236, 2359).

2233 Colling, James K. *Examples of English mediaeval foliage and coloured decoration.* 1874. See (2230, 2278).

2234 Colvin, Howard M. *The history of the king's works.* 1963, 2 vols. Enormously important, the first two vols. cover 1066–1485, during which the monarch possessed several hundred castles, palaces, fortified houses, and chapels (2189, 2206, 2312).

2235 Crisp, Frank. *Mediaeval gardens, 'flowery medes' and other arrangements of herbs, flowers and shrubs grown in the middle ages, with some account of Tudor, Elizabethan and Stuart gardens,* ed. by Catharine C. Paterson. 1924, 2 vols. See (1414).

2236 Digby, George W. and Wendy Hefford. *The Devonshire hunting tapestries.* 1971. From first half of the fifteenth century with good detail for hunting techniques, also provides list of other surviving tapestries; and (2232, 2359).

2237 Dillon, Harold A.L. and William H. St John Hope (eds.). *Pageant of the birth, life and death of Richard Beauchamp, earl of Warwick, K.G., 1389–1439.* 1914. Or the anonymous ed. for the Roxburghe Club, no. 150, 1908; Beauchamp was born 1382 (2026, 2273).

2238 Gardner, Arthur. *Alabaster tombs of the pre-Reformation period in England.* Cambridge, 1940. More work of alabaster sculpture (2211, 2239, 2297, 2316–21, 2326, 2350, 2351, 2364, 2378, 2379, 2386), on sculpted brass (2245), and generally (2244, 2256, 2261, 2269, 2273, 2325, 2358, 2381).

2239 —— *English medieval sculpture.* Cambridge, 1951, rev. ed. And his original study, written with Edward S. Prior, Cambridge, 1912, on figure-sculpture (2238).

2240 Hobson, Geoffrey D. *English binding before 1500.* Cambridge, 1929. See (2456).

2241 Hope, William H. St John. *The stall plates of the knights of the order of the garter, 1348–1485.* 1901. See (1626).

2242 Lasko, P. and N.J. Morgan. *Medieval art in east Anglia 1300–1520.* Norwich, 1973. See (2238, 2252, 2278); emphasis here is on book and manuscript illumination (2223), but the entire range of artistic work is exhibited.

2243 Little, Andrew G. (ed.). *Franciscan history and legend in English mediaeval art* (British Society of Franciscan Studies, XIX). Manchester, 1937. Essays on glasswork, painting, ms. illumination, and wall painting (1630, 2223, 2251, 2278).

2244 *Medieval catalogue* (London Museum, No. 7). 1954. Splendid, exhaustive collection of archaeological objects including weapons and household items (2238).

2245 *Portfolio of monumental brass society*, vols. I–IV (*c.* 1914) and vol. V, pts. 6–8 (1941–5), 5 vols. in diverse parts. Provides introduction to the variety and detail of sculpted brass likenesses of individuals buried in church tombs, walls, and floors; also, Alfred Hills, in *Essex Review*, XLVII, 1938, pp. 115–20; XLVIII, 1939, pp. 69–78. There are useful monographs for counties, such as: Somerset by Arthur B. Connor, Gloucestershire by C.T. Davis, Cornwall by E.H.W. Dunkin, and Wiltshire by E. Kite. More on sculpted brass (2246, 2294, 2295, 2380, 2387).

2246 Schreiber, Wilhelm L. *Handbuch der Holz- und Metallschnitte des xv. Jahrhunderts.* Stuttgart, 1970, 11 vols. (repr.). Basic reference work, but see also Arthur M. Hinds, *An introduction to a history of the woodcut,* and esp. the books by Campbell Dodgson, Strasbourg, 1934, and 1936; for *Metalwork* generally, see Hanns-Ulrich Haedeke, 1970.

2247 Tristram, Ernest W. *English wall painting of the fourteenth century* (ed. by Eileen Tristram). 1955. Also his monograph, 1944, and James C. Wall's, 1913 (2278).

2248 Varty, Kenneth. *Reynard the fox: a study of the fox in medieval English art.* Leicester, 1967. Thoroughly delightful and scholarly study (2230, 2278).

2249 Wall, Arnold (ed.). *Handbook to the Maude Roll, being a XVth century ms.*

genealogy of the British and English kings from Noah to Edward IV, with a marginal history. Auckland, N.Z., 1919. See (2223).

2250 Wood, Margaret. *The English medieval house.* 1965. Also, Henry A. Tipping's survey, 1920 (2189, 2206).

2251 Woodforde, Christopher. *English stained and painted glass.* Oxford, 1954. Also the monographs by Philip Nelson, 1913; William A. Thorpe, 1949, 2nd ed.; Hugh Arnold, 1939, 2nd ed.; and John D. Le Couteur, 1929. More about glass (2242, 2252, 2270, 2287, 2300, 2301, 2328, 2353, 2362, 2381, 2384, 2392).

2252 —— *The Norwich school of glass-painting in the fifteenth century.* Oxford, 1950. See (2242) and Samuel E. Winbolt on *Wealden glass*, Hove, 1933, and Woodforde's local survey of *Stained glass in Somerset 1250–1830.*

4 Articles

2253 Alcock, N.W. 'The medieval cottages of Bishops Clyst, Devon', *Medieval Archaeology*, IX (1965), 146–53. Includes itemized building costs for a cottage, 1406–70 (2189).

2254 Amphlett, John. 'A Midland architect and his work in the fifteenth century', *Transactions of the Birmingham Archaeological Society*, XXXV (1909), 15–33. See (2206, 2216).

2255 Andrews, Herbert K. and Thurston Dart. 'Fourteenth-century polyphony in a Fountains Abbey ms. book', *Music and Letters*, XXXIX (1958), 1–12, 148–53. See (2188, 2217, 2219).

2256 Bailey, Reginald T. 'The mediaeval Blackburn pax', *Lancs Historic*, LXVIII (1916), 167–76. With a list of others that survive (2324, 2327, 2238).

2257 Baillie, Hugh and Philippe Oboussier. 'The York Masses', *Music and Letters*, XXXV (1954), 19–30. See (2188, 2388).

2258 Barnes, Harold D. and William D. Simpson (eds.). 'The building accounts of Caister Castle (A.D. 1432–1435)', *NA*, XXX (1952), 178–88; *AntiqJ*, XXXII (1952), 35–51. Built by sir John Fastolf and mentioned throughout Paston letters (1011), generally (2189, 2206).

2259 Beaulah, G.K. 'A tile memorial and other medieval tiles at Whalley Abbey', *Lancs Antiq*, XLIX (1933), 95–103. Also, compiler of *Scholastic Arms*, 1936, recording armorials of over 400 schools and colleges; for tiles (2286, 2345).

2260 Bent, Margaret. 'Initial letters in the Old Hall manuscript', *Music and Letters*, XLVII (1966), 225–38; *Early Music*, II (1974), 2–14. And with Andrew Hughes, in *Musica Disciplina*, XXI, 1967, pp. 97–147; see Ramsbotham (2198), and generally (2188).

2261 Binnall, Peter B.G. 'Notes on the medieval altars and chapels in Lincoln Cathedral', *AntiqJ*, XLII (1962), 68–80. See (2238).

2262 Blair, Charles H.H. 'Armorials on English seals from the twelfth to the sixteenth centuries', *Arch*, LXXXIX (1943), 1–26; *ArchAel*, 3rd ser., VI (1910), 89–189, and 4th ser., XII (1935), 277–9. See (335).

2263 Bond, Frederick B. 'Mediaeval screens and rood-lofts', *StPaulS*, n.s., V (1905), 197–220. More about screens and lofts in (2212, 2281, 2282, 2343, 2391), about woodwork (2230) and painting (2278).

2264 Borenius, [Carl] Tancred. 'An English painted ceiling of the late fourteenth-century', *The Burlington Magazine*, LXVIII (1936), 268–76. Church of St Helen, Abingdon, Berkshire (2278).

2265 Bowles, Edmund Q. 'Haut and bas: the grouping of musical instruments in the middle ages', *Musica Disciplina*, VIII (1954), 115–40. French and English usage at court, civic functions, and by wandering minstrels (2347, 2187, 2188).

2266 Brakspear, Harold. 'Burnham Abbey', *Records of Buckinghamshire*, VIII (1903), 517–40. Complete architectural reconstruction in detail (2206).

2267 Bukofzer, Manfred F. 'John Dunstable: a quincentenary report', *The Musical Quarterly*, XL (1954), 29–49, 360–3. See (2190).

2268 —— 'The music of the Old Hall manuscript', *The Musical Quarterly*, XXXIV

(1948), 512—32; XXXV (1949), 36—59, 244—9. See Bent (2260), Ramsbotham (2198).

2269 Butler, L.A.S. 'Medieval cross-slabs in Nottinghamshire', *ThorotonS*, LVI (1952), 25—40. See (2238).

2270 Butterworth, Walter. 'Characteristics of stained glass', *Lancs Antiq*, XLIII (1926), 42—61. Commentary on the technology and science of same (2251).

2271 Carpenter, Nan C. 'The study of music at the university of Oxford in the middle ages [to 1450]', *Journal of Research in Music Education*, I (1953), 11—20; *The Musical Quarterly*, XLI (1955), 191—214. The second article extends the study to 1600, and (2394, 2188).

2272 Charles, Sydney R. 'The provenance and date of the Pepys ms. 1236', *Musica Disciplina*, XVI (1962), 57—71. From Kent in the 1460s.

2273 Chatwin, Philip B. 'The grave of Richard Beauchamp, earl of Warwick [1382—1439], and other burials in the Beauchamp Chapel', *Transactions of the Birmingham Archaeological Society*, LXI (1940), 1—10; *Arch*, LXXVII (1928), 313—34; *Arch*, LXI (1909), 583—614. The second article describes decorations, and the third is by Charles F. Hardy on its music (2237).

2274 Chitty, Herbert. 'Fromond's Chantry at Winchester College', *Arch*, LXXV (1926), 139—58. Built after 1422 and still standing (1955, 2206).

2275 —— and John H. Harvey. 'Thurbern's Chantry at Winchester College', *AntiqJ*, XLII (1962), 208—25. See (1955, 2206).

2276 Clapham, Alfred W. 'Three mediaeval hospitals of London', *StPaulS*, n.s., VII (1911—15), 153—60. See (1481, 1483, 130, 626).

2277 Clay, Charles T. 'The seals of the religious houses of Yorkshire', *Arch*, LXXVIII (1928), 1—36. See (335).

2278 Clemens, J.R. 'Fifteenth-century English recipes for the making of pigments', *Art & Archaeology*, XXXIV (1933), 206—10. From ms. Reginald Rawdon Hastings 417—32 and includes detailed costs for variety of illuminated letters. More on painting in (2213, 2228, 2231, 2233, 2242, 2243, 2247, 2248, 2264, 2288, 2313, 2323, 2341, 2343, 2352, 2366, 2370, 2381, 2389).

2279 Cooper. Ivy M. 'Westminster Hall', *JBAA*, 3rd ser., I (1937), 168—228. With historically reconstructed plans, plus plates and anecdotes (396, 2206, 2280).

2280 Corner, George R. 'Observations of four illuminations representing the courts of chancery, king's bench, common pleas, and exchequer, at Westminster', *Arch*, XXXIX (1863), 357—72. From reign of Henry VI (2223, 127, 158, 255).

2281 Crossley, Frederick H. 'The church screens of Cheshire', *Lancs Historic*, LXIX (1917), 1—63; LXXVI (1924), 1—51; LII (1937), 81—150; XCVII (1945), 59—84. Listed, described, and illustrated for each parish screen, plus detailed descriptions of monumental effigies, timber roofs, and stallworks (2230, 2263).

2282 —— and Maurice H. Ridgway. 'An introduction to the study of screens and lofts in Wales and Monmouthshire with especial reference to their design, provenance, and influence', *ArchCamb*, XCVII (1943), 135—60; XCVIII (1945), 64—112, 153—98; XCIX (1947), 1—56, 179—230; C (1949), 207—52; CII (1953), 48—82; CVI (1957), 9—45; CVII (1958), 72—108; CVIII (1959), 14—71; CXI (1962), 59—102. Mainly fifteenth century, with excellent glossary, attempting to catalogue all known examples of medieval woodwork in Wales (2230, 2263, 97).

2283 Crossley-Holland, Peter. 'Secular homophonic music in Wales in the middle ages', *Music and Letters*, XXIII (1942), 135—62. See (2188, 97).

2284 Druce, George C. 'The stall carvings in the church of St Mary of Charity, Faversham', *ArchCant*, L (1939), 11—32. Superb examples of fifteenth-century misericords, with a discussion of animal figures and various symbols (2499, 2230, 2278).

2285 Durrieu, Paul, 'Les souvenirs historiques dans les manuscrits à miniatures de la domination anglaise en France au temps de Jeanne d'Arc', *Annuaire-Bulletin de la Société de l'histoire de France* (1905), 111—35. See (2223, 911).

2286   Eames, Elizabeth. 'The Canynges pavement', *JBAA*, 3rd ser., XIV (1951), 33—46. Fifteenth-century paving and tiling designs (2259).

2287   Eeles, Francis C. 'Fifteenth-century stained glass at Clavering', *EssexT*, n.s., XVI (1923), 77—87. And see (2251).

2288   Fletcher, John. 'Tree ring dates for some panel paintings in England', *The Burlington Magazine*, CXVI (1974), 250—8. And see (2278).

2289   Flood, William H.G. 'The beginnings of the Chapel Royal', *Music and Letters*, V (1924), 85—90. See (2200, 2420, 2188).

2290   —— 'The English Chapel Royal under Henry V and Henry VI', *Sammelbände der internationalen Musikgesellschaft*, X (1909), 563—7; XV (1914), 64—7. And its master, Gilbert Banaster 1478—90, plus notes on the minstrel gild.

2291   —— 'Entries relating to music in the patent rolls of the fifteenth-century', *The Musical Antiquary*, IV (1913), 225. See (2188, 149).

2292   Floyer, John K. 'English brick buildings of the fifteenth century', *AJ*, LXX (1913), 121—32. See (2189).

2293   Forrest, Herbert E. 'Old timber-framed houses (especially in Essex). Principles of construction', *Essex Review*, XXXV (1926), 14—29. See (2189).

2294   Fryer, Alfred C. 'Monumental effigies made by Bristol craftsmen (1240—1550)', *Arch*, LXXIV (1925), 1—72. Extensive catalogue and photographs of monuments (2245).

2295   Gadd, Margaret L. 'English monumental brasses of the fifteenth and early sixteenth centuries; with special reference *a*) to the process of their manufacture and *b*) to their distribution', *JBAA*, 3rd ser., II (1937), 17—46. See (2245).

2296   Gardiner, Dorothy. 'Some notes on petitions concerning Canterbury monastic houses in the court of chancery', *ArchCant*, XLIII (1931), 199—214; LI (1940), 108—12. See (127, 1866, 2189).

2297   Gardner, Arthur. 'Hair and head-dress 1050—1600', *JBAA*, 3rd ser., XIII (1950), 4—13; *Arch*, LXVII (1916), 163—88. Diverse photographs of statuary; and (1089, 2207, 2238).

2298   Gee, Eric A. 'Oxford carpenters, 1370—1530', *Oxoniensia*, XVII (1954), 112—84. See (1337, 2189, 2230, 2263).

2299   —— 'Oxford masons, 1370—1530', *AJ*, CIX (1952), 54—131. Biographical directory to the men and their buildings (1353, 2189, 2311, 2371).

2300   Gill, Harry. 'The church windows of Nottinghamshire', *ThorotonS*, XX (1916), 93—124; XXI (1917), 1—46. Listed and analysed in detail, similarly for porches and doorways (2251).

2301   Green, Mary A. 'Old painted glass in Worcestershire', *Transactions of the Worcestershire Archaeological Society*, n.s., XI (1934), 33—63; XII (1935), 42—55; XIII (1936), 1—10; XIV (1937), 1—17; XV (1938), 10—26. See (2251).

2302   Greene, Richard L. 'Two medieval musical manuscripts: Egerton 3307 and some University of Chicago fragments', *Journal of the American Musicological Society*, VII (1954), 1—34. See (2188).

2303   Hamilton Thompson, Alexander. 'Building accounts of Kirby Muxloe Castle, 1480—1484', *Transactions of the Leicestershire Archaeological Society*, XI (1915), 193—292. See (2189).

2304   —— 'Cathedral builders of the middle ages', *History*, n.s., X (1926), 139—150; *SomersetP*, LXVI (1920), 1—25. Emphasis on the important value of fabric rolls (2189, 2206).

2305   Hamm, Charles. 'A catalogue of anonymous English music in fifteenth-century continental manuscripts', *Musica Disciplina*, XXII (1968), 47—76. See (2219, 2188).

2306   Harrison, Frank L. 'Ars nova in England: a new source', *Musica Disciplina*, XXI (1967), 67—85. See (2188, 2217).

2307   —— 'Faburden in practice', *Musica Disciplina*, XVI (1962), 11—34. Fifteenth-century vocal music (2187, 2188, 2227).

2308   Harvey, John H. 'The architects of English parish churches', *AJ*, CV (1948), 14–26. Listed for 1270–1545, indicates great activity in fifteenth century church construction (2206, 2216).

2309   —— 'Great Milton, Oxfordshire; and Thorncroft, Surrey: the building accounts for two manor-houses of the late fifteenth century [1474–77, 1497]', *JBAA*, 3rd ser., XVIII (1955), 42–56. See (2189, 2206).

2310   —— 'Henry Yevele reconsidered', *AJ*, CVIII (1951), 100–8; *ArchCant*, LVI (1943), 48–53. Details his properties in London, 1361–1400, see his biography of Yevele, 2nd ed., 1946; and (2206).

2311   —— 'The masons of Westminster Abbey', *AJ*, CXIII (1956), 82–101. See (2299, 2189, 1740, 1353).

2312   —— 'The medieval office of works', *JBAA*, 3rd ser., VI (1941), 20–87. See (2189, 2234).

2313   —— 'The Wilton diptych – a re-examination', *Arch*, XCVIII (1961), 1–28. Argues that it was Richard II's creation, 1394–5, symbolizing the rededication of royal prerogative to God's will; reviews entire controversy, begun by William Constable, *The Burlington Magazine*, LV, 1929, pp. 36–45; Martin Conway, *ibid.*, pp. 209–12; Maude V. Clarke, *ibid.*, LVIII, 1931, pp. 283–94; Joan Evans, *AJ*, CV, 1948, pp. 1–5; Ernest W. Tristram, *The Month*, n.s., I, 1949, pp. 379–90, II, 1949, pp. 18–36, and III, 1950, pp. 234–8; Margaret Galway, *AJ*, CVII, 1950, pp. 9–14; Francis Wormald, *Journal of the Warburg and Courtauld Institutes*, XVII, 1954, pp. 191–203; and generally (2278).

2314   —— 'Winchester College', *JBAA*, 3rd ser., XXVIII (1965), 107–28. Built after 1387 (2206).

2315   Higgins, A. 'An illuminated and emblazoned copy of the statutes from Edward III to Henry VI, illustrating the genealogy of the family of Fitzwilliam of Mablethorpe, Lincs. [*c.* 1460]', *Arch*, LVII (1900), 1–10. See (2223, 280).

2316   Hildburgh, Walter L. 'English alabaster carvings as records of the medieval religious dramas', *Arch*, XCIII (1949), 51–101. Extensive illustrations, mostly fifteenth-century work (2238).

2317   —— 'A group of medieval English alabaster carvings at Nantes', *JBAA*, 3rd ser., XI (1948), 1–12.

2318   —— 'Medieval English alabaster figures of the Virgin and Child', *The Burlington Magazine*, LXXXVIII (1946), 30–5, 63–6; LXXXIX (1947), 129–31; XCVII (1955), 338–42.

2319   —— 'Notes on some English medieval alabaster carvings', *AntiqJ*, III (1923), 24–36; IV (1924), 374–81; VI (1926), 304–7; VIII (1928), 54–68; X (1930), 34–45; XVII (1937), 181–91; XXIV (1944), 27–37; XXXV (1955), 182–6.

2320   —— 'Some English alabaster tables', *Proceedings of the Society of Antiquaries of London*, 2nd ser., XXXII (1920), 117–29; XXVIII (1916), 63–8; XXXI (1919), 57–63.

2321   —— 'Studies in medieval English alabaster carvings', *JBAA*, 3rd ser., XVII (1954), 11–23; XIX (1956), 14–19. See (2238).

2322   Hogg, Alexander H.A. and David J.C. King. 'Masonry castles in Wales and the Marches', *ArchCamb*, CXVI (1967), 71–132. Extensive catalogue for fourteenth and fifteenth centuries (1595, 2372–4, 97).

2323   Hollaender, Albert E.J. 'The doom-painting of St Thomas of Canterbury, Salisbury [*c.* 1480]', *WiltsMag*, L (1944), 351–70. See (2278).

2324   Hope, William H. St John. 'English medieval chalices and patens', *StPaulS*, n.s., II (1890), 81–100. Includes photographs and list of known items (2256, 2327).

2325   —— 'The funeral monument, and chantry chapel of Henry V', *Arch*, LXV (1914), 129–86. See (689, 1955, 2238).

2326   —— 'On the early working of alabaster in England', *AJ*, LXI (1904), 221–40. See (2238).

2327   —— 'On the English medieval drinking bowls called mazers', *Arch*, L (1887), 129–93. See (2256, 2324).

2328   Hudson, Henry A. 'The ancient glass of the cathedral church of Manchester',

Lancs Antiq, XXV (1907), 119–45; XXXVI (1918), 1–31. Also, E.F. Letts in *ibid.*, IV, 1886, pp. 130–44; and Hudson's *The mediaeval woodwork of Manchester Cathedral*, 1924; and (2251, 2230).

2329 —— 'The mediaeval roofs of Manchester Cathedral', *Lancs Historic*, LXXII (1920), 1–17; LXXIII (1921), 100–26; LXXIV (1922), 83–90. With descriptions of wood screens and carved musical instruments (2230, 2263).

2330 Hughes, Andrew. 'Mensural polyphony for choir in fifteenth-century England', *Journal of the American Musicological Society*, XIX (1966), 352–69. And see (2188).

2331 Hunter, Michael. 'The facsimiles in Thomas Elmham's History of St Augustine's, Canterbury', *Library*, 5th ser., XXVIII (1973), 215–20.

2332 Jacob, Ernest F. 'The building of All Soul's College, 1438–1443', in John G. Edwards, Vivian H. Galbraith, and Ernest F. Jacob (eds.), *Historical essays in honour of James Tait*. Manchester, 1933, pp. 121–35. See (2189, 2394).

2333 Jope, Edward M. 'Cornish houses, 1400–1700', in Edward M. Jope (ed.). *Studies in building history: essays in recognition of the work of Bryan H. St John O'Neil*. 1961, pp. 192–222. See (2189, 2206).

2334 Kenny, Sylvia W. 'Contrafacta in the works of Walter Frye', *Journal of the American Musicological Society*, VIII (1955), 182–202. See (2188).

2335 —— ' "English discant" and discant in England', *The Musical Quarterly*, XLV (1959), 26–48. And E.H. Salter, *Musica Disciplina*, XIX, 1965, pp. 7–52 (2227, 2187).

2336 Kingsford, Charles L. 'A London merchant's house and its owners, 1360–1614', *Arch*, LXXIV (1925), 137–58. With floor plan, 1463 (2189, 2206, 1481, 1484).

2337 —— 'Historical notes on mediaeval London houses', *London Topographical Record*, X (1916), 44–144; XI (1917), 28–81; XII (1920), 1–66. Individual buildings listed and described by name (2189, 2206, 130).

2338 Kingsford, Hugh S. 'The epigraphy of medieval English seals', *Arch*, LXXIX (1929), 149–78. Meticulous guide to lettering styles, 1072–1500 (335).

2339 —— 'Some English medieval seal-engravers [1200–1485]', *AJ*, XCVII (1941), 155–79. See (335).

2340 Kuhn, Charles L. 'Herman Scheere and English illumination of the early fifteenth century', *Art Bulletin*, XXII (1940), 138–56. See (2223).

2341 Lethaby, William R. 'The Westminster portrait of Richard II', *The Burlington Magazine*, LXV (1934), 220–22. See John G. Noppen in *ibid.*, LX, 1932, pp. 82–7, and Harvey (2313), and (692, 813); for painting (2278).

2342 Levy, Kenneth J. 'New material on the early motet in England: a report on Princeton ms. Garrett 119', *Journal of the American Musicological Society*, IV (1951), 220–31. See (2188).

2343 Long, Edward T. 'Screen paintings in Devon and East Anglia', *The Burlington Magazine*, LIX (1931), 169–76; LVI (1930), 223–32. And W.W. Lillie, in *JBAA*, 3rd ser., IX, 1944, pp. 33–47; and (2230, 2263, 2278).

2344 Mann, James G. 'Four lectures on medieval armour', *JBAA*, 3rd ser., III (1938), 171–8. Extensive bibliography appended (1528).

2345 Martin, Robert H. 'Medieval tiles in Worcestershire', *Transactions of the Worcestershire Archaeological Society*, n.s. X (1933), 33–42; and, *ThorotonS*, LIX (1955), 84–97. See (2259, 2286).

2346 Meech, Sanford B. 'Three fifteenth-century English musical treatises', *Speculum*, X (1935), 235–69. See (2188).

2347 Montgomery, Franz. 'The musical instruments in *The Canterbury Tales*', *The Musical Quarterly*, XVII (1931), 439–48. See (2265, 2187, 2188).

2348 Müller, Hermann. 'Der Musiktrakt in dem Werke des Bartholomaeus Anglicus De proprietatibus rerum', in *Riemann-Festschrift; gesammelte Studien*. Leipzig, 1909, pp. 241 ff. See (2188, 1458).

2349 Myres, John N.L. 'Recent discoveries in the Bodleian Library', *Arch*, CI (1967), 151–68. Concerning the original fifteenth-century construction work (2189, 2332, 2394).

2350 Nelson, Philip. 'Ancient alabasters at Lydiate', *Lancs Historic*, LXVII (1915),

21—6. And Edward Powell, *ibid.*, XLVI, 1894, pp. 157—74 on the same topic; the numerous articles and notes by Nelson on English alabaster can be found in *AJ* between 1914 and 1927; and (2238).

2351 —— 'Some unusual English alabaster panels', *Lancs Historic*, LXIX (1917), 80—90; LXXI (1919), 85—8; LXXII (1920), 50—60; LXXIII (1921), 149—52; LXXIV (1922), 128—31; LXXV (1923), 208—12. See (2238).

2352 Noppen, John G. 'The Westminster apocalypse and its source', *The Burlington Magazine*, LXI (1932), 146—59. In Chapter House, begun between 1394 and 1400 (1740, 2278).

2353 Oldfield, Edmund. 'On the portraits of Edward, prince of Wales (afterwards Edward V) and his sisters in the east window of Little Malvern Church, Worcestershire', *AJ*, XXII (1865), 302—25. See John A. Knowles, *AntiqJ*, XXXIX, 1959, pp. 274—82 (2251); and L.A. Hamand's description of the windows, St Albans, 1947.

2354 Pantin, William A. 'Medieval English town-house plans', *Medieval Archaeology*, VII (1963), 202—39, 173—81. The second article describes houses in King's Lynn (2189, 2206).

2355 —— 'Medieval inns', in Edward M. Jope (ed.), *Studies in building history; essays in recognition of the work of Bryan H. St John O'Neil*. 1961, pp. 166—91.

2356 —— 'Medieval priests' houses in south-west England', *Medieval Archaeology*, I (1957), 118—46; III (1959), 216—58. Numerous floor plans and designs (2189, 2206).

2357 Piper, Edwin F. 'The miniatures of the Ellesmere Chaucer', *Philological Quarterly*, III (1924), 241—56. See (2223).

2358 Radford, (Mrs). G.H. [Cecily]. 'The Courtenay monument, in Colyton Church', *DevonA*, XXXIX (1907), 144—55; LIII (1921), 216—25; LXVII (1936), 291—8. See (2238).

2359 Read, Charles H. 'On a panel of tapestry of about the year 1400 and probably of English origin', *Arch*, LXVIII (1917), 35—42. See (2232, 2236).

2360 Reaney, Gilbert. 'The *Breviarium regulare musice* of ms Oxford, Bodley 842', *Musica Disciplina*, XI (1957), 31—7; IX (1955), 73—104. The second article describes a ms. of mainly French music (2188).

2361 —— 'Some little-known sources of medieval polyphony in England', *Musica Disciplina*, XV (1961), 15—26. See (2188, 2204).

2362 Ridgway, Maurice H. 'Coloured window glass in Cheshire [to 1500]', *Lancs Antiq*, LIX (1947), 41—84; LX (1948), 56—85. See (2251).

2363 Rigold, Stuart E. 'Two types of court hall', *ArchCant*, LXXXIII (1968), 1—22. Canterbury Guildhall and Milton Regis Court Hall, both *c.* 1450 (2206).

2364 Rostand, André. 'Les albâtres anglais du XVe siècle en Basse-Normandie', *Bulletin Monumental*, LXXXVII (1928), 257—309; XCII (1933), 230—1. See (2238).

2365 Rowe, Benedicta J.H. 'Notes on the Clovis miniature and the Bedford Book of Hours', *JBAA*, 3rd ser., XXV (1962), 56—65. And Eleanor P. Spencer, *The Burlington Magazine*, CVIII, 1966, pp. 607—12 (2223).

2366 Rushforth, Gordon M. 'Seven sacraments compositions in English medieval art', *AntiqJ*, IX (1929), 83—100. See (2278).

2367 Russell, Janet. 'English medieval leatherwork', *AJ*, XCVI (1939), 132—41. Numerous illustrations and examples.

2368 Salter, Herbert E. 'An Oxford hall in 1424', in Henry W.C. Davis (ed.), *Essays in history presented to Reginald L. Poole*. Oxford, 1927, pp. 421—35. See (2206, 2332, 2394).

2369 Schmidt, Gerhard. 'Two unknown English *Horae* from the fifteenth century', *The Burlington Magazine*, CIII (1961), 47—54.

2370 Shaw, William A. 'The early English school of portraiture', *The Burlington Magazine*, LXV (1934), 171—84. Fifteenth-century (pre-Holbein) portraits and their painters; see similar article by him in *Connoisseur*, XXXI, 1911, pp. 72—81; and (2278, 2288).

2371 Shelby, Lon R. 'The role of the master mason in mediaeval English building', *Speculum*, XXXIX (1964), 387—403. See (2299, 2311, 2189).

2372 Simpson, William D. 'The affinities of Lord Cromwell's tower-house at Tattershall', *JBAA*, n.s., XL (1935), 177–92. See (2201, 1595, 2322, 762, 2189).

2373 —— 'Buckden Palace', *JBAA*, 3rd ser., II (1937), 121–32.

2374 —— 'The castles of Dudley and Ashby-de-la-Zouch', *AJ*, XCVI (1939), 142–58. See (1595, 2206).

2375 Smith, John T. 'Medieval roofs: a classification', *AJ*, CXV (1958), 111–49; CXXII (1965), 133–58. Mainly fifteenth-century variations, with maps of their geographical distribution, and the second article similarly examines timber-framed buildings (2208); generally (2329, 2230, 2189).

2376 Squire, William B. 'Notes on an undescribed collection of English fifteenth-century music', *Sammelbände der internationalen Musikgesellschaft*, II (1901), 342–92. At St Edmund's College, Ware, Hertfordshire (2188).

2377 Stevens, Denis. 'Processional psalms in Faburden', *Musica Disciplina*, IX (1955), 105–10. See (2227, 2307, 2335, 2383, 2188).

2378 Tavender, Augusta S. 'Medieval English alabasters in American museums', *Speculum*, XXX (1955), 64–71; XXXIV (1959), 437–9. See (2238).

2379 —— 'Three mediaeval English alabasters in French churches', *Speculum*, XXIV (1949), 397–402. See William H. Stevenson, *ThorotonS*, XI, 1907, pp. 89–98 (2238).

2380 Thacker, Francis J., Ettwell A.B. Barnard and J.F. Parker, 'The monumental brasses of Worcestershire', *Transactions of the Worcestershire Archaeological Society*, n.s., III (1925–6), 107–27; IV (1926–7), 129–56; XI (1934), 139–43; XV (1938), 1–9. See (2245).

2381 Thompson, Daniel V., Jr. 'Trial index to some unpublished sources for the history of mediaeval craftsmanship', *Speculum*, X (1935), 410–31. With a word-list of the materials of art-technology (2230, 2238, 2251, 2278).

2382 Tolhurst, John B.L. 'The hammer-beam figures of the nave roof of St Mary's Church, Bury St Edmunds', *JBAA*, 3rd ser., XXV (1962), 66–70. See (2230).

2383 Trowell, Brian. 'Faburden and fauxbourdon', *Musica Disciplina*, XIII (1959), 43–78. See (2227).

2384 Truman, Nevil. 'Ancient glass in Nottinghamshire', *ThorotonS*, XXIX (1935), 92–118; XLIII (1939), 27–32; LI (1947), 50–65; LII (1948), 58–68. See (2251).

2385 Turner, Edmund. 'Description of an ancient castle at Rouen in Normandy, called Le Château du Vieux Palais, built by Henry V., king of England', *Arch*, VII (1785), 232–5. See (1595, 2322, 689).

2386 Vesly, Léon de. 'Les albâtres anglais du XVe siècle au Musée de Rouen', *Bulletin archéologique. Comité des travaux historiques et scientifiques* (1919), 48–52. See (2238).

2387 Wagner, Anthony R. and James G. Mann. 'A fifteenth-century description of the brass of sir Hugh Hastings at Elsing, Norfolk', *AntiqJ*, XIX (1939), 421–8. See (2245).

2388 Wall, Carolyn. 'York Pageant XLVI and its music', *Speculum*, XLVI (1971), 689–712. See (2188, 2257).

2389 Williams, Ethel C. 'Mural paintings of the Three Living and the Three Dead in England (*circa* 1400)', *JBAA*, 3rd ser., VII (1942), 31–40; XII (1949), 19–36; XIX (1956), 20–33. And diverse murals of St George and of St Catherine in England (2278).

2390 Wolf, Johannes. 'Early English musical theorists', *The Musical Quarterly*, XXV (1939), 420–9. Particularly John Hothby, a fifteenth-century English musician in northern Italy, died 1487 after recall by Henry VII (2188).

2391 Wolfgang, A. 'Ancient screens in Cheshire and Lancashire churches', *Lancs Historic*, LXIII (1911), 79–87; LXIV (1912), 20–42. See (2230, 2263, 2278).

2392 Woodforde, Christopher. 'The medieval stained glass in East Harling and North Tuddenham churches, Norfolk', *JBAA*, 3rd ser., III (1938), 1–63; IV (1939), 193–6; V (1940), 1–32. And at Long Melford, Suffolk (2251).

2393 Woodruff, Charles E. 'The rebuilding of the south-west tower of Canterbury

Cathedral in the fifteenth century', *ArchCant*, XLV (1933), 37–47. See (2189, 1866).

XIV. INTELLECTUAL HISTORY

1 Printed sources

2394 Anstey, Henry (ed.). *Epistolae academicae Oxon.: Registrum F. A collection of letters and other documents illustrative of academical life and studies at Oxford in the fifteenth century* (Oxford Historical Society, XXXV, XXXVI). 1898, 2 vols. More about Oxford university in (2070, 2103, 2271, 2332, 2395, 2399, 2410, 2427, 2432, 2437–41, 2443, 2448, 2458, 2477, 2492), about Cambridge and others (1475, 2457).

2395 —— (ed.). *Munimenta academica, or documents illustrative of academical life and studies at Oxford* (Rolls Series, L). 1868, 2 vols. Includes acts of the chancellor's court, a catalogue of the library of Duke Humphrey of Gloucester, and a register of convocation (724, 2394).

2396 Banks, Mary M. (ed.). *An alphabet of tales: an English 15th-century translation of the Alphabetum narrationum of Etienne de Besançon* (EETS, CXXVI, CXXVII). 1904–5, 2 vols.

2397 Baxter, James H., Charles Johnson and James F. Willard (eds.). 'An index of British and Irish Latin writers, 400–1520', *Bulletin Du Cange*, VII (1932), 110–219 (repr. separately 1972). See (41, 2474, 2475, 1, 877).

2398 Blakiston, Herbert E.D. (ed.). 'Some Durham college rolls [1315–1542]', *Collectanea III* (Oxford Historical Society, XXXII). 1896, pp. 1–76. See (1692).

2399 Boase, Charles W. and Andrew Clark (eds.). *Register of the university of Oxford*. Oxford, 1885–9, 2 vols. in 5 pts. See (2394).

2400 Borsa, Mario (ed.). 'Correspondence of Humphrey, duke of Gloucester and Pier Candido Decembrio', *EHR*, XIX (1904), 509–26. And W.L. Newman in *EHR*, XX, 1905, pp. 484–98; Decembrio was Humphrey's book agent in Italy, twenty letters; also Mandell Creighton's ed. of letters with Piero del Monte and Alfonso V of Aragon, in *EHR*, X, 1895, pp. 99–104; B.L. Ullman in *EHR*, LII, 1937, pp. 670–2; see (724, 2444, 2469).

2401 Bowers, Robert H. (ed.). 'A middle English treatise on hermeneutics: Harley ms. 2276, 32^V·–35^V·', *Proceedings of the Modern Language Association*, LXV (1950), 590–600.

2402 Brentano, Robert (ed.). 'The *Jurisdictio spiritualis*: an example of fifteenth-century English historiography', *Speculum*, XXXII (1957), 326–32.

2403 Brown, Carleton F. and Rossell H. Robbins (eds.). *The index of middle English verse*. New York, 1943. And see (20, 46, 54, 2453).

2404 Chambers, Raymond W. and Beatrice M. Daunt (eds.). *A book of London English, 1384–1425*. Oxford, 1931. And Basil Cottle, *The triumph of English 1350–1400*, 1969; the major linguistic students of Middle English syntax are Karl Brunner, Fredericus T. Visser, and Tauno F. Mustanoja (46, 54).

2405 Chitty, Herbert and Ernest F. Jacob (eds.). 'Some Winchester College muniments [1389–1390]', *EHR*, XLIX (1934), 1–13. See (2461); the standard college history is by Arthur F. Leach, 1899.

2406 Corrie, George E. (ed.). 'A catalogue of the books which were given to the library and chapel of St Catherine's Hall, Cambridge, by Dr Woodlark, the founder of the college [1475]', *Cambridge Antiquarian Society, Quarto Publications*, I, no. I (1840), 1–11. And (2419).

2407 De Boüard, Michel (ed.). 'Quelques données nouvelles sur la création de l'Université de Caen (1432–1436)', *Le Moyen Âge*, LXIX (1963), 727–41. Founded by Henry VI (2457).

2408 D'Evelyn, Charlotte (ed.). *Peter Idley's Instructions to his son [1445–50]*. Boston, 1935. See (998, 1031).

2409 Gabriel, Astrik L. and Gray C. Boyce (eds.). *Auctarium chartularii univer-*

sitatis Parisiensis, VI, *Liber receptorum nationis Anglicanae (Alemanniae) 1425–1494*. Paris, 1964. See (93, 2457).

2410 Gibson, Strickland (ed.). *Statuta antiqua universitatis Oxoniensis.* Oxford, 1931. See (2394).

2411 Halliwell, James O. (ed.). 'A catalogue of the books bequeathed to Corpus Christi College, Cambridge (A.D. 1439), by Thomas Markaunt, with their prices', *Cambridge Antiquarian Society, Quarto Publications,* II, *Miscellanea III* (1847), 15–20. See (2419).

2412 Hamilton Thompson, Alexander (ed.). 'Catalogue of the library of Leicester Abbey', *Transactions of the Leicestershire Archaeological Society,* XIX (1936–7), 111–61, 377–440; XXI (1941), 1–88.

2413 Hearne, Thomas (ed.). *J. Lelandi antiquarii de rebus Britanicis collectanea.* Oxford, 1715, 6 vols. This, and his better known *Itineraries,* ed. by Lucy T. Smith, 1906–10, 6 vols., provides a reporter's glimpse of everything from topography to library lists, admittedly, viewed from the 1530s; also (17, 2419).

2414 Herbert, John A. (ed.). *The Sherborne missal [inter 1396 et 1407]* (Roxburghe Club, 176). 1920. See (2101, 1642).

2415 Herrtage, Sidney J.H. (ed.). *Catholicon Anglicum, an English–Latin wordbook, dated 1483* (EETS, XLIX). 1881. Also published by Camden Society, n.s., XXX, 1882; and see (2428).

2416 Heywood, James (ed.). *Early Cambridge university and college statutes in the English language.* 1855. See (2457).

2417 —— and Thomas Wright (eds.). *The ancient laws of the fifteenth century for King's College, Cambridge, and for the public school of Eton College.* 1850. See (2455, 2457, 2461).

2418 Hibbard, Laura A. (ed.). 'The books of sir Simon de Burley, 1387', *Modern Language Notes,* XXX (1915), 169–71. See (2469).

2419 James, Montague R. (ed.). *The ancient libraries of Canterbury and Dover.* Cambridge, 1903. Also ed. of separate ms. lists for various Cambridge college libraries. More about books (2469) and libraries (2035, 2406, 2411–13, 2434, 2445–7, 2467, 2468, 2473, 2495, 2497, 2498).

2420 Johnson, Charles (ed.). 'John Plummer, master of the children', *AntiqJ*, I (1921), 52–3. The Royal Chapel, 1451; edits royal privy seal grant of 40 marks to maintain 8 choral scholars, and (2289).

2421 Leach, Arthur F. (ed.). *Documents illustrating early education in Worcester 685 to 1700* (Worcestershire Historical Society). 1913. Mainly extensive excerpts from monastic obedientiary accounts (2461, 1605).

2422 —— (ed.). *Early Yorkshire schools* (YorksRS, XXVII, XXXIII). 1899–1903, 2 vols.

2423 —— (ed.). *Educational charters and documents.* Cambridge, 1911. See (2461).

2424 Leathes, Stanley M. (ed.). *Grace Book A, containing the proctors' accounts and other records of the University of Cambridge for the years 1454–1488.* Cambridge, 1897. Mary Bateson edited Book B, 1488–1544, in 2 parts, 1903–1905; and (2457).

2425 Leggatt, N.J.S. (ed.). '*The Book of St Albans* and the origins of its treatise on hawking [B.M., Bibl. Sloane, 3488, xviii. F.]', *Studia Neophilologica,* XXII (1950), 135–45. See Rachel Hands, *Review of English Studies,* n.s., XVIII, 1967, pp. 373–86, with regard to Juliana Berners (1104).

2426 Lyell, Laetitia (ed.). *A mediaeval post-bag.* 1934. Letters from diverse fifteenth-century families

2427 Macray, William D. (ed.). *A register of the members of St. Mary Magdalen College, Oxford,* I. *Fellows to the year 1520.* 1894. See (2394).

2428 Mayhew, Anthony L. (ed.). *The promptorium parvulorum: the first English–Latin dictionary* (EETS, e.s., CII). 1908. Or the ed. by Albert Way *et alii* for Camden Society, XXV, LIV, LXXXIX, 1843–65, 3 vols. (2415).

2429 Meech, Sanford B. (ed.). 'A collection of proverbs in Rawlinson ms. D 328', *Modern Philology,* XXXVIII (1940), 113–52. From Edward IV's reign, with detailed commentary (687).

2430 —— (ed.). 'An early treatise in English concerning Latin grammar', *The*

University of Michigan, Language and Literature, XIII (1935), 81–125. See (2471).

2431 Nelson, William (ed.). *A fifteenth-century school book*. Oxford, 1956. See (2461, 2488).

2432 Pantin, William A. (ed.). *Canterbury College Oxford* (Oxford Historical Society, n.s., VI–VIII). 1947–50, 3 vols. College accounts 1379–1520, and diverse statutes and administrative records (2394).

2433 Pearce, E.C. (ed.). 'College accounts of John Botwright, master of Corpus Christi, 1443–74', *Proceedings of the Cambridge Antiquarian Society*, XXII (1918), 76–90. See (2457).

2434 [Raine, James (the elder)] (ed.). *Catalogues of the library of Durham Cathedral at various periods from the Conquest to the Dissolution* (Surtees Society, VII). 1838. Especially the 1391–5 and the 1416 catalogues (1692, 2419).

2435 Rickert, Edith (ed.). 'King Richard II's books', *Library*, 4th ser., XIII (1932), 144–7. See (692, 2469).

2436 Robbins, Rossell H. (ed.). 'The fraternity of drinkers', *Studies in Philology*, XLVII (1950), 36–41. Dedicated to fifteenth-century professional tipplers.

2437 Salter, Herbert E. (ed.). *Medieval archives of the university of Oxford* (Oxford Historical Society, LXX, LXXIII). 1920–1, 2 vols. See (2394).

2438 —— *Registrum cancellarii Oxoniensis, 1434–1469* (Oxford Historical Society, XCIII, XCIV). 1932, 2 vols.

2439 —— and G.C. Richards (eds.). *The dean's register of Oriel, 1446–1661* (Oxford Historical Society, LXXXIV). 1926.

2440 —— and Charles L. Shadwell (eds.). *Oriel College records* (Oxford Historical Society, LXXXV). 1926. Particularly property muniments; for cartulary of Christ Church college, see Noel Denholm-Young, *Oxford Historical Society*, XCII, 1931; and (2394).

2441 Shadwell, Charles L. (ed.). 'The catalogue of the library of Oriel College . . . [1375]', *Collectanea I* (Oxford Historical Society, V). 1885, pp. 57–70.

2442 Sterry, Wasey (ed.). *The Eton College register, 1441–1698*. Eton, 1943. The standard history of the college is by H.C. Maxwell Lyte, 1899, 3rd ed.; and (2461).

2443 Tait, James (ed.). 'Letters of John Tiptoft, earl of Worcester, and archbishop Neville to the university of Oxford', *EHR*, XXXV (1920), 570–4. See (2394).

2444 Weiss, Roberto (ed.). 'New light on humanism in England during the 15th century', *Journal of the Warburg & Courtauld Institutes*, XIV (1951), 21–33. Literary correspondence of Humphrey, duke of Gloucester (724, 2400); more about English humanism (1060, 2445, 2459, 2466, 2481, 2494).

2445 —— (ed.). 'Piero del Monte, John Whethamstede, and the library of St Albans Abbey', *EHR*, LX (1945), 399–406. Also, *Piero del Monte: ein Gelehrter und päpstlicher Beamter des xv. Jahrhunderts: seine Briefsammlung* (Bibliothek des deutschen historischen Instituts in Rom, Band XXIX), 1941; and (2073, 2419).

2446 Williams, Thomas W. (ed.). *Somerset mediaeval libraries . . . prior to the dissolution of the monasteries*. Bristol, 1897. See (1935, 2419).

2447 Wilson, Richard M. (ed.). 'The medieval library of Titchfield Abbey [listed in 1400]', *LeedsS*, V (1943), 150–77, 252–76. See (2419).

2448 Wordsworth, Christopher (ed.). *The ancient kalendar of the University of Oxford* (Oxford Historical Society, XLV). 1904. See (2394).

2449 Worth, Richard N. (ed.). ' "William of Worcester" Devon's earliest [died 1484?] topographer', *DevonA*, XVIII (1886), 462–87. See Harvey's ed. (1013).

2450 Wright, Thomas (ed.). *De regimine principium, a poem, by Thomas Occleve, written in the reign of Henry IV* (Roxburghe Club, 79). 1860. See (595, 688, 1051).

2451 Wright, William (ed.). *Femina* (Roxburghe Club, 152). 1909. Treatise for instructing English children in French, see (2496).

2 Monographs

2452   Bennett, Henry S. *English books and readers 1475–1557*. Cambridge, 1952. Focussed on Tudor era, so read Wormald (2467); also (2469).

2453   Chambers, Edmund K. *English literature at the close of the middle ages*. Oxford, 1947, 2nd ed. corrected. See (2, 20, 46, 54, 1631, 2403).

2454   —— *The medieval stage*. Oxford, 1903, 2 vols. Fundamental reference work, and see Glynne Wickham's study, 1959; the most recent revisionist is Alan H. Nelson, *The medieval English stage*. 1974; and (2192, 2194).

2455   Cobban, Alan B. *The King's Hall within the university of Cambridge in the later middle ages*. 1969. See (2417, 2457).

2456   Duff, Edward G. *The English provincial printers, stationers and bookbinders to 1557*. Cambridge, 1912. Complements his 1906 monograph on Westminster and London, as well as his 1905 survey of the book trade; also ed. bibliography 1917 that is now largely replaced by Pollard and Redgrave (41); and (2240).

2457   Emden, Alfred B. *A biographical register of the University of Cambridge*. Cambridge, 1963. Provides similar register for Oxford to 1500, publ. 1957–9 in 3 vols.; and see Venn (2464). More about Cambridge (2105, 2416, 2417, 2424, 2433, 2455, 2460, 2464), about Oxford (2394), and universities generally (1475, 2081, 2085, 2407, 2409, 2484, 2490, 2500); for schools (2461).

2458   Mallet, Charles E. *A history of the university of Oxford*, Vol. I. *The mediaeval university and the colleges founded in the middle ages*. Oxford, 1924. Or see Henry C. Maxwell Lyte's 1886 survey; the standard reference on medieval universities in general is Hastings Randall's, esp. vol. II, part II for England (2394).

2459   Mitchell, Rosamond J. *John Free: from Bristol to Rome in the fifteenth century*. 1955. Over-inflated but useful study of a minor English humanist (2444).

2460   Mullinger, James B. *The university of Cambridge*. Cambridge, 1873–1919, 3 vols. The first volume is most relevant, to 1535 (2457).

2461   Orme, Nicholas. *English schools in the middle ages*. 1973. Excellent detailed synthesis (2405, 2417, 2421–3, 2442, 2456, 2472, 2486).

2462   Plimpton, George A. *The education of Chaucer*. 1935. Interesting, valuable, general reconstruction from primers and *summae* of the formal knowledge taught in the *trivium* and *quadrivium* (1031, 2461); about Chaucer (2191).

2463   Plomer, Henry R. *William Caxton (1424–1491)*. 1925. Also Nellie S. Aurner's book, 1926, and Norman F. Blake, 1969; Caxton's publications are studied in (2452, 2467) and his translation of *Aesop's Fables* popularized one type of educational literature (1031, 2462).

2464   Venn, John and J.A. Venn (eds.). *Alumni Cantabrigienses . . . [to 1751]*. Cambridge, 1922–7, 4 vols. See (2457, 2460).

2465   Watson, Foster. *The English grammar schools to 1600: their curriculum and practice*. Cambridge, 1908. Now read Orme (2461), and Albert W. Parry's 1920 monograph; for song-schools, see A. Hamilton Thompson, Oxford, 1942; for Welsh schools, read Lewis S. Knight (2486, 97). Watson's book is preferable to Arthur F. Leach, *English schools at the Reformation, 1546–8*, 1896, but both focus mainly on the Tudor era.

2466   Weiss, Roberto. *Humanism in England during the fifteenth century* (Medium Aevum monograph, 4). Oxford, 1967, 3rd ed. Basic, scholarly, and essential survey (2444).

2467   Wormald, Francis and Cyril E. Wright (eds.). *The English library before 1700*. 1958. On the content, composition, and consumption of medieval books and libraries, preferable to Bennett (2452); also (2419). Of prime value, see essays in James W. Thompson, *The medieval library*, Chicago, 1939.

3 Articles

2468   Allen, Percy S. 'Bishop Shirwood of Durham and his library', *EHR*, XXV (1910), 445–56. For Leicester Abbey see Maude V. Clarke, *EHR*, XLV, 1930, pp. 103–7; for John Tiptoft's library (719, 2498); and (2419).

2469 Bell, Henry E. 'The price of books in medieval England', *Library*, 4th ser., XVII (1936), 312—32. And Wilburt L. Schramm in *Modern Language Notes*, XLVIII, 1933, pp. 139—45; Francis A. Gasquet *Transactions of the Bibliographical Society*, IX, 1906, pp. 15—30; and Henry R. Plomer, *Library*, 3rd ser., III, 1912, pp. 412—18. More about books (2400, 2418, 2435, 2452, 2463, 2470, 2474—6, 2482, 2491, 2493, 2494) and about libraries (2419).

2470 Bennett, Henry S. 'The production and dissemination of vernacular manuscripts in the fifteenth century', *Library*, 5th ser., I (1946), 167—78; *Essays and Studies*, XXIII (1938), 7—24. For a fifteenth-century catalogue of books, in BM, Sloane ms. 3548, see Ramona Bressie in *Modern Language Notes*, LIV, 1939, pp. 246—56; and (2419, 2469).

2471 Bonaventure, (Brother). 'The teaching of Latin in later medieval England', *Medieval Studies*, XXIII (1961), 1—20. Also George H. Fowler in *History*, n.s., XXII, 1937, pp. 97—109 (2430).

2472 Bulkeley-Owen, (Mrs). 'The founder and first trustees of Oswestry grammar school', *ShropsT*, 3rd ser., IV (1904), 185—216. See (2461).

2473 Campbell, Lily B. 'Humphrey, duke of Gloucester, and Elianor Cobham, his wife, in the *Mirror for Magistrates*', *Huntington Library Bulletin*, V (1934), 119—55. His contribution to the Oxford library, 1439—44, is indexed by Herbert Craster in *Bodleian Quarterly Record*, I, 1917, pp. 131—5; and see (724, 2419).

2474 Crous, Ernst. 'The inventory of incunabula in Great Britain', *Transactions of the Bibliographical Society*, XII (1911—13), 177—209. Usefully organized by library locations (35, 36, 41, 2397, 2456, 2467).

2475 Deanesley, Margaret. 'Vernacular books in England in the fourteenth and fifteenth centuries', *Modern Language Review*, XV (1920), 349—58. See (2419, 2469).

2476 Dunning, Robert W. 'The muniments of Syon Abbey: their administration and migration in the fifteenth and sixteenth centuries', *BIHR*, XXXVII (1964), 103—11. Also, Robert Whitwell, *EHR*, XXV, 1910, pp. 121—3 (2419, 2469).

2477 Emden, Alfred B. 'Northerners and southerners in the organization of the university to 1509', in *Oxford studies presented to Daniel Callus* (Oxford Historical Society, n.s., XVI). 1964, pp. 1—30. See (2394).

2478 Ferguson, Arthur B. 'Reginald Pecock and the Renaissance sense of history', *Studies in the Renaissance*, XIII (1966), 147—65. And (1060, 1612, 1965).

2479 Field, P.J.C. 'Sir Thomas Malory, M.P.', *BIHR*, XLVII (1974), 24—35. And see William Mathews, *The ill-framed knight*, California, 1966.

2480 Flynn, Vincent J. 'Englishmen in Rome during the Renaissance', *Modern Philology*, XXXVI (1938), 121—38. Describes lists of names, 1449—1514, in the minutes of Confraternity of the Most Holy Trinity and St Thomas of Canterbury, in ms. 17 of the Venerable English College of Rome; see Mitchell (2490).

2481 Galbraith, Vivian H. 'John Seward and his circle. Some London scholars of the early fifteenth century', *Mediaeval and Renaissance Studies*, I (1941), 85—104. See (2444).

2482 Gasquet, Francis A. 'The bibliography of some devotional books printed by the earliest English printers', *Transactions of the Bibliographical Society*, VII (1902—4), 163—89. See (1610, 2419, 2469).

2483 Hay, Denys. 'History and historians in France and England during the fifteenth century', *BIHR*, XXXV (1962), 111—27. Valuable historiographical essay with comparative insights (1569, 2478).

2484 Hays, Rhŷs W. 'Welsh students at Oxford and Cambridge universities in the middle ages', *WHR*, IV (1968—9), 325—61. See (2394, 2457, 97).

2485 James, Montague R. 'Twelve medieval ghost stories', *EHR*, XXXVII (1922), 413—22; XXXVIII (1923), 85—7. The second is an addendum from Herbert E.D. Blakiston.

2486 Knight, Lewis S. 'The Welsh monasteries and their claims for doing the education of later medieval Wales', *ArchCamb*, 6th ser., XX (1920), 257—76.

Especially for moral and religious didacticism; Knight also edited Welsh school charters before 1600, publ. 1926; on Welsh monastic libraries, read David R. Phillipps' survey in *Library Association Record*, XIV, 1912, 288—316 and 374—98; also (2461, 2465, 97).

2487 Leach, Arthur F. 'St Paul's school before Colet', *Arch*, LXII (1910), 191—238.

2488 Mead, Herman R. 'Fifteenth-century schoolbooks', *Huntington Library Quarterly*, III (1939), 37—42. See (2431, 2461, 2469).

2489 Meech, Sanford B. 'John Drury and his English writings', *Speculum*, IX (1934), 70—83. Schoolmaster in Beccles, Suffolk in 1434 (2461).

2490 Mitchell, Rosamund J. 'English law students at Bologna in the fifteenth century', *EHR*, LI (1936), 270—87; *TRHS*, 4th ser., XIX (1936), 101—17; *Italian Studies*, I (1937), 75—82; VII (1952), 62—81. The second article studies English students at Padua, the third at Ferrara, and the fourth is a synthetic description of English students in Italy. She wrote similarly about Scottish law students, *Juridical Review*, XLIV, 1937, pp. 19—24, which was expanded by Annie Dunlop's Historical Association Pamphlet, no. 124, in 1942; and see (2480, 2457).

2491 Owst, Gerald R. 'Some books and book-owners of 15th-century St Albans: a further study of the Stoneham Register', *Transactions of the St Albans and Hertfordshire Architectural and Archaeological Society*, (1928), 176—95. See (2419, 2469).

2492 Richardson, Henry G. 'Business training in medieval Oxford', *AHR*, XLVI (1941), 259—80; *BJRL*, XXIII (1939), 436—57. With appended ms. list for Thomas Sampson, died *c*. 1409; the second article studies Simon O. and his treatise on *dictamen*, *c*. 1420; and (2394).

2493 Robbins, Rossell H. 'English almanacks of the fifteenth century', *Philological Quarterly*, XVIII (1939), 321—31; XIX (1940), 411—12. Another example, from 1478, is noticed by V. Scholderer, *Library*, 4th ser., XIX, 1938, pp. 99—102 (2469).

2494 Savage, Ernest A. 'A monastic humanist of the fifteenth century: a study in English Renascence book-collecting', *Library Association Record*, XXII (1920), 185—97. William Selling's 1464 visit to Italy, afterwards ambassador for Henry VII and prior of Canterbury (2419, 2444, 2469).

2495 Schulz, H.C. 'The monastic library and scriptorium at Ashridge', *Huntington Library Quarterly*, I (1938), 305—11. See (2419).

2496 Suggett, Helen. 'The use of French in England in the later middle ages', *TRHS*, 4th ser., XXVIII (1946), 61—83. And William Rothwell, *Modern Language Review*, LXIII, 1968, pp. 37—46, as well as Mary D. Legge, in *Studies in French language and literature presented to Professor Mildred K. Pope*, Manchester, 1939, pp. 241—6; also (2451).

2497 Watkin, Aelred. 'Some manuscripts in the Downside Abbey Library', *Downside Review*, LVIII (1940), 438—51; LIX (1941), 75—92. See (2419).

2498 Weiss, Roberto. 'The library of John Tiptoft, earl of Worcester', *Bodleian Quarterly Record*, VIII (1936), 157—64, 234—5; VIII (1937), 343—59; and, *EHR*, LVII (1942), 102—5. The second article studies Lincoln College's 1474—6 library catalogue, and the third notes Henry VI's relations with All Soul's College; and (719, 2419).

2499 White, Beatrice. 'Medieval beasts', *Essays and Studies* (1965), 34—44. Attitudes toward animals, real and imaginary (2284).

2500 Young, Robert F. 'Bohemian scholars and students at the English universities from 1347—1750', *EHR*, XXXVIII (1923), 72—84. See (2457, 2107).

INDEX OF AUTHORS, EDITORS AND
TRANSLATORS